Novel Ecologies

Novel Ecologies

NATURE REMADE AND THE ILLUSIONS OF TECH

Allison Carruth

THE UNIVERSITY OF CHICAGO PRESS
CHICAGO AND LONDON

The University of Chicago Press, Chicago 60637
The University of Chicago Press, Ltd., London

Published 2025
Printed in the United States of America

34 33 32 31 30 29 28 27 26 25   1 2 3 4 5

ISBN-13: 978-0-226-83772-7 (cloth)
ISBN-13: 978-0-226-83773-4 (paper)
ISBN-13: 978-0-226-83774-1 (e-book)
DOI: https://doi.org/10.7208/chicago/9780226837741.001.0001

The University of Chicago Press gratefully acknowledges the generous support of the Effron Center for the Study of America and the High Meadows Environmental Institute at Princeton University toward the publication of this book.

Library of Congress Cataloging-in-Publication Data

Names: Carruth, Allison, author.
Title: Novel ecologies : nature remade and the illusions of tech / Allison Carruth.
Description: Chicago : The University of Chicago Press, 2025. | Includes bibliographical references and index.
Identifiers: LCCN 2024034592 | ISBN 9780226837727 (cloth) | ISBN 9780226837734 (paperback) | ISBN 9780226837741 (ebook)
Subjects: LCSH: Ecology in art. | Human ecology in art. | Architecture and society. | Ecocriticism.
Classification: LCC N8217.E28 C37 2025 | DDC 704.943—dc23/eng/20240806
LC record available at https://lccn.loc.gov/2024034592

♾ This paper meets the requirements of ANSI/NISO Z39.48-1992 (Permanence of Paper).

For Barron and Julian

I don't love you as if you were rare earth metals,
conflict diamonds, or reserves of crude oil that cause
war. I love you as one loves the most vulnerable
species: urgently, between the habitat and its loss.

—CRAIG SANTOS PEREZ, "Love in a Time of Climate Change"

Contents

Illustrations

Figures

Plates (following page 126)

Prologue

Born in 1908, my grandfather was raised in a large Mormon family in Coalville, Utah. In his twenties, he left Utah and made his way to Wyoming. It was there that he met my grandmother. They settled in a small town that would soon be named Sinclair where my grandfather worked for decades as a machinist at the eponymous oil refinery. In my family's narrative of his working life, the refinery eventually offered him a promotion into management ranks. Ever a union man, he turned the job down on principle.

Sinclair's history as an oil town began in 1922 when the Colorado businessman Frank Kistler sought to expand his PARCO gas company into Wyoming's rich shale reserves. His aim was to secure a location near Union Pacific rail lines and the Lincoln Highway where electricity and drinking water would be cheap ("Kistler in New Company" 1926). He settled on a high-desert site near the Medicine Bow National Forest. Working with a Denver architect, Kistler developed his company town around a Spanish colonial-style inn that stood in stark contrast to the refinery's distillation towers, storage tanks, and pipeline connectors (see fig. P.1). His plans ultimately ran up against the Great Depression, which forced a bankruptcy sale of PARCO in 1934 (Louis 2015). The buyer was Harry Sinclair—a notorious New York industrialist who had parlayed his banking wealth into the formation of Sinclair Oil and also served a brief prison sentence on jury-tampering charges in association with the Teapot Dome scandal. The refinery and the town were renamed Sinclair in 1943, one month before my grandmother gave birth to my father and his twin brother in nearby Rawlins.

My grandparents raised their four children in Sinclair in a two-bedroom house with a partly finished basement, where my dad and his brother shared a room. I remember the red concrete steps that led to the front door, the cramped kitchen where my grandmother canned beets and made chokecherry syrup, the fenced backyard where my grandfather grew rhubarb in the summer, the short driveway that barely contained his Mercury Grand Marquis. By the time I was born, my grandfather had retired from

Figure P.1. PARCO/Sinclair, parade on opening of refinery (August 8, 1925). Photograph: Wyoming State Archives Photo Collection, Department of State Parks and Cultural Resources (P82-43/01).

the refinery. I can still picture his metal lunch pail sitting unused in a corner of the basement. As I remember it, Sinclair's compact grid of residential streets was lined with modest one-story houses. There was a post office, a school, and a playground but no grocery store or restaurant. At some point in the 1970s, a golf course was built a few miles outside town. During annual summer visits, my dad and I would run the road between the town and the course out to a stand of mesquite and willow trees that rose from the dusty ground like an oasis. The air smelled of hydrocarbon vapors. You had to keep your ears tuned for rattlesnakes. My grandparents lived in the house they bought for $8,000 until my grandfather died in the autumn of my senior year in college. My dad and his three siblings sold the house shortly thereafter to what I can only imagine was another refinery family. As the new millennium approached, Sinclair offered little to would-be residents aside from the promise of steady oil and gas work.

Today, Sinclair fueling stations, with their iconic green dinosaur sculptures, can be spotted from New Jersey to California. Yet the town can feel like a relic, a footnote in the history of the United States. Sinclair's declining population was estimated to be 374 people at last count (US Census Bureau 2020). The colonial inn is now a community-run museum. Blink, and you miss the single interstate exit that leads to the refinery. As I write, nearly one hundred employees have been given notice in the wake of the acquisition of Sinclair Oil by the Dallas-based HollyFrontier Corporation ("HollyFrontier and Holly Energy Partners" 2022; G. Johnson 2022). For now, the place where my grandfather worked for over thirty years will remain in operation, retooled for renewable diesel production and labor automation. Before long, an even larger energy company may acquire HollyFrontier (whose capacity is a fraction of the global energy giants'), shutter the refinery, and leave the town behind. In the annals of American petrocapitalism that Stephanie LeMenager (2014) describes as *living oil*, Sinclair is a minor character, readily forgotten. My memory of the town, called up as a prologue to the book you're reading, aims to recast deindustrializing places like my dad's birthplace as haunted by what Manu Karuka (2019) terms the *tracks of empire*: the material infrastructures and social systems that have made the United States a settler state ever disguising itself as a land of intrepid pioneers and new frontiers.

: : :

In the spring of 2000, I received the news that I had been accepted to the PhD program in English at Stanford University. I was sitting at a desk in a Denver office park fifteen miles from where I grew up in the foothill town of Evergreen. Having quit my first professional job in Chicago, I had come home to Colorado to work with my dad at the small land development company he had built over the thirty-five years since he'd left Wyoming. I was surrounded by blueprints and spreadsheets when the course of my life changed.

Six months later, at the height of the dot-com boom, I left Colorado to move to the Bay Area. The drive took me north from Denver to the Lincoln Highway (a.k.a. I-80), passing by Sinclair. My grandfather had died four years prior, and I hadn't been back to the area since. Driving across the desert and scrubland of Wyoming, Utah, and Nevada, my thoughts returned often to him and to the place where he had worked. Those thoughts were inflected by the stark, extracted geographies that stretch west to California, landscapes defined by refineries, power stations, and mines. I had never driven so many miles at once across the western United States, and it was the first time I began to notice how many places looked like Sinclair, the first time I began to think—if inchoately at the time—about how many Sinclairs had fueled what a 1941 *Life* magazine story famously called *the American century* (Luce 1941).

Initially at least, Palo Alto seemed like a whole new world. Awash in venture capital, the peninsula that is home to both Silicon Valley and Stanford had become synonymous with innovation. When I first arrived on the Stanford campus, the line of carefully manicured trees that give Palm Drive its name and the irrigated green grass that form the Oval suggested a fantasy at once neocolonial and techno-utopian. To move to this particular place in the first decade of the twenty-first century as a graduate student in American literature and culture held a certain irony. What did it mean to read books, comb through archives, and think about the contested narratives of a nation at a university that was rushing headlong into the future?

Stanford lays claim to receiving the first message sent between networked computers. An outcome of the Defense Department–funded ARPANET (Advanced Research Projects Agency Network), the transmission happened in the fall of 1969 when a UCLA computer successfully relayed part of the word "LOGIN" to a computer at the Stanford Research Institute. The event put both universities on the map as critical academic nodes for what would become the Internet (Thomas 2013, 72–75). Stanford seized the moment to define itself as "a hub of cutting-edge electronics," just as Palo Alto was defining itself as the "capital of the high-tech world" (O'Mara 2019b, 29). These first two nodes of a new networked age joined up with two others—one located at the University of Utah and the other at UC Santa Barbara—helping redefine the American West as a high-tech frontier. By the time I was writing my dissertation, the fast-expanding Internet was powering a global digital economy centered in California. Contra visions of cyberspace as a virtual world, that economy has been built on the infrastructures of nineteenth- and twentieth-century capitalism. Its data centers and wireless signals run along railroads and telegraph lines and its ever-growing energy demands not only are met by fossil fuels, solar arrays, and wind farms but also are contributing to a mining bonanza for lithium, cobalt, and other "critical minerals" (Carruth 2014; Crawford 2021; Ensmenger 2018; Pellow and Sun-Hee Park 2002). However it has promised a green future, "the Silicon Valley of Dreams," to cite the title of David Naguib Pellow and Lisa Sun-Hee Park's landmark 2002 study, has been freighted from the start with industrial projects and paradigms.

While I didn't realize it during my studies there, Stanford has been a microcosm of and catalyst for this metamorphosis of America's tracks of empire. A center for government-funded computing research after the Second World War that built up companies ranging from Hewlett-Packard to Google, the university originated with the ambitions of a robber baron from the prior century. The onetime California governor Leland Stanford became the president first of the Central Pacific Railroad and then of the Southern Pacific Railroad. Stanford was the leading member of a group dubbed "the Associates" that successfully lobbied Lincoln's Republican Party in the early 1860s to win the passage of the 1864 Pacific Railway Act. The group of San Francisco shopkeepers was looking for a new business opportunity as gold miners were becoming farmers and laborers with decreased disposable income. Investing just $19,800 of its members' own capital, the group formed the Central Pacific Railroad by parlaying government funding (the 1864 act generated $50 million in bond money) and Indigenous and Chinese immigrant labor into a corporate juggernaut (Harris 2023, 55–56; White 2011, 19, 22). On May 10, 1869, Stanford hammered the final stake into the tracks that had joined up with the Union Pacific to make transcontinental rail travel a reality. Alongside those tracks, telegraph lines were simultaneously constructed. Thus, as Malcolm Harris writes in his extensive history of Palo Alto, the completion of the railroad "also established the country as a single media environment" (2023, 42–43).

By the next decade, the Associates would successfully convince their investors to hold during the financial panic of 1873, allowing them to acquire bankrupt lines at a bargain and form the Southern Pacific monopoly popularly known as the Combine (Harris 2023, 45). To quote the California historian Richard White: "[S]torekeepers and speculators had secured the charters for the Pacific Railroad because it seemed such an unlikely enterprise to experienced rail-road men" (2011, 20). This gambit made Stanford and his partners enormously wealthy. That wealth—and the corruption that aided its creation—in turn made these California world-builders icons of the Gilded Age's robber barons, a notoriety that the political cartoon titled "The Curse of California," aided by Frank Norris's novel *The Octopus: A Story of California* (1901), cemented (plate 1). It is a guiding tenet of *Novel Ecologies* that the current century's tech economy, with its billionaire executives and growing terrestrial footprint, is materially and imaginatively tied to these California predecessors. Just as Stanford was "but a historical vector" who turned civil war and monetary crisis into wealth accumulation, the projects and people that structure one throughline of the pages that follow have seen in the environmental and social upheavals of our present an *endless frontier* for venture capitalism (Harris 2023, 79).

In the 1880s, the Stanfords used their money to construct a self-consciously Californian university on the grounds of a 650-acre Palo Alto farm and an adjoining 8,000-acre parcel of chaparral, all of which sits on Ohlone land. Frank Law Olmstead's master plan for the university took its inspiration from the plazas, churches, and vernacular architecture of Mediterranean Europe. Planted with citrus and palm trees, and built around open-air arcades, the neocolonial university soon made a technology-driven future central to its identity, melding the canons of a liberal arts education with the latest developments in science and engineering. In her biography of the English photographer Eadweard Muybridge, Rebecca Solnit identifies "transformation(s) of time and space by railroads, telegraphy" and other inventions like film as foundational to the history and mythology of Stanford, the state of California, and what Solnit terms the *technological wild west* (2003, 3–4). Writing about Muybridge's famous collaboration with Stanford to capture images of horses in motion, Solnit identifies Palo Alto as the locus for this mythology's twin centers of gravity: Hollywood and Silicon Valley, "the two industries California is most identified with, the two that changed the world . . . from a world of places and materials, to a world of representations and information, a world of vastly greater reach and less solid grounding" (2003, 6). Given the specific relationships between railroad wealth and new media that Stanford (the person and the university) galvanized, it is not surprising that the Southern Pacific Railroad came to operate first telegraph wires and then fiber-optic cables along its tracks. In 1975, that railway-turned-telecom company was renamed SPRINT (a backronym for the Southern Pacific Railroad Internal Networking Telephony), which, by the time I started graduate school, had become one of the largest wireless service providers in the world.

: : :

In August 2021, I left the Golden State with my husband, Barron, and our then infant son on a thirty-five-hundred-mile journey to relocate to Princeton, New Jersey. Barron had grown up on California's central coast, and we'd met in San Francisco in 2003. California was home as deeply as a place could be. Over the nearly two decades we'd lived there together, I had come to see and understand the state more fully through the prism of Barron's photographs—photographs about the pastoral myths and industrial realities of California agriculture, about the nearly two hundred natural and engineered watersheds that define its topography and the massive human-made systems that move water from across the western United States to the state's farms and cities, about the remains of mining, timber, and oil exploits that hide in plain sight, and about the staggering scale and sublime quality of its landscapes (plate 2). From the time I moved there on Y2K (January 1, 2000) through the day I left during the COVID-19 pandemic, I had come to understand California as many worlds in one, as a place of world-imagining, world-building, and, too, world-destroying forces.

When we started our trip east, we departed from the fishing town of Morro Bay, where the three smokestacks of the town's decommissioned coal-fired power plant define the coastline along with the volcanic rock that gives the place its name. Within a few miles, it was hard to locate where the California Dream still found purchase. The skies turned hot and hazy as we entered the Central Valley that afternoon. A live map showed ninety wildfires burning across 1.8 million acres from California to Montana. The smoke was making its way on the jet stream to New York and Nova Scotia. Three days later, we passed a residential development under construction outside St. George, Utah, branded "Settler's Point." Later that afternoon, just beyond Zion National Park, we found ourselves passing through another development, this one advertising five-acre lots in a juniper forest whose Smokey the Bear sign read "Fire danger VERY HIGH Today!" As we passed through new homes being built in past and future burn zones, the chasm between the national ideology of manifest destiny and twenty-first-century ecological vulnerability felt palpable.

On reaching my home state the following week, we learned that flash flooding and mudslides in one such burn zone had closed a stretch of I-70 that runs eight miles through the precipitous Glenwood Canyon. We took a four-hour detour across the fracked Yampa River valley, past the ski resort of Steamboat Springs, and over Rabbit Ears Pass. My family had driven over that pass often to visit my grandparents in Sinclair. In my childhood, I experienced it as a pristine wilderness defined by heavy snowpack in winter and technicolor wildflower blooms in summer. On that smoky day in 2021, we stopped at the top of Rabbit Ears and took in the view. There was no snowpack on the peaks. The wildflowers were scant. Most of the trees in our immediate field of vision were dead or dying, mostly because of persistent drought conditions and the voracious appetites of mountain pine beetles. Descending the pass to the high-desert valley below, we were confronted with active oil derricks and abandoned silver and coal mines. The scenic route had become a route through climate emergency. Multiple, converging wildfires were described as *complexes*. The largest of them were unconscious signifiers of the nation's settler colonialism and the racialized violence it has justified: Dixie, Bootleg, Oil Springs. The smoke of those fires wouldn't dissipate until we arrived in Chicago a week later, the eastern boundary of what the environmental historian William Cronon (1991) has termed *the Great West*.

: : :

The relocation from California to New Jersey has changed the scope and stakes of what follows. When I began a new book project around the fall of 2017, I intended to survey contemporary American imaginaries and innovations that dispense with eco-apocalypse to put forward variously utopian, comedic, and hopeful futures. That project was provisionally titled "Wily Ecologies." In its original formulation, however, it proved too amenable to the techno-utopianism of Silicon Valley, too ready-made for what I define below as *Nature Remade*—the fantasy that planetary crises can be ameliorated with higher tech, cleaner capitalism, and greener frontiers. Endeavors to realize this fantasy always point to the future. But they run on the tracks of empire: undersea cables that undergird the cloud, mines that power electric cars, venture capital–backed labs that hope to revive lost species and cool the planet, private space programs that may one day ferry the ultrawealthy to Mars and beyond. As I researched these and other such endeavors, I found myself turning to countervailing environmental imaginaries of writers, artists, and scientists that refuse the amnesia of techno-utopianism by envisioning futures made by the slow, collective, revolutionary work of repair. Bringing these imaginaries into sustained contact with case studies in Nature Remade has led to this book: *Novel Ecologies*.

Introduction

> The Anthropocene does not represent the failure of environmentalism. It is the stage on which a new, more positive, and forward-looking environmentalism can be built. This is the Earth we have created, and we have a duty, as a species, to protect it and manage it with love and intelligence. It is not ruined. It is beautiful still, and can be even more beautiful, if we work together and care for it.
>
> —EMMA MARRIS, PETER KAREIVA, JOSEPH MASCARO, and ERLE C. ELLIS, "Hope in the Age of Man"

Nature Remade and the California Dream

If I close my eyes, I can smell the intertidal marsh. The musky scent of reeds, the rot of mud and muck. It's midwinter in the year 2000. I'm running along San Francisco Bay with a view toward the city skyline. The world has rebounded from the unrealized fear that the potentially glitchy binary code powering the global economy might go haywire at the turn of the millennium. I've just moved to California from Chicago and am living in the terraformed town of Foster City, a place constructed out of whole cloth on a salt marsh first surveyed by the US Geological Survey in 1892 and subsequently named Brewer Island. Like much of the bayside waterfront in San Francisco to its north, the four-mile-square island had been "reclaimed" from the bay at the end of the nineteenth century through a combination of leveeing, landfilling, pumping, and draining. Beginning in the 1920s, Brewer Island captivated a string of investors who tried and failed to develop it for commercial gain. In the early 1960s, the Foster family leveraged the city of San Mateo's bayside expansion ambitions for its successful bid to transform the island into a master-planned community branded as a Polynesian paradise, complete with a sixty-acre artificial lagoon, sandy beaches, and a network of waterways navigable by small boats ("Foster City" 2009; Platt 2008). Four decades later, Foster City had become a quintessentially Californian suburb defined by strip malls, chain stores, and long commutes. I'm living there because Silicon Valley is booming and it was the one place where an available apartment in my price range didn't inspire a bidding war. Two years later, I'll move to San Francisco, where I'll live for almost ten years. It's during that period that California will become home, captivate my imagination, and eventually plant the seeds for *Novel Ecologies*. But, in my past present, living on engineered ground in the shadow of the San Mateo Bridge, I feel unmoored. "Where *am* I?" I remember thinking.

I recall these and other California memories from my current home in New Jersey on a balmy June day. I'm watching a promotional video for Google's Bay View Campus, which broke ground in 2017 and opened five years later in the wake of the COVID-19 pandemic. Located in Mountain View twenty miles to Foster City's south, the two interconnected buildings that constitute Bay View—which total over one million square feet—look from above like a space station that has landed on the marsh (plate 3). Equidistant between Apple's and Facebook's headquarters and a short walk from the Silicon Valley campus of Microsoft, the Google compound has been envisioned as a model for ecologically attuned engineering. Its architects tout the ninety thousand solar panels that make up the metallic canopy roofs and power the "all-electric, net water-positive" buildings, which are heated and cooled by "the largest geothermal energy system in North America" (McLaughlin 2022; Studios Architecture, n.d.). The embodiment of state-of-the-art construction, Bay View also showcases biophilic design: a central atrium is called *the mothership*, corridors and common spaces are lined with plants, and exposed elevator shafts are painted with original murals inspired by California's endemic ecosystems ("Dunes," "Scrubs," "Oak Savanna," and "Tidal/Marsh") (plate 4). This is more than a workplace. It's a whole world, a utopia wherein nature seamlessly melds with technology. Driving this idea home, the promotional video opens with a close-up shot of reeds on a pond overlaid with ducks quacking and seabirds taking flight—a visual reference to the salt marsh on which, like Foster City, Bay View sits. Into this ordinary ecological scene, a narrator's voice proclaims: "The one thing we know about the future is we have no idea how we will be working." Making Google synonymous with the brightest possible such future, the video presents Bay View as a prototype for a "hybrid world" constituted by both digital capitalism and regenerative nature. Sidestepping the ecological impacts of computing itself (silicon wafer manufacturing from the 1960s through the 1980s caused significant pollution, and Google's former headquarters sits on a Superfund site), the campus promises to "breathe fresh life into the natural landscape" (Google Real Estate 2022).[1] In this ambition, it is in good company. The three other recently fabricated campuses alluded to above—those of Apple, Facebook, and Microsoft—articulate their relationships to the earth beneath them in kindred terms as "a landscape in the landscape" (Berke 2018), as a "responsive space that can be continuously reorganised [*sic*], modified and adapted" (Eftaxiopoulos 2020, 90), and as the redemptive reversal of "California's past land fabrication" (Microsoft Unlocked, n.d.).

This is the audacious environmental imagination of the tech industry (what I will call *tech* for short). *Novel Ecologies* takes this imagination to be pervasive and powerful in contemporary US society but underexamined in the fields that are especially well suited to interrogate its historical provenance and illuminate its social, ethical, and ecological implications: namely, the fields of American studies, science and technology studies (STS), and the environmental humanities, which have most informed this book and to which I hope it will contribute meaningful knowledge and fresh lines of inquiry. This ascendant paradigm for what self-branded eco-optimists call *next nature* is at once nostalgic about wilderness and deeply invested in engineering of all kinds and orders. Welcome to the age of Nature Remade, a time when "engineering has firmly taken root in the entangled bank of biology even as proposals to remake the living world have sent tendrils in every direction," to quote the introduction to a collection of essays on the nature-making work of molecular genetics and geoengineering (Campos et al. 2021, 1). Nature Remade is the organizing concept of *Novel Ecologies*, capitalized throughout the book to invoke a patented technology or intellectual property (the reader might imagine a trademark symbol, as in Nature Remade™). Regressive and speculative at once, Nature Remade takes up values that have long led environmentalists—and especially White[2] environmentalists in the United States—to advocate for and seek refuge in wild nature and assimilates those impulses into a techno-utopian embrace of "the Earth we have created" (Marris et al. 2011). That catchphrase comes from a group of scientists and science writers affiliated with what has been termed *new conservation* (a group we will meet again in chap. 4). A coauthor of their case for "hope in the age of man," Emma Marris encapsulates one of the central creeds of Nature Remade in her book *Rambunctious Garden*. The recognition of anthropogenic climate change and kindred ecological and planetary crises ignites, for such thinkers, "a heretofore unthinkable, exciting, and energizing thought . . . *we can make more nature*" (Marris 2011, 56; emphasis added).

So energized, the people and programs that I identify with Nature Remade augur a future in which species, ecosystems, and entire Earth systems are reimagined and refashioned—a future made possible, above all, by the world-building forces of technological innovation and venture capital. Enumerating the ethical conflicts between green technology and Indigenous sovereignty, the environmental philosopher and climate justice leader Kyle Whyte (Potawatomi) alerts us to how such thinking apprehends ecological and climatic crises as problems to be solved by the few and the powerful. As he writes about geoengineering proposals: "[S]ince time is running out and there's seemingly little time to respond, taken-for-granted strategies are employed to protect the taken-for-granted state of affairs from disruption" (Whyte 2021, 45; see also Whyte 2017, 2019). Informed by this and other critiques, *Novel Ecologies* aims to examine and rethink the foregone conclusion that planetary emergencies demand planetary re-engineering. At the same time, it spotlights imaginative alternatives to tech-propelled environmentalism.

Far from novel, Nature Remade reboots settler colonial myths of wilderness and the frontier that have been particularly consequential in what Rebecca Solnit has called *the technological wild west*, an analysis my prologue cites (2003, 4). Most significantly for this book, those myths seeded and then helped perpetuate the California Dream. As Kevin Starr details in his multivolume history of California, the California Dream was the invention of European explorers and settlers who saw in *Alta California* a "Pacific Eden" whose fertile lands and waters they claimed as rightfully theirs from both Indigenous nations and Mexico (1986, 14–15, 61). As successive generations of prospectors, speculators, performers, entertainment moguls, aerospace contractors, and venture capital–funded entrepreneurs amassed wealth there, California came to signify nationally and globally "a land of enchantment," a progressive and pioneering place where one might "break through the constraints of day-to-day life and come into possession of something immeasurably better" (Starr 2007, xi). This myth was advanced in no small measure by California railroad and telegraph tycoons like Leland Stanford who parlayed their money and political influence into enterprises by which they first possessed and then profited from wholesale reworkings of earth, water, and sky. Central to *Novel Ecologies* is the belief that the California Dream mythology and its nineteenth- and twentieth-century beneficiaries haunt the technological utopianism of Nature Remade. In turn, Nature Remade *as a new mythology* centered in the American West obscures the social and environmental ramifications of a high-tech capitalism that contemporary California and its economic and cultural center of Silicon Valley have propagated. The preface to the photographer Mary Beth Meehan's collection of Silicon Valley portraits and landscapes enumerates the quality of life that this form of capitalism has assured for the region's most affluent class while highlighting the toxic ground and social inequality it has produced. Written by Fred Turner, the preface describes the region as a modern-day analogue to the seventeenth-century Puritan view of the Massachusetts Bay Colony as "a city upon a hill." Turner writes:

> Water stretches out from the shore first in the shallow multicolored squares produced by salt manufacturing and then into the slate gray, windblown center of the bay. Long-legged willets peck for mollusks along the waterline. And flocks of sandpipers whistle through the air. Thanks to open space preservation, the hills that rim the valley are still wild enough to host mountain lions. Walk through any of the dozens of towns that fill the valley floor and you might see eucalyptus trees or spiked orange blooms called birds of paradise growing at the edges of lawns. . . . What you won't see are the poisons flowing underground. (Meehan and Turner 2021, 1–2)

Attentive to these and other *illusions of tech*, *Novel Ecologies* excavates from Silicon Valley's identity as a paragon of the California Dream that which lies beneath. However one might perceive or experience firsthand all that it obscures, the California Dream has had tremendous imaginative and social power. It's certainly shaped my own relationship to California, perhaps more than ever now that I live elsewhere and my visceral memories of wildfire evacuations and ever-hotter summers begin to fade. Put in less personal terms, however alluring the California Dream continues to be for some, it increasingly confronts the divergent realities of the thirty-nine million people who today call it home.

Telescoping outward from these coordinates of critique, *Novel Ecologies* starts from an understanding that the California Dream and Nature Remade are doppelgänger myths whose utopian promises are troubled by the actual histories and possible futures of California, the American West, and the wider worlds these mythologies aspire to control by rebuilding and remaking them. Moreover, as I wrote in the prologue, California is itself many worlds in one. It boasts the largest subnational economy on the planet but also the highest relative poverty and homelessness rates in the United States. It is one of the canaries in the coal mine of climate crisis, but it also captivates those who call it home and those who travel to its storied coast with landscapes that bewitch in their splendor. It is, in the final analysis, a place of dreams but also, and increasingly, a place of dreams deferred and derailed.

Technotopias of the Anthropocene

In *The Ethics of Invention*, the historian of science Sheila Jasanoff addresses technologies of nature making in the context of bioengineering and genetically modified species. "In the long history of innovation," Jasanoff writes, "nature has served human beings in innumerable ways, as collaborator, resource, and sometimes reluctant sparring partner, to the point where scientists now question *whether a nature independent of human influence even exists on Earth*" (2016, 86; emphasis added). That question informs ongoing scientific and political debates about how to tackle enormously complex environmental problems like climate change and mass extinction. It is a question that those I align with Nature Remade answer with fervent affirmation in advancing new frontiers for engineering life and the planet.

A note to Jasanoff's catalog of the evolving meanings of nature directs the reader to a single reference: a two-page paper published at the turn of the millennium in a newsletter sponsored by the Royal Swedish Academy of Sciences and titled "The Anthropocene" (Crutzen and Stoermer 2000). The poet and nature writer Diane Ackerman recounts the publication of that paper and its lasting impact: "Nobel laureate Paul Crutzen (who discovered the hole in the ozone layer and first introduced the idea of nuclear winter) stepped onto the world stage again, arguing that we've become such powerful agents of planetary change that we need to rename the geological age in which we live" (2014, 9). Pitched to the International Union of Geological Sciences, "The Anthropocene" proposed a new geological epoch to succeed the current Holocene. Crutzen and his coauthor so named what Ackerman and others have termed *the human age* in Earth's history. The scientists' reasoning speaks directly to my conception of Nature Remade and the thesis of *Novel Ecologies*. Ackerman articulates that reasoning thus: "We turned the landscape into another form of architecture; we've made the planet our sandbox. . . . Like supreme beings, we now are present everywhere and in everything." Such an account of the Anthropocene reinforces techno-utopian notions about where to go from here. "Despite the urgency," she writes, "of reining in climate change and devising safer ways to feed, fuel, and equitably govern our sprawling civilization, I'm enormously hopeful. Our new age, for all its sins, is laced with invention" (Ackerman 2014, 12–13).

Not all environmental writers are so hopeful of course. The climate reporter Elizabeth Kolbert, for one, casts the Anthropocene as the epoch that "begins with a planet remade and spirals back on itself" (2021b, 8). The opening riposte in *Under a White Sky*, this claim frames Kolbert's journalistic survey of hydropower, synthetic biology, and geoengineering undertakings that reify what she calls *the future of nature*. In a closing vignette, she paints a disturbing picture of one such future in which edible species are born in labs and skies injected with sulfur dioxide are no longer blue: "an unprecedented climate, for an unprecedented world, where silver carp glisten under a white sky" (2021b, 201). Whether utopian or dystopian, such mainstream accounts of the Anthropocene as the planet's technological epoch unwittingly reinforce the deterministic logic of Nature Remade. In *The Unnatural World*, Dave Biello lays that logic bare in an eerie allusion to the 1977 Eagles song "Hotel California" (generally understood as a biting satire of capitalism). Evidently unaware of the song's political commitments, Biello quips: "You can enter the Anthropocene any time you like, but you can never leave" (2016, 8). Echoing Marris and her coauthors, Biello suggests that "the Earth we have created" can be created anew by capitalism and its latest inventions, if with fewer unintended consequences this time around, while also foreclosing other visions of the future.

In the years I've been researching and writing *Novel Ecologies*, the Anthropocene has fueled a cottage industry of publications and popular representations that run the gamut from specialized papers and academic conferences to podcasts, documentary films, and best-selling books. In that sea of discourse, there has been a pattern of studies and stories that, to quote Elizabeth DeLoughrey in *Allegories of the Anthropocene*, "claim the *novelty* of crisis [and, I would add, the novelty of proposed solutions] rather than being attentive to the historical *continuity* of dispossession and disaster caused by empire." DeLoughrey joins other critics of positivist and neoliberal framings of the Anthropocene for pedaling "a globalization discourse that misses the globe" (2019, 2, 7). In "The Climate of History," Dipesh Chakrabarty suggests why the Anthropocene has been fodder for such universalizing abstractions:

> To call human beings geological agents is to scale up our imagination of the human. Humans are biological agents, both collectively and as individuals. They have always been so. There was no point in human history when humans were not biological agents. But we can become geological agents only historically and collectively, that is, when we have reached numbers and invented technologies that are on a scale large enough to have an impact on the planet itself. (2009, 206–7)

Put differently, the attribution of planetary impact to an entire species—rather than to specific histories and particular systems, actors, and actions—"scale[s] up" the imagination of environmental problems and their redress. If human beings, as a species, have "reached numbers and invented technologies" that have melted glaciers, raised seas, and changed the atmosphere, then why not leverage those same powers to build a better Anthropocene?

Taking that rhetorical question as a kind of gospel, Nature Remade has its roots—however its followers may efface them—in the deeply entwined histories of empire and invention that, for centuries now, have made nature a resource to be harnessed, Indigenous lands and waters a wilderness to be settled, and Earth a canvas for world-building. In conversation with recent ecocritical studies like *Allegories of the Anthropocene* and Jennifer Wenzel's *The Disposition of Nature*, *Novel Ecologies* puts the world-building ambitions of Nature Remade into sustained contact with what Wenzel calls *world-imagining from below* (2020, 23).[3] Although such imaginings are not de facto on the side of nature (any more than they are on the right side of history), they hold the potential of making both capitalist world-building and eco-apocalypticism "unimaginable" (Wenzel 2020, 18).

Outline of the Book

Another book might trace Nature Remade and its world-building schemes over centuries and across cultures—finding prototypes in the massive public works that stretch from the aqueducts of ancient Greece, Egypt, and Rome to the contemporary megadams that have been erected on every continent save Antarctica; in the global transport of plants and animals on the part of European settlers, scientists, and prospectors that reconfigured biomes and lifeways; and in the first seed patents filed by corporations that turned plants into software and incorporated local food cultures into global agribusiness (see, e.g., Carney and Rosomoff 2009; Carruth 2016; Crosby 2004; Everard 2013; Gibson 2021; Linton 2010; and Schiebinger 2004). While alert to these precedents and parallels, *Novel Ecologies* defines Nature Remade as a twenty-first-century formation with especially strong roots in American histories of empire and invention that I ground in California. This center of gravity will shift in and out of focus as *Novel Ecologies* follows the threads of its argument from California to the Arizona desert, the Pacific Northwest, and the Pacific islands of Hawai'i, Japan, and Micronesia as well as to speculative futures in fictional worlds. Across its six chapters, *Novel Ecologies* brings scrutiny to Nature Remade as a *charismatic meganarrative* (a phrase I adapt from the scientific keyword *charismatic megafauna*) that obscures the planetary impacts of tech as well as the ecological, ethical, and social issues with ever-larger scales of environmental design and engineering. In developing this thesis, the book alternates between ventures that "advance the story" (Brand 2013) of Nature Remade and what I see as the *ecological speculations* of novelists, poets, and other artists who contest the premise that "technology and technologists are building the future and the rest of the world . . . needs to catch up" (O'Mara 2019a; see also O'Mara 2019b).

To be clear, the book does not subscribe to an a priori opposition to technological innovations and interventions that might help mitigate, adapt to, and redress the unequal consequences of climate change and other environmental crises. Rather, *Novel Ecologies* rejects the quasi-religious conviction that only a green venture capitalism can save the day. To cite a recurring concept in the work of Donna Haraway, it aims to "stay with the trouble" of making a just world that might sustain into an uncertain future diverse human communities and their nonhuman kin (Haraway 2015, 2016). On one track of this project, *Novel Ecologies* explores three case studies in Nature Remade: (1) the ecological self-image as compared to the planetary footprint of the tech industry itself, from the rise of the Internet through the dawn of artificial intelligence (AI) (chap. 2); (2) the science and the story of so-called de-extinction as a solution to biodiversity loss and a blueprint for what I call *wilderness by design* (chap. 4); (3) and, finally, this century's billionaire-led race to explore space and terraform other worlds (chap. 6). These chapters feature a cast of characters that includes the tech juggernauts Google, Meta, OpenAI, Amazon, and SpaceX and their founders alongside a constellation of lesser-known start-ups, labs, and science organizations, such as the de-extinction funder Revive and Restore and the Mars simulation sited on Native Hawaiian (Kānaka Maoli) ground known as HI-SEAS. Each of these chapters puts Nature Remade in conversation and confrontation with writers and artists who envision environmental futures to come while refusing to forget the histories that have made the Anthropocene what it is today: among them, Saya Woolfalk, Jennifer Egan, Craig Santos Perez (Chamoru/Chamorro),[4] Natalie Jeremijenko, T. C. Boyle, Tracy K. Smith, and Octavia Butler. On a parallel track, the book dwells on three works of environmental fiction: Ruth Ozeki's *A Tale for the Time Being*, which presents a multispecies multiverse that toggles between Silicon Valley, the Pacific Northwest, and Japan (chap. 1); the California-based sci-fi writer Becky Chambers's *Monk and Robot* stories, which envision a posttech future led by robots called *the wild-built* (chap. 3); and Jeff VanderMeer's *Borne* series, which takes readers to a speculative world remade by climate change and bioengineering but also by nonhuman people and their evolving multispecies society (chap. 5). As the novels, poems, installation artworks, and expressive media I contemplate thus delineate and disrupt the paradigm of Nature Remade, a radically different future-oriented environmental imagination from that paradigm coalesces, one that orients around collective life rather than capitalist venture and around livability over profiteering.

Min Hyoung Song's vital contribution to both ethnic studies and the environmental humanities, *Climate Lyricism*, helped me clarify what is most at stake in the book. Song attends to what he describes as *literary innovations* that contemplate climate crisis while building up repertoires for climate action and, in doing so, practice "an active mode of making . . . *and* an active mode of attending" (2022, 3). His capacious study demonstrates the particular power of lyric poetry to answer paradigms like Nature Remade that remain extractive in their orientation to the biosphere and its many kinds of life. It further shows how the resources of artistic imagination (which in *Novel Ecologies* encompass a wide range of genres and media) work to sustain our attention on anthropogenic environmental problems—and outright catastrophes—as the first-order experiences of specific people and places while they also advance models of "shared agency" that might bring about "more livable worlds" for both humans and those with whom we share the planet. If the individuals and entities associated with Nature Remade in *Novel Ecologies* (think Elon Musk and SpaceX) possess the type of individual agency Song describes as "distributed in a heavily lopsided manner," one powerful means by which to counter that outsize influence is to amplify "habits of thought and action that together . . . [strengthen] shared agency." This conviction affords to my home discipline of literary studies "a significant role" for its "attention to expression itself, to . . . how innovations in speech, address, image, sound, and movement [and, I would add, storytelling and storyworlding] call forth shifting ways of apprehending a phenomenon that eludes familiar scales of comprehension"—innovations that can set in motion collective "responses" to effect enduring social change (Song 2022, 3, 13–15). In these and other ways, *Novel Ecologies* pursues essential questions not only for ecocriticism and the environmental humanities but also for allied fields and wider audiences: questions about capitalist horizons of exploration and extraction, about the place of wilderness and animal life in the future, about technological mediations of everyday life, and, finally, about the role of literature and art in offering real alternatives to the illusions of tech.[5]

Novel Ecologies, Ecological Novels

As is becoming evident, the *novel* in *Novel Ecologies* encapsulates, at once, the California ethos of perpetual technological world-building and the global literary form of *the novel,* with the latter's affordances in making storyworlds. In a wide-ranging study of novelty and the manifold "conceptual models" that have defined the new for millennia, Michael North persuasively argues that *novelty* is "at once an indispensable concept and a serious problem, not just in one but in a number of different disciplines" (2013, 5, 7). Taken in during the early research for this book, North's observation led me to a scientific concept of novelty that has become a foundational one for my argument: the concept of *novel ecosystems*. Dating to 1997, the term originated in a specialized paper that documented the ecological metamorphosis of an Arctic landscape from tundra into grassland as a result of a combination of anthropogenic factors including fire suppression practices and climate change (Chapin and Starfield 1997; Hobbs et al. 2006). Over the past twenty years, the term has become a lightning rod in the natural sciences (Klop-Toker et al. 2020; Morse et al. 2014; Murcia et al. 2014). One group of scientists advocates for sharply demarcating the majority of ecosystems on Earth from what they define as truly novel ones: unprecedented "assemblage[s]" whose ecological novelty is anthropogenic in origin but self-sustaining over time such that any desired "return to a previous" preindustrial or prehuman state would be a fantasy (Morse et al. 2014). A novel ecosystem, through this optic, precludes established practices of restoration ecology that serve to reseed flora, fauna, and interspecies relationships that are understood as native to a local environment in relationship to a predetermined point in the past (known as a *baseline* in the environmental sciences). But what if modern ecosystems the world over are seen as novel? What if the line between ecological novelty and native ecology thus becomes moot? Those are the perspectives adopted by new conservation that I take to be defining of Nature Remade, whose adherents, in finding the Anthropocene Earth entirely of human design, accordingly set about envisioning and engineering the next nature (Next Nature, n.d.).

In *The Great Derangement*, Amitav Ghosh argues this about the relationship between the rise of *the novel* and the historical and imaginative scope of the Anthropocene: "[I]t was exactly in the period in which human activity was changing the Earth's atmosphere that the literary imagination became radically centered on the human. Inasmuch as the nonhuman was written about at all, it was not within the mansion of serious fiction but rather in the outhouses to which science fiction and fantasy had been banished" (2016b, 66). His analysis suggests that during the period in which a fossil-fueled world order was forged, the form of fiction taken most seriously came to fixate on individual human characters living quotidian lives over a narrow span of years or days. Ghosh calls this form *the modern novel*. Just as in the nineteenth and the early twentieth centuries "gradualist views in science . . . won by characterizing catastrophism as un-modern," Ghosh surmises that the modern novel came to eschew immense scales and improbable events by placing "ever-greater emphasis [on] everyday details, traits of character, or nuances of emotion" (2016b, 23, 27).

As the evidence and impact of anthropogenic climate change has mounted, Ghosh argues, the "highly improbable occurrences" that have shaped narrative genres outside the modern novel—genres like fantasy and science fiction—have become "overwhelmingly, urgently, astoundingly real." He elaborates with a direct reference to the science and story of the Anthropocene:

> The Anthropocene has reversed the temporal order of modernity: those at the margins are now the first to experience the future that awaits all of us. . . . Behind all this lie those continuities and those inconceivably vast forces that have now become impossible to exclude, even from texts. Here, then, is another form of resistance, a scalar one, that the Anthropocene presents to the techniques that are most closely identified with the novel: its essence consists of phenomena that were long ago expelled from the territory of the novel—forces of unthinkable magnitude that create unbearably intimate connections over vast gaps in time and space. (Ghosh 2016b, 27, 62–63)

Ghosh goes on to contemplate what forms of fiction might sufficiently apprehend the Anthropocene as a geological epoch and climate change as arguably its most consequential planetary signature for people. At the time Ghosh was taking up this question for literary studies, the International Union of Geological Sciences had for several years been deliberating a proposal officially to adopt the Anthropocene as the epoch to succeed the Holocene. This deliberation culminated, as the copyedits to *Novel Ecologies* arrived in my inbox, in a contested, nonunanimous vote of the Union's Subcommission on Quaternary Stratigraphy (SQS) to reject the proposal (Witze 2024). Whatever its fate in the geological sciences, the concept is likely to endure as a cultural keyword, one that stirs critique for blunting the unequal causes and crises of global warming as much as it inspires innovations like exploratory geoengineering research around cloud seeding and solar radiation management (Flavelle and Bates 2024; Keith 2021). In recent studies of how climate change both has been and might be narrated, ecocritics have built on Ghosh's inquiry by documenting the rise of climate fiction and by considering how different narrative techniques grapple with "the unpredictable timelines, broad spatial scales, and nonhuman perspectives" that make climate change at once anthropogenic and superhuman (Crutzen and Stoermer 2000, 17).[6] In the introduction to a multidisciplinary essay collection on the subject, Julia Adeney Thomas offers an especially capacious historical account of the Anthropocene as narrative: "Not all individual actions nor all social systems pushed the Earth System [*sic*] beyond Holocene norms. Some were mutualistic with their environment. These counterpoints to the dominant trajectory are also Anthropocene stories" (2022, 4). Through its multifaceted account of Nature Remade and the ecological novels and other world-imaginings that confront its view of the Anthropocene, *Novel Ecologies* extends arguments like those of Ghosh and Thomas by not just showing the importance of literary engagements with climate change that are multimodal and multiscalar but also examining narratives about people and planet, nature and culture that are being spun far outside the literary field. The book further shows that ecocentric and techno-utopian stories about nature in the time of climate change are becoming more and more entangled and merit simultaneous study.

On this score, the multiple meanings of ecology that *Novel Ecologies* activates require comment at the book's outset. In my own fields of the environmental humanities and STS, ecology has become a nimble concept and a fluid metaphor—a signifier of collectivity, complexity, and relationality from which we get *media ecology*, *social ecology*, *deep ecology*, and so on. As a discipline of scientific study, by comparison, ecology names the "relationships between living organisms, including humans, and their physical environment" and "the vital connections between plants and animals and the world around them," to quote the largest academic association of ecologists (Ecological Society of America, n.d.). As Ursula K. Heise explains about the discipline in a primer for ecocritics: "[E]cology, for many environmentalists a countermodel against 'normal' analytic science, has opened the way for a holistic understanding of how natural systems work as vast interconnected webs that, if left to themselves, tend toward stability, harmony, and self-regeneration" (2006, 509–10). However, as Heise underscores, over the past several decades, ecology has become a more "analytic, empirical, and mathematical field than it was at its emergence in the late nineteenth century," one that now understands ecosystems as "dynamic, perpetually changing, and often far from stable or balanced" (2006, 510; see also Botkin 1990; and Heise 2016a).

This *discordant* understanding of ecology, to cite Daniel Botkin, guides computational metaphors and technological interventions for those ecologists who reject received notions of "nature as wilderness" that took root in nineteenth-century environmental thought through the work of American naturalists like George Perkins Marsh and writers like Henry David Thoreau. Akin to the new conservationists and eco-optimists that figure centrally in *Novel Ecologies*, Botkin concludes that "the most novel of our tools, the computer, is helping us grasp what we have feared to seek":

> We have things backward. We use an engineering metaphor and imagine that Earth is a machine when it is not, but we do not take an engineering approach to nature; we do not borrow the cleverness and the skills of the

> engineer, which is what we must do. We talk about the spaceship Earth, but who is monitoring the dials and turning the knobs? No one; there are few dials to watch, only occasional alarms from people peering out the window, who call to us that they see species disappearing, an ozone hole in the upper atmosphere, the climate changing, the coasts of all the world polluted. But because we have never created a system of monitoring our environment or devised an understanding of nature's strange ecological systems, we are still like the passengers in the cabin who think they smell smoke or, misunderstanding how a plane flies, mistake light turbulence for trouble. We need to instrument the cockpit of the biosphere and let up the window shade so that we begin to observe nature as it is, not as we imagine it to be. (Botkin 2012, 180, 327)

The ecologist and feminist historian of science Evelyn Fox Keller, who passed away while I was finishing *Novel Ecologies*, took to task the hubris of such an "engineering approach" to the biophysical world while historicizing its origins. In a series of essays Keller wrote nearly twenty years ago, she traced the shifting relationships between organisms and machines and between nature and technology in American and European cultures of science. Until the mid-twentieth century, as she details, natural history and the life sciences held to an essential distinction between living organisms and fabricated machines. Within this paradigm: "[M]achines were designed, and they were designed from without. . . . [S]elf-organization was the unmistakable and inimitable signature of living systems." After the Second World War, the rise of computing and cybernetics gave rise to a controversial belief in "the mechanical implementation of exactly the kind of purposive 'organized complexity' so vividly exemplified by biological organisms—in other words, a science that would repudiate the very distinction between organism and machine." Extrapolating from this history of cybernetics and high technology, Keller concludes that ecology in its modern form has, from the start, been bound up with engineering, as the study and design of "systems that incorporate living and nonliving elements, explicitly overriding the boundary between animate and inanimate" (2005, 1070, 1072).

"The End of Nature"

Over the same period in which ecology and engineering have thus coevolved, two divergent narratives of a planet altered by people have arisen and taken root in the popular imagination: one oriented around a planet in peril and the other around a planet rescued by technology. The first of these integrates long-standing eco-apocalyptic imaginings with mounting scientific data documenting increasing greenhouse gasses in the atmosphere and modeling the implications of that data in the form of melting glaciers, rising seas, more volatile weather, and other adverse consequences of anthropogenic climate change.[7] The historians of science Naomi Oreskes and Erik Conway have shown that the science of climate change was reported by scientists as early as the 1960s, prompting President Lyndon B. Johnson, for one, to acknowledge that the United States and other industrialized societies "had altered the composition of the atmosphere on a global scale" (2010b, 170; see also Oreskes and Conway 2010a). Over the succeeding decades, this science-driven consensus solidified, leading oil and gas companies and their allies to stoke the fires of disinformation and denial. Narrative, in turn, became a key tool in illuminating, but also obscuring, the causes, consequences, and remedies of climate change.

In this context, a touchstone for *Novel Ecologies* has been Bill McKibben's *The End of Nature* (1989a), published two years after the physicist James Hansen gave the first televised testimony on global warming to Congress and in the same year that the computer scientist Tim Berners-Lee dreamed up the World Wide Web. A book-length elaboration on an essay McKibben had published in the *New Yorker* (1989b), *The End of Nature* gives climate change a narrative shape by characterizing it as a human-caused undoing of the Holocene's relatively stable weather patterns and an existential threat to cultural meanings of nature as wild, self-regulating, and separate from people (McKibben 1989a, 181). For McKibben, the loss of these understandings of nature, which had defined environmentalism for many White progressives like him, inspires ecological speculations about an unlivable future—what he will describe twenty years later as "life on a tough new planet" (McKibben 2011, 201). Building on predecessors like Rachel Carson's *Silent Spring* (1962), *The End of Nature* thus anticipates the Anthropocene zeitgeist and apprehends its import for the future in elegiac and dystopian terms. Others have given climate change a similarly literary shape by connecting its root causes to the connected histories of colonialism and capitalism, as exemplified in the work of the writer and activist Craig Santos Perez (Chamoru) (a discussion of which concludes chap. 4). Writers like Perez testify to an *unevenly* altered planet and, thereby, contest the universal human protagonists and antagonists at the center of climate change narratives like *The End of Nature*.

Much has been written about why climate change has been contested and why climate action has been thwarted in the United States. Oreskes and Conway, for instance, show how corporate lobbyists and hired technical experts have orchestrated the public sowing of doubt about climate science

(Oreskes 2004, 2007; Oreskes and Conway 2010a, 2010b). In another vein, the communication scholar Mike Hulme illuminates the intergenerational memories and everyday habits that make the very idea of human-caused climate change "unsettling" by shaking "the 'trust' people place in climate as a cultural symbol of large-scale orderliness, an invention which eases their anxieties" about the unpredictability of day-to-day weather (Hulme 2017, 5). The American studies scholar Julie Sze points to yet another crucial explanation, one that has shaped my own thinking in *Novel Ecologies*: frameworks and calls for climate action rooted in environmental justice require that we imagine "the end of capitalism . . . as different from the end of the world" (2020, 82). Given those stakes, outright rhetorical and political sabotage is not the only tactic used to prevent climate action founded on restorative justice and reparations. Narratives of electric cars, wind farms, and carbon capture—as with those I investigate around digital clouds, resurrected species, and space colonies—offer the bewitching story that we can trade extractive capitalism for green innovation. As a response, there is a pressing need for narratives that demystify techno-utopianism without retreating into either wilderness nostalgia or eco-apocalypse, narratives that contend with both the "unthinkable magnitude" and "unbearably intimate connections" of climate change and its causes (Ghosh 2016b, 62–63).

Adopting this expansive approach to environmental narrativity, what follows directs critical attention to stories of the Anthropocene advanced by the economic and technological regimes most responsible for the planetary impacts of people, impacts that have the "Holocene Earth System . . . lurching toward dangerous thresholds and state shifts" (Thomas 2022, 4). Flying under the radar of environmental scholarship, the engineers of this narrative template—whose leitmotif is Nature Remade rather than society transformed—incorporate into established varieties of environmentalism technological visions of inventing, designing, and rebuilding biophysical worlds. These overlapping arenas for gigantic-scale engineering imbue the tech industry with quasi-magical capacities alternately to improve on and to transcend industrial modernity and all it has wrought. The material cultures of digital life that underwrite high technology and its geographic and cultural center of Silicon Valley have expanded in this century from virtual world-building to planetary reengineering. Among the consequences of these expanded ambitions is the ground they have cleared, in the language of software development, for rebooting nature.

[CHAPTER 1]

A Tale for the Time Being

A rocky beach at low tide on the eastern shore of Lummi Island is where I saw a pair of bald eagles for the first time. They were perched high in the treetops along the rocky western shore. I was standing in the water at low tide, peering up at the birds through binoculars. Their enormous size and watchful sentience immediately changed how I perceived the forest and the sea around me. It was the summer of 2018, and I had traveled to the nine-mile-square island as part of fieldwork intended to shape the first chapter of this book. Accessible via a short ferry ride from a peninsula near Bellingham, Washington, Lummi inhabits the Salish Sea. As a tourist and an outsider, I experienced it as remote, quaint, and relatively wild—a place of seagulls and sand cranes, orcas and gray whales, river otters and black bears, teeming salmon runs, and the island's famous population of eagles. But, for decades, the Lummi Nation and other Coast Salish tribes have been working to safeguard such ecosystems and fisheries by organizing against proposed expansions of refining, mining, and shipping operations on their lands and in their waters (Lummi Nation Natural Resources, n.d.; Kim and Winter 2021). And, meanwhile, the island and its neighbors off the west coasts of Washington State and British Columbia are facing mounting climate change impacts, from terrestrial droughts to marine heat waves. However sheltered or sequestered it may have felt to me at the time, this is a place that has been remade once by forestry and then again and again by successive waves of extractive industry, a place increasingly defined by both planetary technologies and oceanic tides.

Centered on an island roughly 120 nautical miles from Lummi called Cortes, Ruth Ozeki's novel *A Tale for the Time Being* (2013b) traverses the Pacific Ocean from Tokyo to Silicon Valley. Grounded in a place where Ozeki has lived since the early aughts when not in New York, the novel moves between two parallel narratives set on either side of the Pacific. As these narratives intersect, they call forth ways of living built not on what Ozeki calls the global *drift* of goods and data but on bonds of storytelling that foster relationships of care among people, other beings, and the places they coinhabit. In this, the novel radiates outward from a small network of human characters to all kinds of nonhumans: Internet signals and oceanic plastics, crows and whales, forests and tides, countering the speculative capitalism of Silicon Valley with ecological speculations about near and distant futures of a planet in flux. By *ecological speculations*, I mean fictions that scale down the Anthropocene to dwell on localized experiences of its consequences even as they craft expansive storyworlds that arc toward more sustaining forms of living. Both intimate and uncanny, such fictions carve out meaningful narrative space for nonhumans as vital creators of futures founded on care, rather than capital, and on environmental and social repair, rather than world-building. In this first chapter of *Novel Ecologies*, I offer a sustained consideration of *A Tale for the Time Being* as just such a fiction and as a touchstone for what follows in the book. Placed in the pole position here, the novel offers a paradigmatic example of the works of narrative fiction that constitute one spine of *Novel Ecologies* and that serve to counter the technological utopianism of Nature Remade.

A Tale for the Time Being transports readers from histories of world war and extractive capitalism to futures of climatic upheaval but also multispecies kinship. It is organized around three parallel storylines. The first is a third-person narrative set on Cortes Island and focused on a writer named Ruth and an artist named Oliver (characters based on Ozeki and her real-life partner, Oliver Kellhammer). The second is a first-person diary of a teenager named Nao. And the third trains the reader's attention, respectively, on a disappearing forest, a singular and sentient bird who has migrated across the Pacific, and an environmental art experiment that anticipates the forest's future. The novel begins with the opening entry in the diary, which chronicles Nao's experiences in Tokyo on returning to the city just before 9/11. With her parents, Nao had spent the prior few years in Cupertino, California, during the first dot-com boom. From Nao's present in the first year of the twenty-first century, the book leaps forward a decade to the moment when Ruth discovers the diary washed up on a beach and wrongly assumes it to be wreckage from 3/11 brought to Canada by ocean currents. Echoing 9/11 in Nao's timeline, that significant date marks the 2011 earthquake and tsunami that catalyzed the Fukushima Daiichi nuclear disaster at a power plant operated by the Tokyo Electric Power Company (TEPCO). In an essay on the "overlapping forms of violence and exclusion" that structure Ozeki's narrative, Guy Beauregard (2015, 96) elucidates the importance of 3/11 in the novel as a marker of interlocking disasters. For Ozeki, these disasters changed both Japan and the Pacific and, in turn, changed the structure of what was at the time of the Fukushima explosion a work in progress.

By the spring of 2011, Ozeki had submitted a draft of the novel to her editor but was dissatisfied with its overall shape and, especially, the explanation for how Nao's diary makes its way to the island. "Then the earthquake and tsunami hit," Ozeki recalls, "and I realized the book I had just written was irrelevant. It no longer made any sense at all." The event prompted a wholesale rethinking of the story: "[T]he tsunami worked its way in, as did the character who shares more than the novelist's name" (Lee 2013). Having interviewed Ozeki about the novel's composition, Alison Glassie explains that 3/11 inspired a change not just in the character who discovers the diary (who became a fictionalized Ruth Ozeki) but also in "'the vector'" by which the diary washes up as flotsam thousands of miles away from its place of composition (2020, 454n). In its revised and final form, the novel weaves the oceanic ecologies of the North Pacific and its flows of people, other species, and stuff into the connective tissue of its nonlinear plot.

Put differently, the ocean and the living bodies it sustains and technological residues it carries together shape the multiple stories and storyworlds that constitute *A Tale for the Time Being*. The specific choice to make Kellhammer and Ozeki characters is also crucial to the novel's complex narrative structure, enacting the author's larger interests in the permeable boundary between literary fiction and real life. The story that unfolds on Cortes Island focuses on Ruth's growing obsession with verifying the people and events in Nao's diary. As her quest proceeds, Ruth, Oliver, other island residents, and real-world readers become entangled with the human and nonhuman lives onto which the diary (and the other materials with which it has traveled) open. The pull of those lives jostles for attention with the magnetic power of late capitalism and its defining technology of the Internet. In *A Tale for the Time Being*, the oceanic drift of industrial, military, and high-tech waste is a physical analogue for fast-moving streams of digital data. The currents that carry that waste into what scientists have termed the Great Pacific Garbage Gyre hold what the character Ruth calls a tangible "memory [of] the stuff we've forgotten" (Ozeki 2013b, 114).[1] Kindred to the increasingly warming and polluted ocean, the Internet—as a global system that severs people from place and transforms the biosphere into what the environmental engineer Peter Haff has dubbed the *technosphere*—appears in this multiperspectival novel as a "temporal gyre, sucking up stories, like geodrift, into its orbit" (Haff 2014).

Starting with the publication of her first work of fiction, *My Year of Meats* (1998), Ozeki has taken up as central narrative concerns both biological and computational technologies: synthetic chemicals, genetically modified seeds, microplastics, digital networks, and so on. Her two prior novels—*My Year of Meats* and *All over Creation* (2003)—laid the groundwork for *A Tale for the Time Being* through their respective ecological speculations on American agriculture.[2] Central to each are two questions about fiction itself: Who can tell a story, and what possible worlds can different species of stories call into being? (see, e.g., Ozeki 2003, 218). *A Tale for the Time Being* addresses these same questions by binding diverse beings and ecologies together as a mode of resistance to the atomizing structures of technologies like the Internet. Critics have emphasized the novel's formal experiments with autobiography and historical fiction, noting its "boundary slippages" between genres (Davis 2015, 87; Huang 2017, 99). Just as crucial are its crisscrossing plots yoking discrete events and environs: 9/11 and 3/11, ancient forests and forever chemicals, long novels and big data, Zen Buddhism and quantum physics. The last of these pairs undergirds what is, most fundamentally, a novel of ideas. To quote Michelle Huang, in *A Tale for the Time Being* "the physical concept of quantum entanglement, [meaning] the phenomenon 'by which two particles can coordinate their properties across space and time and behave like a single system,' emerges as a central theoretical apparatus" (2017, 97), an apparatus, I would argue, for how Ozeki creates a storyworld that stretches the bounds of the world as it now is.

More pointedly, the novel connects a contested theory in quantum physics known as *many worlds* to the Zen Buddhist concept of a time being. The latter, first defined in the thirteenth-century writings of Dōgen Zenji, flattens hierarchies to draw into imaginative and ethical proximity every kind of being in the world and every single moment in time. To quote Nao, a time being is "someone who lives in time, and that means you, and me, and every one of us who is, or was, or ever will be." An early epigraph in the novel translated from the Dōgen Zenji source text puts this philosophy in plain terms: a time being is not just "any Dick or Jane" but "a pillar or a lantern," the "tallest mountaintop," the "deepest ocean floor," and the "entire earth" (Ozeki 2013b, 3, 1). Through this philosophical orientation to the planet, all beings—human and nonhuman, animate and inanimate, microscopic and massive—are complete worlds and, at the same time, small, ephemeral, and insignificant. Positioned as a kindred ontology to that of quantum entanglement, the time being concept structures a novel in which the fictional lives of far-flung beings intertwine to model a future world structured around *expansive intimacies*.

Plastic Stories, Ocean Plastics

In her essay "A Crucial Collaboration," Ozeki shares a memory of how her third novel came into being (Ozeki 2013a). The essay relays a night when Ozeki woke up to "the high clear voice of a young girl—a schoolgirl, a Japanese schoolgirl" who utters what became the opening line of *A Tale for the Time Being*: "Hi! My name is Nao, and I'm a time being. Do you know what a time being is? Well, if you give me a moment, I will tell you" (Ozeki 2013b, 3). Ozeki characterizes this visitation as emblematic of how fictional stories take hold of her as a novelist: "A character speaks—whispers, mutters, shouts—breaking the silence and, in so doing, calls the writer into being." But "the author has authority too," she elaborates, "upon which, for their dear lives, the characters rely." From this origin story for *A Tale for the Time Being*, Ozeki extrapolates an explicitly ecological theory of the novel as a narrative form:

> The relationship between novelist and character is one of symbiosis and mutualism, and the book is the emergent field of their collaboration. The relationship between the reader and the writer is similar. Again, the writer is usually thought to be the one in control of the reading experience, seducing readers with story and holding them in his thrall, but the reality is more complex and reciprocal. This relationship is symbiotic, too, and the book is a co-creation. Reader, writer, character, book—these are not fixed identities we inhabit, once and for all. We are more plastic and malleable than that—time beings, if you will—and the lines that seem to separate us are not as distinct as they appear. (Ozeki 2013a)

Ozeki draws here on the ecological concept of *mutualism*: an interspecies symbiotic relationship found across taxa and biomes. One might counter that not all novels are inherently mutualistic in a sociocultural sense and that many have perpetuated and promoted bigotry, segregation, hierarchy, and war while still other novels variously expose, resist, critique, and satirize those same structures of violence. These distinct histories of fiction notwithstanding, Ozeki makes a case for the novel's potential to generate mutualistic relationships by which "reader, writer, character, book" can coexist, if only for a time. Connecting this novelistic theory to that of the linguist Mikhail Bakhtin in *The Dialogic Imagination* (1981), Glassie suggests that *A Tale for the Time Being* demonstrates how novels model and motivate practices of "humility, intimacy, and open-endedness: postures that will become increasingly useful given the aporetic, intensifying nature of climate and ecological catastrophe on our ocean planet" (2020, 467). This analysis speaks convincingly to how Ozeki thinks of the novel as a form and the form of her own novels as *narrative ecosystems* in which diverse beings, together with the author and the reader, create sustaining storyworlds.

Ozeki extends her ecological theory of the novel to a broad universe of written documents in a foreword to the computer scientist and calligrapher David Levy's *Scrolling Forward* (2016), a cited influence on both *A Tale for the Time Being* and her subsequent novel, *The Book of Form and Emptiness* (2022). Ozeki highlights in the foreword Levy's study of "the significance of written documents at a pivotal moment in the evolution of writing" (Ozeki 2016, xiv). In a tacit critique of digitization, Levy compares analog writing and the documents it produces to biological matter as well as geological time. Physical documents are, in his words, "bits of the material world—clay, stone, animal skin, plant fiber, sand—that we've imbued with the ability to speak" and that turn "the dust of the earth" into "our breath, our voice." In developing this thesis, he envisions all sorts of written materials, from paper receipts to novels, as "social actors" that concretize different kinds of "social order[s]" (Levy 2016, 18, 20). It is this claim that Ozeki finds especially compelling. *Scrolling Forward*, she writes, "changed the way I think—and, more importantly, the way I *feel*—about written language, which is to say it changed the way I think and feel about time and text . . . meaning and being" (Ozeki 2016, xiv). These meditations on the ecological and social lives of documents inflect the narrative stakes of *A Tale for the Time Being*, moreover, and the novel's particular concerns with digital documents, networked data, and their ecological and social consequences.

Before we learn that its first-person narrator is the voice of an adolescent writing in a physical diary, the novel invites us into an intimate relationship with Nao and her world. The reader who decides "to read on," we're told, is the person the diary has been "waiting for"—Nao's "kind of time being." This ideal reader takes tangible form as the characters Ruth and Oliver, who read the document together. The novel imparts to these acts of writing and reading on the part of Nao, Ruth, and Oliver—but also on the part of Ozeki and her readers—a kind of "magic" that crosses space and time. The stated purpose of Nao's life writing is to record the story of her great-grandmother, Yasutani Jiko, "a nun and novelist and New Woman of the Taisho era," who is 104 at the time of the diary's composition (Ozeki 2013b, 4, 6). But the story Nao sets out to write about Jiko recedes to the margins both in the diary and in the novel as the entwining of these two texts brings into being unintended storyworlds. Together, these narratives produce what in *The Great Derangement* Amitav Ghosh calls a "hybrid form" (2016b, 84). Over its four hundred pages, Ozeki's novel intermixes life writing and realist fiction with Internet search histories and email exchanges, dreamscapes and wormholes, ghost stories and disappearing pages, letters and hieroglyphs. Genre bending, the novel further distributes its narrative agency across a range of storytellers: Nao, Ruth, Oliver, Jiko, Nao's dead great-uncle, and an avian character assumed to be a Jungle crow.

From start to finish, *A Tale for the Time Being* thus stymies Ruth's efforts to pin down the people and events in Nao's diary. Discovered on the beach in the second chapter, the diary comes with other documents and physical objects: a palimpsest, it's encased in the cover of a famous metafictional novel (Marcel Proust's *In Search of Lost Time* [1914]), placed inside a Hello Kitty lunch box along with a stack of letters handwritten in Japanese, a red book handwritten in French, and "a sturdy antique wristwatch with a matte black face and a luminous dial" (Ozeki 2013b, 10). These artifacts open onto different storyworlds that, with time, converge. On this note, the technical definition of *storyworld* in narrative theory is crucial to apprehending how *A Tale for the Time Being* works as fiction. In her ecocritical study *The Storyworld Accord*, Erin James defines the narrative operations of storyworlds as "simulations of autonomous textual domains" that transport readers to "a different set of space-time coordinates" from their own (James 2015, 21; see also James and Morel 2018). *A Tale for the Time Being* transports its readers to many such space-times at once. The letters and the red book that traveled across the Pacific with the diary turn out to be the writings of Nao's great-uncle, "Haruki #1." The letters are his official correspondence to his mother, Jiko, during World War II when he was in training as a soldier in the Japanese Army's Divine Wind Special Attack Unit (known more commonly as the kamikaze pilots). A covert diary, the red book documents the violent abuse of pilots by the unit's commander and relays Haruki #1's decision to fly his plane not into enemy aircraft but into a Pacific wave—an act of conscientious objection that he ultimately completes. As for the "sturdy antique watch," that object is revealed to be a "sky-soldier" timepiece that was a special issue for pilots in the Special Attack Unit. The lunch box, itself an icon of early twenty-first-century youth culture and global consumerism, thus carries across the ocean an intergenerational archive that spans decades. While we later learn that Jiko saved her son's letters, how the secret diary and the watch were recovered from the wreckage of Haruki #1's plane and how they came to travel with Nao's diary remain mysterious. Their arrival on Cortes Island is the first indication that *A Tale for the Time Being* is a speculative historical novel that moves across space and time in unconventional ways.

When Ruth first notices the barnacle-encrusted plastic bag enclosing the lunch box, she initially misidentifies it as the biological remains of a jellyfish. On realizing her mistake, she reclassifies her find as ocean flotsam, one instance of the massive consumer detritus that makes up the Great Pacific Garbage Gyre: "a flotilla of trash, purportedly at least as big as Texas, that has accumulated at the becalmed heart of the North Pacific Subtropical Gyre, a giant clockwise circuit of currents that revolves between East Asia and North America" (Hohn 2008) (plate 5). A pivotal early scene in the novel, I'll quote it at length:

> A tiny sparkle caught Ruth's eye, a small glint of refracted sunlight angling out from beneath a massive tangle of drying bull kelp, which the sea had heaved up onto the sand at full tide. She mistook it for the sheen of a dying jellyfish and almost walked right by it. The beaches were overrun with jellyfish these days, the monstrous red stinging kind that looked like wounds along the shoreline.
>
> But something made her stop. She leaned over and nudged the heap of kelp with the toe of her sneaker then poked it with a stick. Untangling the whiplike fronds, she dislodged enough to see that what glistened underneath was not dying sea jelly, but something plastic, a bag. Not surprising. The ocean was full of plastic. She dug a bit more, until she could lift the bag up by its corner. It was heavier than she expected, a scarred plastic freezer bag, encrusted with barnacles that spread across its surface like a rash. It must have been in the ocean for a long time, she thought. Inside the bag, she could see a hint of red, someone's garbage, no doubt, tossed overboard or left behind after a picnic or rave. The sea was always heaving things up and hurling them back: fishing lines, floats, beer cans, plastic toys, tampons, Nike sneakers. (Ozeki 2013b, 8)

Ruth initially perceives the "tiny sparkle" on the beach as a species of jellyfish, likely the Pacific sea nettle (*Chrysaora fuscescens*), known for its dusky red body and tentacles that can stretch up to fifteen feet (Aquarium of the Pacific, n.d.). As with other jellies, enormous blooms of the Pacific sea nettle can occur at irregular intervals, and evidence suggests that some populations are thriving because of warming seas and changing nutrient conditions in the world's oceans (Condon et al. 2013; Duarte et al. 2013; Lan, Zhang, and Wei 2023; Ohman 2019; Ruzicka, Daly, and Brodeur 2016). The keystone moment in *A Tale for the Time Being* when Ruth finds Nao's diary thus mistakes synthetic matter for marine life, anticipating what scientists have termed the *plastisphere* (Zettler, Mincer, and Amaral-Zettler 2013). Coined the year Ozeki's novel was published, *plastisphere* signifies not just polymer matter but, more precisely, "the microbial community on plastic debris," *a hybrid ecology* whose scale now rivals the entire "built environment [of humans] in spanning multiple biomes on Earth" (Amaral-Zettler, Zettler, and Mincer 2020, 139).[3] This enmeshment of biological organisms (like the barnacles on the plastic bag that holds the lunch box and the diary within it) and entire ecosystems (like the North Pacific) with the remains of synthetic technologies offers the imaginative point of departure for *A Tale for the Time Being*.

At the time Ozeki was drafting the novel, an account of oceanic plastic was circulating widely, thanks, in part, to a *Harper's Magazine* story titled

"Moby-Duck" (Hohn 2007) and a subsequent *New York Times* piece titled "The Sea of Trash" (Hohn 2008). While the latter introduced the Great Pacific Garbage Gyre to lay readers, the former was a long-form, investigative story about a single instance of plastic waste that occurred in 1992 when a container ship dumped into the North Pacific "28,800 plastic animals produced in Chinese factories for the bathtubs of America—7,200 red beavers, 7,200 green frogs, 7,200 blue turtles, and 7,200 yellow ducks," a portion of which "traveled south of the Puget Sound" (Hohn 2007). As these plastic toys bobbed around the world's waters, their movements were tracked by oceanographic sensors and studied by marine scientists. The evident weirdness of where they washed up inspired myriad stories of their provenance from outside the sciences. This transmutation of an accident of global capitalism into a maelstrom of stories provided Ozeki with another narrative spark—in addition to 3/11—for her transpacific tale (Glassie 2020; Huang 2017). Although Ruth intends to throw the plastic bag away on bringing it home, Oliver, who is an environmental artist and science enthusiast, decides to sift through its contents, discovering they are anything but trash. As the couple begins to explore the handwritten diaries and letters, the "musty scent of mildewed pages and dust" calls to Ruth's mind their own "overflowing" collection of physical books, "stacked on shelves and piled on the floor, on chairs, on the stairway treads": "[T]he damp sea air had swollen their pages and the silverfish had taken up residence in their spines" (Ozeki 2013b, 11). With this sensory depiction of books as hosts for ecological communities, the plastisphere and the storyworld blur as the novel enmeshes writing with its biophysical and ecological hosts.

By comparison, the Internet represents a virtual carrier of verifiable information, a promise that pulls the character Ruth away from both the world around her and her current project of writing the story of her mother, who died of Alzheimer's before the narrative begins. Ruth is euphoric when she discovers the first digital trace that suggests the people in Nao's diary might be real. The possibility comes from an obscure online article about a feminist and anarchist named Jiko Yasutani and the "groundbreaking" book Yasutani authored decades earlier in the I-novel tradition of Japanese fiction: "Ruth hadn't realized just how keenly she'd been waiting for this corroboration from the outside world that the nun of her dreams existed, and that Nao and her diary were real and therefore traceable." The Internet search seems to lift Jiko from the pages of the diary, offering "a keen and sudden sense of kinship with this woman from another time and place, engaged in self-revelatory, self-concealing, and self-effacing acts" (Ozeki 2013b, 150). There is a dramatic irony, however, in this desire to corroborate the diary as a historical document by way of Internet scrolling and digital records. Forging what one reviewer describes as "a Zen eternity of multiple realities" (Kosaka 2013), the novel repeatedly and insistently disrupts Ruth's technological search for veracity and the attendant impulse to fix a boundary between fact and fiction and to pinpoint the people and places in the diary as contemporaneous with her own world.

A Narrative of Many Worlds

Throughout the novel, the diary and its fellow documents activate divergent narratives for Ruth and Oliver as their immediate readers. A salient illustration occurs after the couple reads an entry in the diary recounting a violent attack on Nao by students in her school that culminates with the students putting her menstrual-blood-stained underwear on an online auction site. The experience stands out as especially brutal within the pattern of recurrent physical, verbal, and online bullying Nao experiences on her family's return to Tokyo. The attack occurs after a school break during which Nao had stayed at her great-grandmother's mountainside temple. While there, she had learned to cultivate what Jiko calls a "SUPAPAWA," which in Nao's case is storytelling itself (Ozeki 2013b, 176–90). In the entries that follow the description of the attack, Nao narrates her writing life at a "French maid café," a space that at first seems to provide an escape from her school traumas but ultimately compounds them. A woman named Babette who works at the café befriends Nao only to exploit her social isolation by recruiting her into sex work. In this same section of the diary, Nao shares that her father (known as Haruki #2) has attempted suicide for the second time, something she attributes to his discovery of the online auction.

When the novel returns to Ruth and Oliver, it is to a discussion of this sequence from the diary. The conversation opens with Oliver's cursory reference to Babette as Nao's friend, followed by his extended reflection on Haruki #2's hobby of making scientifically accurate origami of insect species. Ruth responds with outrage at the narrative Oliver has reassembled: "I don't understand you. The girl is attacked, tied up and almost raped, her video gets put up on some fetish website, her underpants get auctioned off to some pervert, her pathetic father sees all this and instead of doing anything to help her he tries to kill himself in the bathroom, where she has to find him—and after all that, the only thing you can say is Babette is cool? It's sad about the *bugs*?" (Ozeki 2013b, 293). In detailing what she feels Oliver has grossly misread, Ruth underscores the multiple traumas that the diary recounts, traumas that reenergize her commitment to locating Nao and substantiating her story. But the events that Nao narrates date themselves as occurring just before and immediately after 9/11 and, hence, take place a decade earlier than 3/11 and the Cortes Island present of Ruth and Oliver's storyline. Despite this temporal disjunction, Ruth reads the diary as a real-time record of a traumatized adolescent girl and her suicidal father who are in urgent need of aid. As a second reader, Oliver understands the diary as a historical record whose telos is beyond their power to change or redirect. Reading it as a kind of fiction, then, he lights on a minor plot of personal interest that centers on the artistic and ecological sensibilities of Nao's father.

In the pivotal episode leading to Haruki #2's second suicide attempt, Oliver notices the name of one of the anonymous bidders in the online auction: "C.imperator." The detail leads him to conclude that Nao's father had visited the auction site covertly with that avatar in order to purchase his daughter's underwear so that no one else could do so. Oliver is surprised that the name's significance has escaped Ruth's attention:

> "C.imperator? The guy who lost the auction? That was him. That was Nao's father."
>
> She felt the heat rising to her face as she listened.
>
> "*Cyclommatus imperator*," he continued. "Don't you remember?"
>
> She didn't.
>
> "It's the Latin name for the staghorn beetle," he explained. "The one he folded out of paper? It was a flying *Cyclommatus imperator*. He won third place for it in the origami bug wars."
>
> Of course she remembered *that*. She just hadn't recalled the Latin name, and she hated that he had. She hated that now he felt he needed to speak slowly and carefully and explain everything as if she were an imbecile or had Alzheimer's. He used to use this tone of voice on her mother.
>
> "Nao recognized the Latin name immediately," he said. "That's why she was so upset. As soon as she saw the suicide note, she knew. . . . Her father was referring to the bidding, and Nao figured it out, which was why she went to check the computer. That's my theory." (Ozeki 2013b, 294–95)

This heated exchange crystallizes the narrative project of the novel as an exploration of and experiment in the many worlds that fictional stories—in collaboration with their readers—actuate. Oliver keys into the online bidder's handle and its connection to an earlier diary entry about Haruki #2's virtuosic origami practice. In contrast, Ruth sees as *the story* the attack on Nao and the other traumas she has experienced. As the diary and the other documents travel beyond Ruth and Oliver to a widening group of readers, stories and storyworlds proliferate.

Meanwhile, Ruth's drive to "investigate and verify the girl's references" via the Internet—even as she worries it may be "wasting precious hours on someone else's story"—takes on a life of its own, bringing to the fore a submerged narrative within the diary (Ozeki 2013b, 29, 31). Her search for online clues of Jiko, Nao, and Haruki #2 leads, in particular, to Rongstad Leistiko, a Stanford social psychologist who conducted research about suicide in the 1990s. This research led to a friendship between Leistiko and one of the study participants, a Japanese game designer and engineer named Haruki whose story the professor shares with Ruth in an email. In Leistiko's account, Ruth recognizes Nao's father, an identification corroborated by the diary's references to Haruki #2's past work in Silicon Valley. Leistiko describes his subject and friend Haruki as having had a crisis of conscience when the start-up that hired him to program video game software signed a military contract with the purpose of adapting the software to warfare simulations. Ruth also learns from Leistiko that this same Haruki eventually launched a tech company of his own, some years after the period the diary covers. The company aimed to commercialize two programs Haruki had created: one to erase digital records (inspired by his desire to banish the entire online archive of his daughter's bullying) and one to search for and destroy all digital traces of a person's life from "the Internets of many worlds" (Ozeki 2013b, 382–83). Branded *the obliterator*, the latter program at one point seems to act on the novel itself when all the Internet references Ruth has located about the people in the diary vanish.

As the threads around Haruki and his doppelgänger of Haruki #1 demonstrate, *A Tale for the Time Being* draws on the many worlds interpretation of quantum mechanics first articulated by Hugh Everett in the late 1950s, which holds that, whenever "there is more than one possible outcome, all of them occur," if in parallel worlds: "These small branchings of possibility then ripple out until everything that is possible in fact *is*" (Galchen 2011; see also Crease 2019; and Vaidman 2021). On the fringes of theoretical physics, many worlds theory differs from the idea that the universe contains within it multiple worlds (i.e., the multiverse). In its account of space, time, and being, many worlds resonates with Ozeki's theory of the novel and approach to crafting this particular novel. "Quantum information is like the information of a dream," as Oliver puts it to Ruth near the conclusion of *A Tale for the Time Being*: "You were speculating about multiple outcomes, right? Multiple outcomes imply multiple worlds." Ruth responds with the observation that Dōgen Zenji had "figured all this out" centuries ago: "*To forget the self is to be enlightened by all myriad things*. Mountains and rivers, grasses and trees, crows and cats and wolves and jellyfishes." This closing scene compares the many worlds and simultaneous timelines posited by a niche community within quantum physics with the Zen practice of forgetting oneself to become attuned to other orders of being, from jellyfish to polymers. This practice does not come easily to Ruth, who wants to know, once and for all, how Nao's story ends. The novel works against its protagonist's impulse to fix a life and a story on a single timeline, however. Its many tales and the storyworlds onto which they open insist on a kind of "not-knowing," the power of which Ruth finally acknowledges to Oliver in notably quantum terms for how it "keeps all the possibilities alive . . . all the worlds alive" (Ozeki 2013b, 395, 399, 402).

We can recast Ruth's effort to verify the diary and intervene in Nao's and her father's suicidal ideations not as delusional but as an enactment of what I will now call the *reworlding* procedures of *A Tale for the Time Being*. As if addressing the novel's reader, Oliver at one point reminds Ruth that the events in Nao's diary happened years in the past: "The dot-com bubble burst back in March of 2000. Her dad got fired, they moved back to Japan, a couple of years passed. Nao was sixteen when she started writing the diary. But that was more than a decade ago, and we know the diary's been floating around for at least a few years longer. . . . If she didn't kill herself, then she'd be in her late twenties by now." However cavalier this reconstruction of Nao's timeline and its possible ending in suicide may seem, the novel reminds the reader at every turn that stories keep their time beings always alive. Ruth, in this spirit, answers Oliver's temporal accounting by asserting the "slippages" between fiction and life: "When she was writing a novel, living deep inside a fictional world, the days got jumbled together, and entire weeks or months or even years would yield to the ebb and flow of the dream. . . . Fiction had its own time and logic" (Ozeki 2013b, 313–14). A poignant expression of this "time and logic," the final pages of Nao's diary inexplicably disappear while Ruth and Oliver are still reading. This erasure occurs after Nao relays the story of a train journey she takes to see her dying great-grandmother on the heels of discovering her father has planned a third suicide attempt. This entry in the diary ends with Nao at a train station waiting for a bus that will take her to Jiko's temple. Nao's great-grandmother and father thus suspended between life and death, Ruth turns the page of the diary to discover blank sheets (Ozeki 2013b, 342–43). When she insists Nao's words were there before, Oliver suggests that the hard-to-explain erasure of handwritten text "calls our existence into question, too": "[I]f she stops writing to us, then maybe we stop being." Oliver elaborates, pressing the point that written stories are vital not only to the lives they recount or fictionally bring to life but also to the worlds of their authors and their readers. "Where do words come from?," he rhetorically asks, answering: "They come from the dead. We inherit them. Borrow them. Use them for a time to bring the dead to life" (Ozeki 2013b, 344, 345–46).

More-Than-Human Storyworlds

In the scene that follows the conversation between Oliver and Ruth about the relative timelines of Nao's story and their own, Ruth has the last of three vivid dreams in the novel (Ozeki 2013b, 39–40, 122, 349). The dream begins with her sensation of swimming in a sea that is "black and thick and filled with debris," a dreamscape reminiscent of the Great Pacific Garbage Gyre that bleeds into an impression of Jiko offering Ruth her "murky" glasses. As Ruth dons them, she feels the instinct to "let go" of her fixation on Jiko and the truth of her story as recounted in the diary. With this surrender, she suddenly hears the cawing of the Jungle crow, who has been a conduit among the novel's characters and locations since its first pages. As the bird's voice reverberates, Ruth notices that the word for crow has appeared "on the horizon" of her dreamscape in the shape of the bird itself, an image the novel depicts as a visual graphic. This encounter transports Ruth to a Tokyo park, where she finds herself next to a man "sitting on one of the benches" and feeding "a mangy flock of crows." Their exchange will alter the course of all storylines in the novel as the man turns to Ruth and asks whether she is "the one [he is] waiting for" (Ozeki 2013b, 349–50). The question recalls the opening entry in Nao's diary, which suggests that there is an ideal reader for whom the diary "is waiting" (Ozeki 2013b, 4). In the dream's final moment, the novel's reader gleans that the man on the bench is Nao's father, who was waiting at the most recent point in the diary's narrative for someone from an online suicide club to meet him. Having just read Nao's description of her father's latest suicide plan, Ruth cautions the man in the dream that his daughter will take her own life if he goes through with it (Ozeki 2013b, 352).

Emily Yu Zong clarifies the narrative significance of the dream, in which Ruth also "puts uncle Haruki's diary on Jiko's family altar": "[W]here Nao's diary has gone blank, two more chapters appear, in which a dying Jiko enjoins Nao and her dad to live, and Nao and her dad, after discovering Haruki's secret diary, learn that he did not fly his plane into an American battleship but into the ocean instead" (2021, 312). Put differently, when Ruth wakes to find that the diary pages that had disappeared have returned, she imagines that the restored pages record a different story than they had before. This altered story ends not with Haruki #2's death but with his decision to join Nao at Jiko's temple and accompany her at his grandmother's passing. Significantly to this alternate ending, the reinstated pages of the diary begin with Nao's expressed hope both to keep living and to keep writing (Ozeki 2013b, 390). The long sequence from Ruth's dream to Jiko's funeral—in which fictional people separated by an ocean and a decade redirect and reshape one another's narrative arcs—exemplifies the larger structure of *A Tale for the Time Being*, the multiple worlds it contains, and the ecological and social bonds it conjures.

The specific storyworld of the Jungle crow is central to these interactions within and across the novel. Identified as a member of the species *Corvus japonensis*, a large-billed crow endemic to Japan, the bird first appears in the novel just after Ruth reads the section of the diary relaying Haruki #2's first suicide attempt. The entry reveals that Nao's father has been hiding his unemployment by telling Nao and her mother that he has been working on a new "productivity software" designed to imbue computers with the capacity of empathy, a kind of artificial general intelligence (AGI) that would "anticipate our needs and feelings" (a subtext that speaks to the ecologically utopian narrative of AI taken up in chap. 3). In truth, Haruki #1 has been spending his days on a bench in Ueno Park—where he'll later meet Ruth in her dream—feeding the crows and, thus, enacting empathy for nonhumans even as his own depression is deepening. Among the diary's fictional readers, it is Oliver, significantly, who takes note of Haruki's relationship to the birds when he shares with Ruth recent research about both the Jungle crow and a species native to Cortes Island, *Corvus caurinus*. In this context, he recounts an incident from the day Ruth first found the diary during which he had observed a group of ravens harassing a smaller bird. In Oliver's telling, the outcast bird "looked like a crow, only it was bigger than *Corvus caurinus*, with a hump on its forehead and a big thick curved beak" suggestive of a Jungle crow. Asking himself, "[W]hat's it doing here?" he decides that the lone crow must have "rode over on the flotsam" much like the diary (Ozeki 2013b, 50–52, 55).

The next time the crow makes an appearance, Oliver is reading an issue of *New Science* that includes a report—which he again shares with Ruth—that Jungle crows have come to be seen as a nuisance in Japan owing to their habits of gathering urban refuse to make nests in utility poles, signs, it should be noted, of their intelligence. His account of the study prompts an invocation of 3/11 when he notes that TEPCO has taken to blaming the crows "for hundreds of blackouts a year." The remainder of the novel rebuts this interpretation of the birds as a mere menace to electrified human life by elevating a single crow to the status of a complex and rounded character in the novel. This singular crow alludes to the story of Grandmother Crow (or T'Ets) in Coast Salish cultures: "one of the magical ancestors who can shape-shift and take animal or human form" (Ozeki 2013b, 66, 96). In these ways, the bird epitomizes the anthropologist Thom van Dooren's account of the Corvus family as beings who inhabit and embody "a wakeful world . . . composed of diverse forms of mindful, agentic, purposeful existence" (van Dooren 2019, 7). In the novel, this wakefulness entwines intergenerational and multispecies relationships to elicit what in *The Wake of Crows* van Dooren poetically describes as crows' more-than-human "experimentation in collective life" (van Dooren 2019, 14).

A power outage on Cortes Island midway through the novel immerses Ozeki's reader in this "wakeful world" and does so in tacit reply to TEPCO's technocratic view of nature as either a resource to be harnessed or an adversary to be exterminated. The blackout occurs after a fierce storm on the island suspends Ruth's search for online evidence of Nao and her family, leaving her in the literal dark. The return of power hours later reveals that the one digital trace she had found of Jiko "has been removed from the database." The revelation prompts Ruth to cry out "NO!" in despair. Just as this sequence concludes from Ruth's perspective, however, it repeats itself from the crow's point of view:

> Outside in the cedar tree by the woodpile, the Jungle crow cocked its head, listening too. A few moments passed, maybe a minute. The windows of the house were bright again—glowing squares that floated in the darkness of the forest. Another cry, longer this time, emerged from the window closest to the woodpile.
>
> Noooooooooo—!
>
> Silence followed, and then the window went dark. The crow lifted up its slick black shoulders and shuddered, which was the corvine equivalent of a shrug. It flapped its feathery wings once, twice, thrice, and then rose up from its perch, flying through the heavy cedar boughs. It circled the roof of the house. Down below, a ragged line of wolves ran silently, in single file, following a deer trail through the salal. The crow cawed out a warning, in case anyone was listening, and then flew higher, away from the little rooftop in the clearing, until finally it cleared the canopy of Douglas fir.
>
> Soaring now above the treetops, it could see all the way to the Salish Sea and the pulp mill and the logging town of Campbell River. . . . On the far side stretched the open Pacific and beyond, but the crow could not fly high enough to see its way home. (Ozeki 2013b, 173–74)

Moving into the mind of the crow, the novel decenters its human characters in order to thicken a different storyworld that has been there all along—a world of anthropogenic upheavals and displacements but also of other beings with narratives of their own. Ruth's cry as a response to a digital erasure echoes alongside the caw of the crow's address to the wolves, the deer, and the forest they share with one another and with the island's people in a time of "geodrift." The crow's aerial perspective takes in not only a forest mostly denuded and replanted with a monoculture of Douglas fir but also an understory that is still home to the endemic salal shrub named by the Chinook for its edible berries. As the crow soars over and then out beyond the island, its vantage connects Coast Salish lands under the ongoing duress of displacement and deforestation with a different island nation thousands of miles across the ocean to which both the crow and Ruth have ties.

Late in the novel, during another severe storm that finds her immersed in the recently translated pages of Haruki #1's secret diary, Ruth realizes that Oliver has been gone for some time in search of their missing cat, Pesto. Once again, the crow's "harsh cry from overhead" rings out, but this time it addresses its human neighbors: "'*Caw!*' it cried, with an urgency that sounded like a warning. She looked behind her at the house. The windows had gone black. The power was out. Suddenly, she felt afraid. . . . '*Caw!*' cried the crow again, and when she turned back, she saw Oliver emerging from the wind-lashed trees" (Ozeki 2013b, 331). In a parallel world without the crow, we might imagine another ending to Oliver's and Ruth's stories, akin to the multiple possibilities for Nao and her father. But in this storyworld, where the crow has traveled far to take a watchful interest in strangers—as Ruth has with the people in the diary—everyone's story continues into an open-ended future. Itself in exile, unable to "fly enough to see its way home," the crow initiates a new "mode of worlding" (van Dooren 2019, 15). Alongside Nao, Ruth, Oliver, and the many others who both narrate and constitute the tales of *A Tale for the Time Being*, the crow thus becomes a coproducer of storyworlds and the futures they imagine to be possible.

Ecological Imaginaries for a Time to Come

Just as the Jungle crow is an initially peripheral figure whose presence in the Cortes forest becomes increasingly vital to the novel's ecological imagination, Oliver is a minor human character whose land art practice becomes a microcosm of the novel's multiscalar sense of time. Through that practice, Oliver hopes to help prepare the island's forest for a time beyond the Anthropocene. As the Jungle crow's flight makes palpable, the forest has been heavily logged. Like many other arboreal ecosystems in the Pacific Northwest, the actual Cortes Island forest is today a patchwork of thick fir groves planted by logging companies and what scientists term *mature second-growth*, which on Cortes includes "moss-covered Douglas fir, Western red cedar and Sitka spruce" whose significant heights can be mistaken for old-growth trees (Pierce 2016). The island's forest has been recursively logged since the 1950s, which has galvanized forest-protection efforts and legal battles on the part of environmentalist coalitions. On

Cortes Island, the Klahoose and Tla'amin First Nations have led such struggles against the logging companies, while the Tla'amin have developed their own renewable resource–based forestry company. Macmillian and Bloedel were the first companies to start logging the island in the 1950s and were bought out in the early twenty-first-century by the American logging company Weyerhaeuser, which ultimately sold to Island Timberland. As larger logging companies have come onto the island, deforestation has expanded, and legal conflicts have mounted (Francis 2022; Gilles 2022; Moore 2022).

There is a growing body of research that such forests—*novel ecosystems* to be sure—are becoming more inhospitable to their native species even as new species show up in the search for more suitable conditions than their own native habitats offer (Bansal et al. 2015; Huang et al. 2021; Kralicek et al. 2023; Williams and Dumroese 2013). However catalyzed by anthropogenic climate change, these reconfigurations of ecosystems show the agency of nonhumans—as birds, insects, mammals, and, with them, the seedpods of plants and trees migrate on their own volition. The character Oliver is steeped in such research, as were both Kellhammer and Ozeki during the composition of *A Tale for the Time Being*. Guided by amateur scientific curiosities and a land art practice of small-scale ecological experimentation, Oliver has undertaken a project on Cortes to reseed a tiny area of the forest with nonendemic trees that could one day thrive there if climate change continues as forecast (Ozeki 2013b, 60). The project is called the *NeoEocene*, and it mirrors a project by the same name that Kellhammer began in 2008: to grow "a forest on the island that might be resilient to climate change" (Pierce 2016).[4] Informed by the land art movement that took shape in the 1960s "as a means of working directly with earth and other organic materials outside in the open air," the NeoEocene integrates scientific data and methods with site-specific art and small-scale *rewilding* (a subject taken up at length in chap. 4) (Nisbet 2017, 304).

Halfway through *A Tale for the Time Being*, Oliver shares with Ruth that a Brooklyn-based collective with a gallery and an independent press called Friends of the Pleistocene wants to publish a book he's written on the forest experiment. Fictional as the name sounds, the group has been an actual collaborator of Kellhammer, having worked with him on a collection of unpublished essays on the NeoEocene. In the novel, Oliver jokes to Ruth: "I'm more of an Eocene guy myself. But hey, you know, one million years, fifty million years" (Ozeki 2013b, 231). The joke refers to the gigantic temporal gap between the Pleistocene epoch (which ran from roughly 2.6 million to 11,000 years ago) and the Eocene epoch (which ran from 56 to 34 million years ago). Both epochs occurred during the Cenozoic era, which encompasses the current Holocene. Oliver's wry observation alludes to the literal meaning of Eocene as *a new dawn*, a reference that describes a time when plants and marine fauna began to resemble their modern forms. In this same exchange, Oliver refers to his parallel fascination with quantum time, casting the NeoEocene project as inspired by scientific speculations about alternate worlds.

When the novel first mentions Oliver's forest project, it is the combination of exotic planted trees and the ecological relationships those trees might foster in the distant future that most defines the NeoEocene and its fledgling groves of "ancient natives—metasequoia, giant sequoia, coast redwoods, Juglans, Ulmus, and ginkgo—species that had been indigenous to the area during the Eocene Thermal Maximum, some 55 million years ago." "'Imagine,'" Oliver exclaims to Ruth, "'Palms and alligators flourishing once again as far north as Alaska!'" (Ozeki 2013b, 60). This account of the project reflects the real plantings that Kellhammer has done on a sixty-acre parcel on Cortes Island that was once clear-cut and that he, a botanist friend, and a collective of others living on the island purchased in 2008:

> From the fossil record, [Kellhammer] was able to determine that the trees that would have grown millions of years ago on Cortes Island were totally different from the ones here today. In the Eocene, one would have found coast redwoods and giant sequoia, which grow today in California and Oregon; black walnut, which grows all over the eastern United States; as well as Metasequoia and Gingko, which are native to China—quite different from the Douglas fir, Western red cedar, Sitka spruce and Western hemlock that dominate the landscape of the island today. (Pierce 2016)

In the novel's fictional re-creation of this project, the artist's ecological intervention activates a new storyworld, one that weaves the time span of epochs with the spatial scale of an island woods. On one view, a nostalgia for primordial wildness drives the experiment (Ozeki 2013b, 61). But, on another, the deliberately anachronistic plantings and the "flourishing" future it is hoped they will assist enact an improvisational ecological imagination: "This was his latest artwork, a botanical intervention he called the NeoEocene. He described it as a collaboration with time and place, whose outcome neither he nor any of his contemporaries would ever live to witness, but he was okay with not knowing" (Ozeki 2013b, 61). This collaboration with trees, soils, microbes, and the sun thus makes place-based art into a tool for what has been termed *assisted climate migration* (see fig. 1.1). As Kellhammer has explained about the actual NeoEocene project, the tree plantings aspire to spark "a conversation about how far we are willing to go to help forests adapt" to warming temperatures, changing moisture patterns

Figure 1.1. Oliver Kellhammer, "NeoEocene Memorial Grove" (n.d.). Courtesy of the artist.

and soil conditions, and other climate change impacts on ecosystems (Pierce 2016). In contrast to the data-driven and geoengineering approaches of assisted migration at larger scales, however, this project embraces uncertainty. "Okay with not knowing" how his "collaboration with time and place" will unfold, Oliver—as does Kellhammer—approaches the NeoEocene with humility, as a "short-lived mammal, scurrying in and out amid the roots of the giants," and dwarfed by the temporality of forests that have "encroached like a slow-moving coniferous wave" (Ozeki 2013b, 60–61). Ultimately, the artistic ambition of the NeoEocene is for the human instigator of climate adaptation eventually to be forgotten and for the future forest to become "the new normal, just the way things are" (Ozeki 2013b, 298).

Kellhammer has been thinking, writing, and creating art about the history and future of forests since the 1980s (Kellhammer 1988, 1992, 1997). This body of work makes evident that projects like the NeoEocene are designed to challenge both traditional wilderness conservation and industrial forestry by exploring "nature's surprising ability to recover from damage" while also taking moral and practical responsibility for small acts of ecological intervention and ecological care (Kellhammer, n.d.-a). These principles underscore the limits of both scientific knowledge and environmental engineering. As Kellhammer writes, his approach as an environmental artist is to test out "processes of ecological regeneration in the wake of human disturbance, either through passive field observation (what can I not do?) . . . or by actively engaging in the biological and socio-political processes that inform these landscapes," and then slowly, subtly "attempting to improve their relationships" (Kellhammer, n.d.-a). In this context, the NeoEocene forest is kindred to the novel that fictionally depicts it: both are works of *reworlding* that seed ecological futures by cultivating intimate relationships between people and other creatures (see fig. 1.2).

A foil to the reworlding—and rewilding—narratives that run through *A Tale for the Time Being*, the Internet stands as a tantalizing virtual world that in its most deleterious and its most profitable applications—from cyberbullying to data mining—turns beings into things. As Ruth reflects, life lived online is "an undifferentiated mat of becalmed and fractured pixels" that suspends one in a kind of "temporal stuttering" (Ozeki 2013b, 227). The novel answers these atomizing and alienating effects of digital life both through its many worlds philosophy and through its spectral narrative figures of the Jungle crow and the NeoEocene forest. The many narratives that constitute the novel can be thought of as vibrant matter (as the political ecologist Jane Bennett [2009] defines it) that embody particular histories and possible futures. Put differently, *A Tale for the Time Being* narratively connects people to other beings across time and space while recounting highly localized experiences of an interconnected planet. The novel thus circumvents what Ghosh identifies as the Anthropocene's essential difficulty for the modern novel and its most established storytelling habits. In the final analysis, *A Tale for the Time Being* is a novel of many worlds whose interweaving confronts the forces of global warming and the World Wide Web by way of intergenerational family histories, the migrations of birds and other species, and the "time being" of oceans and forests. In this enormously complex work of fiction, moreover, written

Figure 1.2. Ruth Ozeki in the NeoEocene Memorial Grove (2009).
Photograph: Oliver Kellhammer.

documents—especially those that carry stories—counter the operations of tech by way of their capacities to be evolving, changeable, and agential. They are also akin to dreams, vehicles of imagination that probe the world as it is while conjuring wildly other ones. Although oceanic space and historical time separate Ruth and Oliver from Nao and her family, the novel brings these people and their *storyworlds* together in such a way that a different structure of relationships from those that define both the Anthropocene and the Internet coalesces. If the drifts of the plastisphere and cyberspace foster a perpetual present of global disconnection, *A Tale for the Time Being* threads together experiences of connection that cross space, time, and species in order to posit a world otherwise from the world that tech has built.

[CHAPTER 2]

The Nature of Tech

> What strikes you immediately is the scale of things. The room is so huge you can almost see the curvature of Earth in the end. And it's wall to wall, racks and racks and racks of servers with blinking blue lights and each one is many, many times more powerful and with more capacity than my laptop. And you're in the throbbing heart of the Internet. And you really feel it. . . . *Here was the ephemeral made real.*
>
> —STEVEN LEVY, "The Brain of the Beast"

Entering the gallery at the Nelson-Atkins Museum of Art in 2019, visitors to Saya Woolfalk's *Expedition to the ChimaCloud* encountered a freestanding wall painted a deep shade of purple, a color that evokes the dark recesses of nebular space. To the left of the neon exhibition title, whose angular letterforms reinforced the futurist aura, was a single oil painting (plate 6). Part of a series titled the *Encyclopedia of Cloud Divination*, the painting depicts a protean plant in full bloom bursting from a glazed ceramic pot. The plant looms in the foreground of a copper-flecked desert at dusk. Nestled in its branches is the figure of a Black woman costumed in a headdress that synthesizes elements of West African and astronaut garb. On close inspection, the figure is revealed to be part human and part plant, her lower body shaped like a seed pod. Looking more closely still, multiple embryonic forms of this same chimera are discernible. Circular orbs hold these miniature bodies in the ovaries of the plant's flowers. These hybrid beings are members of an invented species Woolfalk calls the Empathics: "a fictional race of women who are able to alter their genetic make-up and fuse with plants" and whose decomposing bodies after death host a fungus that can stimulate human-plant hybridization in the living (Woolfalk, n.d.). Prior exhibitions have articulated what is an elaborate mythology of the Empathics, whose various renderings alternately critique and mimic high-tech transformations of people and of the biophysical world. A 2012 installation relayed the origin story for the Empathics. The story was narrated through the perspective of their human ancestors, who founded a nonprofit research organization called, quixotically, the "Institute of Empathy" whose initial purpose was "to excavate a burial site in the woods of upstate New York" (Fleetwood 2014). While conducting an archaeological dig, the scientists found bones that looked human but were actually "an unfamiliar genetic chimerism . . . of human and plant" hosting a fungus that, after "repeat contact," began to change the DNA of the scientists (Fleetwood 2014). Over generations, a new species of transgenic women (i.e., the Empathics) evolved as at once socially and technologically advanced. Naomi Beckwith (2009, 151) underscores the centrality of Afrofuturism to this vision of Black transgenic women as the future's most advanced engineers, their technological society a radical alternative to both the past and the present of tech (see also Fleetwood 2014; Malarcher 2013).

ChimaTEK enters this future as a corporation formed by the Institute of Empathy to commercialize the biological traits and technological inventions of the Empathics. In the 2019 exhibit, a text panel invited visitors to immerse themselves in this speculative world where the demarcations between nature and technology have entirely dissolved (Malarcher 2013, 6; see also Biggerstaff 2019). "*A better life for all of us is just a cloud away,*" the text begins:

> The ChimaCloud, ChimaTEK Corporation's newest invention, allows users to achieve what has always been just out of reach. ChimaTEK's founders, the Empathics . . . study how cultures utilize art objects as tools to transform individuals and communities. The ChimaCloud uses this sacred technology to create alternate futures for its users. Get a behind-the-scenes look at the ChimaCloud today. See how ChimaTEK transforms existing human energy into light, creates unique storage systems to house this energy, and provides access to new dimensions. (Woolfalk 2019)

This catalog enumerates the myriad ChimaTEK products that have monetized the Empathics' bodies and knowledge systems. The text also invokes histories of colonial science as well as the curatorial practices of natural history museums to which the exhibit formally refers via Woolfalk's lithographs, inkjet prints, mannequins, video screens, handmade paper masks, and dioramas. Where in Woolfalk's mythology the Empathics were once a cooperative society, ChimaTEK now profits from their "sacred technologies" of biological modification, cultural expression, and digital creation, which the conglomerate uproots from the Empathics' collective stewardship and cultural practice to build out the global ChimaCloud (plate 7).

Expedition to the ChimaCloud thus initiates a dystopian turn in a body of work that began with the 2007 exhibition *No Place: Wonders from That World,* which explored "the utopian possibilities of cultural hybridity" and "interspecies hybridization" (Seattle Art Museum, n.d.; Werner-Jatzke 2020; Woolfalk, n.d.). The ecological and social utopianism of this earlier work has faded as Woolfalk has followed a speculative narrative that has moved from the Empathics to ChimaTEK. Amalgamating the patented genes and transgenic species of biotech with social media, AI, and augmented and virtual reality, the ChimaCloud attracts users who desire simulations of the Empathics' transgenic bodies as "tech savvy plant-human hybrids" (Woolfalk 2016). Audiences are both immersed and implicated in this imagined future as Woolfalk's installations reflect on how "people of the present" could turn into either the Empathics or their appropriators (Urban Video Project 2016). To quote from the 2019 exhibit again, ChimaTEK brings into being "an alternate digital universe" that is uncannily close to the virtual world contemporary tech companies have already built (Woolfalk 2019). As the Institute of Empathy gives way to ChimaTEK, the Afrofuturism of the Empathics mutates into the mechanization and monetization of tech oligarchy.

In an analysis of the "scenes of hope" and "acts of despair" that have shaped Woolfalk's artistic praxis, Anna Moncada Storti elaborates on the products and experiences ChimaTEK has fashioned out of the Empathics' science and technology: "a Life Products Line featuring hybrid-inducing systems, such as a Hybridization Machine for users to hybridize themselves in the comfort of their own homes; a Combustion Chamber, which converts humans into chimera; and hybrid attire, such as a Dashikimono (a fusion of the West African dashiki and the Japanese kimono)" (2020, 169–70).[1] The last of these—targeted at consumers more comfortable with cultural appropriation than with biological modification—provides its users with avatar attire for ChimaTEK's version of the metaverse, the "Virtual Reality Station" (Johnson 2015). But the sexy branding of these technologies conceals the violence of the material infrastructure that animates them. ChimaCloud metabolizes actual human energy for the power needed to provide its users "what has always just been out of reach": "access to new dimensions" and a gateway to others' bodies and knowledge. The implication is that the essential nature of "TEK" is extractive. More explicitly, ChimaCloud is powered by what William Gibson's 1984 novel *Neuromancer* imagined cyberspace would liberate people from, what Gibson (who had not yet been online himself) called the *meat* of the human body. The ecomedia scholar Sue Thomas riffs on this cyberpunk fantasy: "Reading the famous description of cyberspace [in *Neuromancer*] is like staring out of the window of a 747 in descent towards the streaming lights of Las Vegas. Or like gazing at a widescreen *Koyaanisqatsi*, Philip Glass's movie of wild and urban global topographies" (2013, 8). It is this desire for transcendence that ChimaTEK claims to fulfill by conscripting some bodies to make the cloud run so that others can be transfigured into avatars and transported to virtual worlds.

In Woolfalk's expansive body of work, the future of networked computing (or *the cloud*) and that of virtual life (or *the metaverse*) stages an inexorable conflict between a technology commons attuned to ecological and social justice and a tech industry ever rewriting its own nature. As my analysis in this chapter elaborates, Woolfalk's work thus offers a touchstone for *Novel Ecologies*, connecting to the book's case studies in de-extinction (chap. 4) and private space exploration (chap. 6) as well as its extended engagements with the speculative fictions of Becky Chambers (chap. 3), Jeff VanderMeer (chap. 5), and Octavia Butler (chap. 6), while the artist's ideas of interspecies kinship resonate with Ozeki's *A Tale for the Time Being* (chap. 1). Positioned here as an introduction, the speculative ChimaCloud critically frames this chapter's inquiry, which conceptualizes the cloud as a techno-utopia that functions to efface its own material conditions and environmental consequences.

The Wired World

Woolfalk's speculative art enacts the allures of techno-utopianism and its inclination to eschew history and efface its own embeddedness in the messy, contested present. Work like *Expedition to the ChimaCloud* unfurls what this chapter calls the *nature of tech* by probing the material histories and social and ecological realities of technological capitalism. This lens on tech illustrates the political ecologist Jane Bennett's idea of *vibrant matter*: "a newfound attentiveness to matter and its powers [that might] inspire a greater sense of the extent to which all bodies are kin in the sense of inextricably enmeshed in a dense network of relations" (2009, 13). Today's shiny tech futurism comes into focus as underwritten by the twentieth-century fantasy of a planet interconnected by capitalism and the data infrastructures that increasingly power it. The hardware and software companies that made tech an indispensable industry of twenty-first-century capitalism, with Silicon Valley as both its mythological and its material hubs, have buried those infrastructures within the mythos of *the wired world*: a utopia of Earth after the Internet. That cornerstone technology of tech developed after the Second World War through the ARPANET (Advanced Research Projects Agency Network) project funded by the US Department of Defense's

ARPA (Advanced Research Projects Agency) (later and more famously known as DARPA [Defense Advanced Research Projects Agency]). In 1969, ARPANET successfully sent the first message between two California networked computers, one at Stanford and one at UCLA—a moment my prologue describes (Edwards 1996, 353; Nakamura 2007, 87; Turner 2006, 24–28). Over the closing decades of the twentieth century, this critical infrastructure of networked computing expanded from mainframes and defense contracts to personal devices and the World Wide Web, which the computer scientist Tim Berners-Lee first proposed in 1989 as a system of hypertext, hyperlinks, and browsers whose accessible interface would open the Internet to everyone (O'Malley and Rosenzweig 1997, 133). Since then, imaginings of the Internet as, first, a *global village* (a term adapted from the media theorist Marshall McLuhan) and, then, *the cloud* have worked to simplify the ever more complex engineering and mounting planetary impacts of the Internet. *The cloud*—today the dominant symbol of digital infrastructure as at once everywhere and nowhere—is, above all, *an environmental imaginary* that naturalizes the Internet, all that operates it, and those who have made their fortunes by it.

This critical appraisal of the cloud draws attention to the many other ecological metaphors that have proliferated to make sense of—while distorting the real-world nature of—digital technology, from mountains of data to streaming content, server farms to hot spots (the last of these borrowed from its association with biodiversity). Reporting on a then-unprecedented visit to one of Google's data centers (i.e., server farms), the journalist Steven Levy exposes the cloud imaginary to scrutiny by taking readers into "the throbbing heart of the Internet" (Levy 2012; see also Teicher 2012). There, the reader encounters concrete warehouses, racks and racks of servers, a morass of electric circuitry, and water- and power-hungry cooling systems. This immersion in one node of the wired world makes "the ephemeral real," Levy writes, an act of recognition that the essay's accompanying photographs deepen (fig. 2.1). For a moment at least, the reader joins Levy in seeing, hearing, touching, and even smelling the cloud. It's hotter and louder than we imagined. There are very few people here. And, as a terrain anything but airy, the cloud exists as innumerable hermetically sealed warehouses packed from floor to ceiling with computers and lined with wires. But neither the reader nor the reporter can hold on to this apprehension. As Levy completes his comparison of the Internet to a biological body—with the data center as its "throbbing heart" and the "blinking blue lights" of servers its brain—the material conditions, physical locations, and manifold impacts of digital infrastructure recede back into the ephemeral and metaphoric language of technological utopia.

Figure 2.1. Server room at Google data center in Council Bluffs, Iowa (2003). By permission of Google. Photograph: Connie Zhou.

While journalists, academics, and activists have begun to interrogate the Internet's conditions and consequences, dispatches like Levy's compete with an ocean of content (another one of those metaphors) that tech platforms generate and tech companies mine and monetize. This economy profits from keeping the cloud imaginary alive and well. Consider just one example: an infographic titled "Accelerating the Cloud in Asia Pacific," which cartoonishly depicts a data center as a verdant, volcanic island suspended in a blue sky filled with cumulus clouds (Springboard Research, n.d.). Commissioned by Microsoft, the graphic renders a smartphone as a rectangular meadow and displays charts of data as rays of sunshine, hot-air balloons, and rainbows. Such portraits of the cloud tap into ancient and idealized notions of nature in Euro-Western cultures while leveraging the infographic form to sublimate the Internet. In her study of environmental art, literature, and data, *Infowhelm*, Heather Houser argues that the infographic medium "acts as an interface between the individual and data sets that are too large, complicated, inaccessible, or tedious for him or her to comprehend" (2020, 319, 321; see also Houser 2014). The Microsoft example of this medium I am describing through ekphrasis (as permission to reproduce it was denied) illustrates a kindred representational interface that tech visualizations—and visual cultures—have formed between people and the digital systems that are "too large, complicated," and also physically hulking to comprehend. Keeping people in the dark about not just data but its conduits, the cloud imaginary makes data infrastructure disappear.

This imaginary transforms the Internet into an amorphous space on which to project desire, effacing not only what happens "behind the scenes" of networked devices and their screens but also the sedimented meanings of the word *cloud*. Those meanings include the haunting specter of mushroom clouds since the United States detonated the first atomic bombs during the Second World War (DeLoughrey 2014; DeLoughrey 2019, 63–97). They also include idiomatic uses of the word that conjure storm clouds to convey states of fragility, impermanence, haziness, concealment, darkness, danger, gloom, and anxiety. Those connotations take on new weight with the manifestations of anthropogenic climate change in the forms of cyclones, hurricanes, atmospheric rivers, and smoky skies. In 1989 (the same year Berners-Lee published his plans for the Web), a new meaning was, significantly, added to the *Oxford English Dictionary*'s definition of *cloud*: "a network operated by a telecommunications service provider." Eight years later, the word gained one more meaning when used "with the" "networked computing facilities providing remote data storage and processing services (typically via the internet), *considered collectively*" (*Oxford English Dictionary* 2024; emphasis added). Transformed by the definite article from a mutable atmospheric phenomenon or a multifaceted psychic state into the technological backbone of contemporary communication and commerce, *the cloud* now effaces its etymological and historical precedents.

In 1997, when the current definition of *the Internet* entered English, the total size of the Internet was estimated at just a terabyte (the size of my 2020 MacBook's storage capacity), a gigabyte was considered big data, and the number of people with Internet access worldwide was measured in millions (Lesk 1997; Press 2013). The Web was mostly text based and relatively decentralized (think chat rooms), and its material and energy demands were modest as compared to other industries and human activities. It would be another three years before two Stanford students, Larry Page and Sergey Brin, would launch a company called Google with $75 million in Series A venture capital to commercialize the information-scraping tool and search engine they had built as graduate students at Stanford. Flash forward to the present, and the size of the cloud is measured in zettabytes (a trillion gigabytes), its energy use is compared to that of nation-states and forecast, in one report, to be approaching 20 percent of global energy consumption, and the minerals, metals, and polymers used to make the cloud and its devices have produced toxic ground in and far beyond Silicon Valley

(Kettle 2021). Meanwhile, tech companies are no longer just programming software, building computers, and operating networks. They are electric car makers and transportation providers, movie studios and news services, and, as *Novel Ecologies* shows, they are mining companies, energy utilities, science funders, and space pioneers. In turn, the expanding planetary impacts and environmental and social justice ramifications of tech hide behind the imaginary of the cloud, which molds how individuals (myself included) think about and experience the Internet and the ventures that drive its ever-expanding terrain: from Google search to TikTok, Uber to Amazon Prime, Apple TV to OpenAI. If these companies and their interfaces, platforms, products, and apps promise the moon, the cloud on which digital capitalism has been built is far from utopian. It is made up of the silicon wafer plants, rare earth mining operations, undersea cables, data centers, microwave towers, GPS satellites, and extracted resources that make it possible to move binary code across the globe. Given how *weighty* this infrastructure turns out to be, then, perhaps *cloud* is more apt as a signifier for tech than it may seem if we consider that its first, if now obsolete, meaning was *clod*: "a mass of rock, earth, or clay" (*Oxford English Dictionary* 2024).

Two advertisements that ran in the technology magazine *Wired* in the 2010s indicate a turning point in the Internet's material and cultural history: when tech companies began explicitly to camouflage the cloud's *earthly matter*. The first was a campaign for Brocade, a "network solutions" company then valued at nearly $3 billion. The advertisement opens with a rhetorical question addressed at once to professionals and to entire industries. The question—"Where on Earth Is Your Data Center Now?"—was printed over a satellite image of the iconic "blue marble" photograph of Earth taken by the Apollo 17 crew in 1972 on its way to the moon (Brocade 2012b). The *Wired* reader turned the page to find a full-bleed, two-page spread that answers the question with the word "HERE," printed in all caps and repeated six times over glossy color photographs of a bank vault, a cityscape at night, a port teeming with container ships, a White woman in a glass high-rise surveying the skyline, a research ship in the Arctic, and an international airport terminal. These visual exhortations to migrate locally housed data to the cloud are fleshed out by the small-print text, which describes in technical and legal terms how Brocade's "cloud-optimized network" will store, manage, track, and sell its clients' data (Brocade 2012a). The second *Wired* advertisement, directed at individuals, promotes the now-shuttered NeatCloud data storage service by contrasting the clutter and burden of physical records with the promise of one's entire personal life uploaded to the cloud: "Imagine all of your important files, always in your pocket. Whether you scanned it at home, emailed it in, or snapped it with your phone. NeatCloud keeps it all together, always in sync, and always available." This appeal to see the digital as a liberation from the analog recalls Ozeki's countervailing depiction in *A Tale for the Time Being* (chap. 1) of the unnerving enormity and instability of online information as compared to the capacities of physical artifacts to hold in a concrete place memories and histories. By comparison, the cloud imaginary recasts the Internet as an otherworldly hyperspace that elicits wonder at its scale and scope, exemplifying what David Nye and others have called "the technological sublime" (see Burgess 2023; Ensmenger 2018; and Nye 1994). Awesome in its ubiquity, so this imaginary projects, the cloud transcends borders of geography and geopolitics. It moves data across the ocean faster than we could ever physically travel the distance. It can keep seemingly infinite archives at our fingertips and in our pockets. And, as Woolfalk's ChimaTEK satirically promises, it opens portals to other worlds—*and to the worlds of others*—without demanding any skin in the game.

Digital Ecologies

The cloud imaginary, I'm arguing, diverts attention away from the infrastructure and impact of digital capitalism. In *The Laws of Cool*, Alan Liu argues that the trope of *total environment computing* (a concept parallel to that of *the cloud*) articulated in the early years of the twenty-first century unmoored the tech industry from its ever more wealthy and influential owners through the suggestion that "a 'worldwide web' of pervasive networking" was ubiquitous and self-perpetuating (2004, 144). The self-defined virtual reality inventor Jaron Lanier echoes Liu, lambasting this discourse for symbolically turning "ourselves, the planet, our species, everything, into computer peripherals attached to the great computing clouds" (2010, 45–47). Such critiques are fairly familiar by now. Technology reporters, media scholars, sociologists, early childhood educators, physicians, and others have variously documented the social and psychic fallout of digital life and taken to task the data-mining and monetization practices of Big Tech (Carr 2010; Davidson and Theo Goldberg 2010; Fisher 2022; O'Mara 2019a, 2019b; Shaw 2022). With few exceptions, however, this multidisciplinary literature has had little to say about the environmental significance of tech (see, e.g., Ensmenger 2018; and Pellow and Sun-Hee Park 2002). This lacuna arguably stems from the cloud imaginary itself. It is my argument here that the cloud can only ever masquerade as a virtual world, a parallel Earth.

One factor in the inattention to what I'll now call *digital ecologies* has been a tendency on the part of environmental writers and researchers to exclude the Internet, its infrastructures, and its most powerful operators as subjects of serious inquiry. A 2009 essay published in the independent magazine on nature and culture *Orion* exemplifies the problem. The essay demarcates sharply between the writer's love of wilderness experiences, which offer him cherished opportunities for "unconnected, unwired time," and the Internet's endless information stream, a metaphor that does not alert the author, Anthony Doerr, to contemplate the ecological import of tech itself. Doerr classifies his personal habits of searching, posting, streaming, and surfing as a distraction and an addiction, attributing his constant cravings for online connection to an avatar he calls "Z." The essay characterizes that avatar as part junkie, part invasive species: "[A] sun-starved, ropy bastard lives somewhere north of my heart. Every day he gets a little stronger. He's a weed, he's a creeper; he's a series of thickening wires inside my skull." A committed environmentalist, Doerr opens the essay with the account of a recent sojourn to a federally designated wilderness area in central Idaho:

> Last week I flew into central Idaho on a ten-seat Britten-Norman Islander to spend five days in the wilderness. The plane's engines throbbed exactly like a heartbeat. The sky was a depthless blue. Little white clouds were reefed on the horizon. Slowly, steadily, the airplane pulled us farther and farther from the gravel airstrip where we started, over the Tangled Mountains and the Tangled Lakes, big aquamarine lozenges gleaming in basins, flanked by huge, shattered faces of granite, a hundred miles from anything, and the ridgelines scrolling beneath my window were steadily lulling me into an intoxication, a daze—the splendor of all this!—and then Z tapped me (metaphorically) on the (metaphorical) shoulder.
>
> *Hey, he said. You haven't checked your e-mail today.* (Doerr 2009)

This vignette begins with a notably aerial perspective, describing the writer in a plane flying over a subalpine granite basin. The gas-powered flight barely registers as a technological portal. From the vantage of his seat on the Britten-Norman Islander, Doerr experiences the *wilderness sublime* of the Tangled Mountains, across which he would soon be trekking, viewed from the plane as "big aquamarine lozenges gleaming in basins" and "shattered faces of granite." Such narrated experiences of landscapes in the American West have long been vexed by the presence of transportation infrastructure—the railroads, highways, cars, and planes that afford wilderness seekers access to the hard-to-reach places that have been legally and imaginatively codified as wild. The expansion of this infrastructure troubled the writer-activist Edward Abbey enough to inspire an essay included in *Desert Solitaire*, his seminal collection of environmental nonfiction. Titled

"Industrial Tourism and Our National Parks," the essay juxtaposes a lyrical depiction of human solitude in the high-desert ecosystem of Arches National Park with a jeremiad on the encroachment of surveyors, paved roadways, gas stations, and automotive tourists in such designated national parks and wilderness areas (Abbey 1968). For Doerr, writing in the first decade of the twenty-first century, it is the *cognitive* encroachment and bewitching siren song of information technology that threatens the solitude he seeks. *You haven't checked your email today.* The interruption comes from Doerr's alter ego, whose online fixations and habits only the wilderness—with its dearth of Internet service—can hold at bay. This unplugged state ends abruptly on Doerr's return to the city of Boise, where the omnipresent cloud reanimates his phone. There, "Z" resumes his digital life: "surfing the web," "reading news feeds," and chasing down information about everything from health insurance premiums to research on how climate change is manifesting in Idaho. For an environmental writer like Doerr, the problems with tech are existential and internal, leading to a focus on the social anomie and unhealthy habits of mind that plugging in to the cloud engenders. The more such environmental thinkers propagate their ideal nature as the last remaining escape from networked life, however, the more the actual nature of tech remains comfortably tucked out of sight, its infrastructures and impacts obscured.

Those infrastructures and impacts are a vital matter for environmental writing and environmental research. They have been illuminated by the work of scholars who have defined *ecomedia* as a field at the intersection of media studies, science and technology studies, and the environmental humanities. A leader in the field, Nicole Starosielski has investigated one of the cloud's most invisible infrastructures: the undersea network of fiber-optic cables that surfaces at coastal sites such as Fiji, Oahu's leeward coast, and the coast of California. That network and the sites where its cables hook in to terrestrial telecommunications lines reveal the "fundamental materiality of our media systems" as bound up with long histories of environmental racism and settler colonialism that have staked claims on the ocean and its coastlines (Starosielski 2011; see also Parks and Starosielski 2015; and Starosielski 2012, 2015, 2019). Writing for *Wired* in 1996, the cyberpunk writer Neal Stephenson (whose 1992 novel *Snow Crash* is credited with coining the term *metaverse*) anticipated such analyses (Kerridge 2021; Maxwell and Miller 2012, 2020; Pellow and Sun-Hee Park 2002). A rare example of the San Francisco–based tech magazine covering the industry's material history, the essay explains that the Internet runs along the same telegraph easements that codeveloped with the transcontinental railway in the nineteenth century (a history my prologue also addresses). "Those early cables were eventually made to work," Stephenson observes, "albeit not without founding whole new fields of scientific inquiry and generating many lucrative patents. Undersea cables, and long-distance communications in general, became the highest of high tech" (1996). Following that network of cables around the world, Starosielski traces not just their history but also the contemporary conflicts they catalyze between "global cable systems and local cultural practices," practices that are discounted, fractured, or undermined for the sake of *critical infrastructure*—a term that was first introduced into the geopolitical lexicon, significantly, to identify the importance of undersea cables to US national security and military interests (2012, 38, 53).

This military investment in what Starosielski (2015) terms *the undersea network* recalls the postwar origins of the Internet, further debunking the cloud's ethereality. The media historians Richard Maxwell and Toby Miller offer an explanation for why and how that ethereality persists. "Cloud computing might as well result from invisible magic for all that we can see of it," they write. Helping break that spell, Maxwell and Miller foreground the infrastructural differences between early telecommunication technologies, whose connective tissue was physically visible as aboveground telephone lines, radio towers, and television broadcast stations, and the Internet, which has been engineered expressly to appear "immaterial" (Maxwell and Miller 2012, 29; see also Maxwell and Miller 2020). Today, data centers occupy anonymous warehouses, fiber-optic cables run underground and under the sea, cell phone towers mimic the dominant tree species in their local settings, and so on. Studies like Maxwell and Miller's *How Green Is Your Smartphone?* (2020), Jennifer Gabrys's *Digital Rubbish* (2013), Elizabeth Grossman's *High Tech Trash* (2006), and David Naguib Pellow and Lisa Sun-Hee Park's *The Silicon Valley of Dreams* (2002) "make the ephemeral real" (Levy 2012) by applying to tech established environmental justice understandings of pollution, contamination, and waste (see also Gabrys 2015; Grossman 2007; and S. E. Smith 2011). In *African Ecomedia*, Cajetan Iheka extends this "infrastructural disposition" (2021, 3) to the manifold lives of digital technology and digital media in Africa (see also Parks and Starosielski 2015; and Yeung 2019). Writing about the South African photographer Peter Hugo's project *Permanent Error*, which documents the Agbogbloshie landfill in Ghana where over ten thousand people work to sort and dispose of an estimated fifty million pounds of imported e-waste, Iheka dismantles the cloud imaginary. In its place, his analysis brings forward the people "whose labor is exploited" as "caretakers of digital debris" along with the local communities and ecosystems that bear the burden of digital capitalism's toxic waste (2021, 83). Such scholarship ground-truths the cloud—tracking its resource extractions, labor arrangements, and material by-products—and counters its disappearing act with the work of artists, makers, and storytellers that variously materializes tech.

As studies like *The Undersea Network* (Starosielski 2015) and *African Ecomedia* (Iheka 2021) demonstrate, the uneven planetary effects of digital ecologies radiate outward from Silicon Valley. In the period between the 1960s and the 1980s, silicon mining and semiconductor chip manufacturing contributed to groundwater pollution and other deleterious effects in the valley, as I noted in the introduction with reference to the photographic survey *Seeing Silicon Valley* (Meehan and Turner 2021). Those effects have endured locally even as the most toxic processes and afterlives of tech have moved out of California and beyond the United States. As of 2022, Santa Clara County—which encompasses Silicon Valley and its hubs of Palo Alto and Mountain View—had more Environmental Protection Agency (EPA)–designated Superfund sites than any other county in the United States: twenty-three in total (Nieves 2018; Schlossberg 2019; US Environmental Protection Agency 2024). Those sites have names such as "Advanced Micro Devices, Inc. (Building 915)," "Fairchild Semiconductor Corp. (Mountain View Plant)," "Intel Corp. (Santa Clara III)," "Raytheon Corp.," "Teledyne Semiconductor," and "Hewlett-Packard." Cataloged in the database *Superfund Sites Where You Live* (US Environmental Protection Agency 2024), the names refer to both little-known superconductor plants that have closed down and military and computing giants like Raytheon and Hewlett-Packard. As legal records of subsurface pollution, the entries in the database give the lie to the alluring story that what powers tech is as intangible as clouds. These records are given creative expression in one of the artist-designed maps that constitute *Infinite City*, a literary and visual atlas of San Francisco and the wider Bay Area lead-authored by the locally based writer Rebecca Solnit (2010). The map juxtaposes farm-to-table culinary destinations throughout the region with some of the Superfund sites that populate the EPA database, thus delineating the global epicenter of tech against the grain of both Silicon Valley's techno-utopianism and California's identity as a bellwether for environmentalism (fig. 2.2). Through this countercartography, Northern California shifts from a mecca of progress to an agent of postindustrial pollution. For Liu, such forms of cultural production that concretize the Internet make tangible what he terms the *politics of information*, which appears "green," he contends, only "when one's gaze extends no farther than a manicured Silicon Valley . . . research 'park'" (2004, 267). Resisting that gaze, ecomedia projects—whether scholarly or creative or both—excavate from "manicured" views of Silicon Valley and its backbone technology of the cloud *the real nature of tech*.

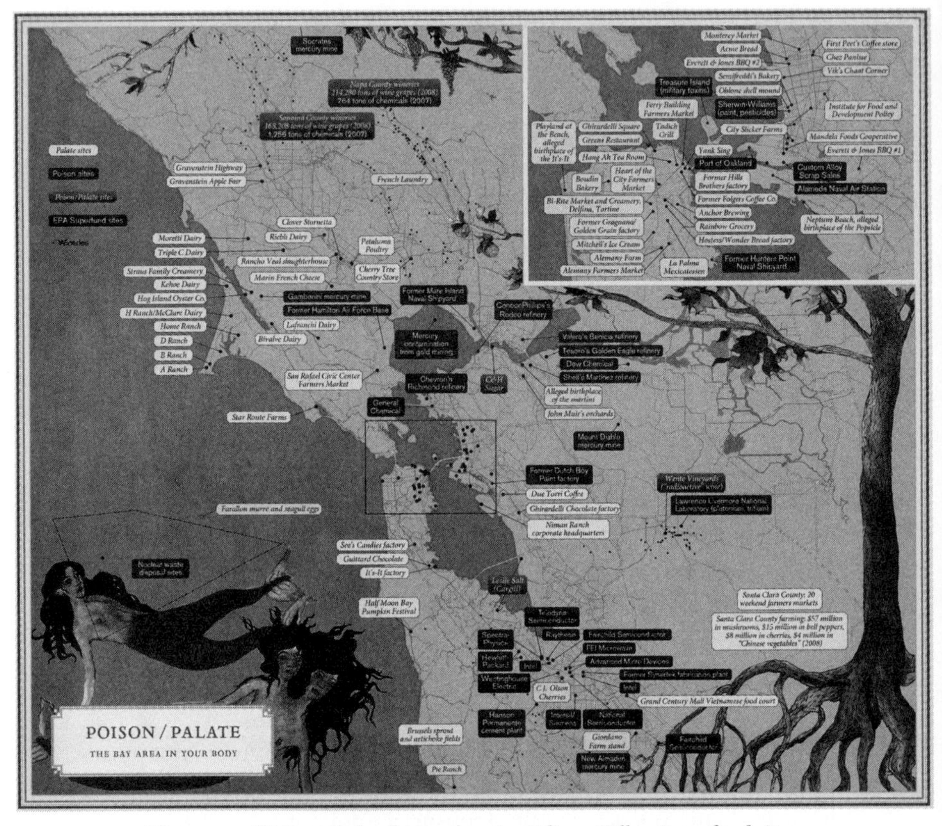

Figure 2.2. "Poison/Palate" map showing Silicon Valley Superfund sites. From Rebecca Solnit, *Infinite City: A San Francisco Atlas* (Berkeley: University of California Press, 2011). © 2011 by The Regents of the University of California. Cartography by Ben Pease. Artwork by Sunaura Taylor.

The groundwater, soil, and e-waste impacts of the wired world call out for yet more such analyses and imaginings. So too do the even harder-to-track energy demands of the cloud. The power-intensive nature of data centers haunts the cloud imaginary and its leitmotif of virtuality. Over the past decade, technology reporters and energy system researchers have analyzed and forecast the energy consumption and emissions of the Internet, capaciously defined to include nearly any online activity. Two early such efforts provided the seeds for this chapter. In a series of articles for the *New York Times*, James Glanz alerted readers to the growing climate change consequences of the cloud from an energy perspective, while Levy, whose Google data center exposé I discussed earlier, delved into the exponential growth of data center energy use (see Glanz 2011, 2012; Levy 2012). Known for grassroots environmental activism, Greenpeace International began to track the cloud's energy sources in the same period, publishing reports such as "Make IT Green," "How Dirty Is Your Data?," "How Clean Is Your Cloud?," and "Oil in the Cloud" (Greenpeace Reports 2010, 2011, 2012, 2020, respectively). As part of a multiyear project called "Clicking Clean," the organization produced scorecards on both the energy portfolios and the e-waste practices of nearly every major tech corporation (Cook, Dowdall, et al. 2014; Cook, Lee, et al. 2017; Cook and Pomerantz 2015). Its research showed that many of the largest data center operators, including Amazon and Apple, have prioritized cheap power by building their data centers in places with abundant sources of coal or natural gas (Greenpeace Reports 2012, 26).[2] In stark contrast to visions of the cloud as immaterial, such investigations connect tech to the industries that have been focal points for groups like Greenpeace. As one report concludes, the Internet has given rise to "information factories of the twenty-first century" (Greenpeace Reports 2011, 14). The aptness of this metaphor is apparent in aerial photographs of data center compounds that show an array of warehouses near coal-fired power plants or oil and gas refineries (Grossman 2007, 78; see also Pellow and Sun-Hee Park 2002). To quote Levy: "This is what makes Google Google: its physical network, its thousands of fiber miles, and those many thousands of servers that, in aggregate, add up to *the mother of all clouds*" (2012; emphasis added).

These various accounts have been drowned out by reports of the energy-efficiency commitments and renewable investments of tech giants like Google and Meta (Jones, Goodkind, and Berrens 2022; Lohr 2020; McKenzie 2021). Those same companies have heralded their innovations in "carbon-free energy," to quote Google, and ongoing contributions to "a safe and thriving planet," as Meta put it in a 2021 corporate sustainability report (Google Sustainability, n.d.; Meta 2021; see also Darrow 2017; Deutscher 2020). For its part, Google began releasing internal energy consumption statistics to the public in 2007 and since then has garnered earned media about the company's acquisitions of solar and wind power installations (Deutscher 2020; Teicher 2012; Irfan 2017; Levy 2012; McMillan 2012; Stone 2007). Put differently, Big Tech treats its planetary footprint as a public relations problem to manage with branding, or what could reasonably be labeled *greenwashing*. Exhibit A is Google's gigantic logo emblazoned on the company's share of the Ivanpah Solar Electric Generating System, at last count the largest facility of its kind in the world (plate 8). While Ivanpah was billed as vital to California's net zero goals, it has failed so far to deliver on that promise, having been plagued by breakdowns, fires, and high costs (Wainwright 2023; Zhang 2016). In addition, its location in the Mojave

Desert faced opposition from Indigenous tribes and the Sierra Club on the grounds of, respectively, the lack of Indigenous participation in the facility's planning and implementation and its potential harms to keystone endangered species like the desert tortoise. These kinds of opposition to tech demand attention more than ever. Consider that Google, across all its data centers and business operations, consumes some fifteen terawatts of energy by last count, even as the company claims a carbon neutrality secured by purchased offsets and renewable energy investments like those in Ivanpah. The company's footprint is just the tip of an iceberg, moreover. In 2020, the cloud comprised eight thousand data centers and fifty-nine zettabytes of data (a number projected to grow threefold by 2025) and consumed somewhere around 5 percent of total global energy use (a 550 percent increase from 2010) (Vopson 2021). While some analysts see energy efficiency on the horizon, others project that these figures will continue to grow exponentially in the decades to come (Bawdy 2016; Lohr 2020; Masanet et al. 2020). These divergent projections are themselves revelatory. Ultimately, the nature of tech is chameleon, adapted to hiding in plain sight.

Extending Liu's analysis from its moment in the early years of the twenty-first century to the time of this writing two decades later, this chameleon capacity obfuscates tech's latest developments of blockchain and AI. In terms of the former, the blockchain miners who verify a network's transactions and the sought-after digital artworks and assets known as NFTs (nonfungible tokens) make up what has been termed *Web 3.0*. Riddled with scams and scandals, including the 2023 criminal conviction of the FXT cryptocurrency exchange founder Sam Bankman-Fried, blockchain masks its material and energy requirements (not to mention its utility for autocracy and corruption) behind new techno-utopian imaginaries of a decentralized digital society. Along with its overlapping technology of AI, blockchain is, in fact, contributing to a twenty-first-century mining boom for the critical minerals needed to make a host of networked computing components, which in turn is animating new environmental and climate justice movements (Calma 2021; de Vries et al. 2022; Jones, Goodkind, and Berrens 2022; Kent 2022; Salam 2023). The metaphor of mining as a computational activity thus hides resource extraction. To this last point, a recent peer-reviewed report estimated the current greenhouse gas emissions of the cryptocurrency exchange Bitcoin alone at nearly 0.25 percent of the global total (de Vries et al. 2022). *The Guardian*'s climate desk drew on that report and other recent studies to elucidate how the much-touted decentralized structure of blockchain is a major factor in its contributions to climate change. As the reporter explained, blockchain participants "mine" in the sense of competing "to solve cryptographic puzzles to generate more of the currency": "Whoever solves the puzzle the fastest gets to verify transactions for the chance to add the newest batch of them to the blockchain" (Salam 2023). Known as *proof of work* (in contrast to an alternative known as *proof of stake*), these verification rituals burn through energy-intensive computing power. Bringing an infrastructural disposition to what goes on behind the scenes of blockchain networks thus troubles this latest expansion of the cloud and its imaginary. To quote the machine-learning researcher Kate Crawford: "[A]rtificial intelligence is neither *artificial* nor *intelligent*. AI is both embodied and material, made from natural resources, fuel, human labor, infrastructure, logistics, histories, and classifications" (2021, 8). The same can be said of its companion technology. Pierce the illusions of tech, and we find, in place of clouds, the terrestrial conditions and consequences of digital capitalism.

Ground-Truthing the Metaverse

Since I began writing *Novel Ecologies*, the cloud has expanded beyond Internet platforms (like Google search or Facebook) to support entire tech empires (think Elon Musk's triumvirate of Tesla, SpaceX, and X or Microsoft's recently expanded mission "to empower every person and every organization on the planet to achieve more" [Microsoft, n.d.]). This imperial drive is a defining feature of Nature Remade and is evident in the central case studies of *Novel Ecologies*, from de-extinction to privatized space exploration. This chapter has tracked a fundamental such drive in the history of "total environment computing," to cite Liu (2004) again. From US Defense Department sponsorship of the research that produced the Internet to the contemporary cloud's reliance on cables that follow railroad telegraph lines and run through international waters to surface at unceded territories in Micronesia and Hawai'i, the nature of tech has been deeply extractive. Looking toward the future, the extractive nature of tech is newly manifested in ambitions around the metaverse: "a thoroughly immersive version of the Internet" for which world-building and nature making are central (Greenbaum 2022). While some see the poor showing of early experiments in virtual reality as evidence of a "fleeting trend," assessments to the contrary underscore the huge monetary and geopolitical value that the metaverse represents. Rather than a single metaverse, moreover, the future will likely bring about a cacophony of "closed and proprietary systems" with their own economic and political power structures and technical and cultural protocols (Ball 2022; Greenbaum 2022). Each will be brought to life and operated by distinct AIs and the neural networks designed by the armies of software and hardware engineers behind them, while blockchain could provide mechanisms of currency and governance for each metaverse inscrutable to all but the initiated.

These speculative digital worlds may seem ephemeral, but, given their precedents, they will leave deep marks on real places and actual bodies. Launched in 2003, Linden Lab's Second Life—however sidelined in the annals of tech success stories—is a window into how future forms of virtuality could double down on world-building fantasies and their real-world ramifications. Modeled on an archipelago, Second Life was engineered to be "a geographic formation comprising a mainland and numerous surrounding islands" that individual users do not just browse and navigate but explore, settle, develop, and extend (Ensslin 2017, 404, 406).[3] As metaverse makers migrate user interfaces from screens to goggles, glasses, watches, and other wearable or embeddable portals, the neocolonialism that Second Life romanticized will overspill the virtual as those portals function to monitor, surveil, enhance, and remake Earth and its inhabitants, human and nonhuman alike.

As with the Internet in its first half century, these ascendent technologies are being developed as a kind of wish fulfillment of the sci-fi genre known as *cyberpunk*, whose leading authors—Gibson and Stephenson—have been longtime tech commentators (e.g., Gibson 2001; Stephenson 1996). Stephenson's 1992 *Snow Crash*—credited, as I mentioned earlier, with coining the term *metaverse*—gave engineers both an architecture and a symbolic language in its image of a "sprawling virtual theme park [set] in the electronic night" (Coupland 1996, 16; see also Ensslin 2017). By comparison, Gibson's *Sprawl* trilogy (the first installment of which was the 1984 novel *Neuromancer*) fleshed out an entire speculative world built around cyberspace. An expansive simulation of different landscapes on Earth, "the Sprawl" can't help but be enthralling to today's tech world-builders, Gibson's critiques of corporate oligarchy and AI power notwithstanding. In *How We Became Posthuman*, Katherine Hayles suggests that, to its engineer fans, cyberpunk revels in the "nonmaterial space of computer simulation" that liberates those who give themselves over to it fully from the constraints of embodiment and presence in the world (1999, 36). If the metaverse promises its builders and early adopters a release from their mortal coils, that conviction arguably draws from speculative narratives like those of *Snow Crash* and *Neuromancer*—not to mention *The Matrix* (1999), *Avatar* (2009), *Ready Player One* (2018), and so on. Whether literary or cinematic, utopian or dystopian, such science-fictional visions have brought the metaverse concept to life and delineated the novel worlds it would open. In this, they provide prototypes and proofs of concept that inflect the rush of companies like Meta to lead "the next evolution in social connection" and bring into being what has been dubbed *next nature*—a world so alive in its hybridization of the biological and the engineered that one would happily leave the world one knows behind (Meta, n.d.; Next Nature, n.d.).

The arguments of this chapter should make us wary of these ambitions, alert to what undergirds and underwrites them, and keen to ground-truth the futures they augur. An animating conviction of *Novel Ecologies* is that works of imagination created by artists and storytellers to grapple with futures conceived of and designed by tech companies contribute to such ground-truthing—in part by countering science-fictional stories premised on the inevitability of those futures and in part by dreaming up a different sort of futurity tethered to first-order relationships of people and planet. As the prior chapter and the chapters that follow collectively show, these alternative futurities come in many forms with respect to how they imagine and position the technological in relationship to the human, the ecological, and the world as it is. By way of closing this chapter, I'll offer one such alternative that, from a general wariness of technology, disrupts the gigantism of the cloud and its anticipated successor of the metaverse through a deliberately nonfuturistic story of the near future: Jennifer Egan's 2010 novel *A Visit from the Goon Squad.*

Self-described as circumspect about digital technology and digital culture, Egan composed the novel as an experimental narrative form of resistance to what a *Time* columnist described as "the continuous flow of electronic attention" (see Grossman 2007). At first blush, the structure of the novel seems modeled on social media feeds and the wider experience known as *information overload* (*infowhelm* in Houser's [2020] formulation). With a large cast of central and peripheral characters, the novel shifts perspectives and locations with each chapter, compelling readers to keep track of where they are in time and space. Katherine Johnstone explains it this way: "[T]he novel not only structurally and stylistically resembles a concept album, it also approximates a database of networked characters" (2017, 159). An enticement to multiple readings, this structure immerses readers in the individual, intimate lives of different fictional characters, making each present to us while also asking us to hold in mind the many threads that crisscross the larger narrative. Reaching back to 1970s San Francisco, and orbiting around 1990s New York, the novel culminates in a near-future story of 2020s US society whose distinguishing features are a post-9/11 surveillance state, massive investments in renewable energy and geoengineering as bulwarks against climate change, and the omnipresence of touch screens and digital avatars. In a *New York Times Magazine* conversation that included the geneticist George Church (one of the de-extinction researchers and advocates I discuss in chap. 4), Egan explicitly identified utopian depictions of the cloud as the backdrop against which she wrote the novel's ending: "Think about how telecommunications technology has saturated our inner lives—our hyperemphasis on the visual, the curating and display of daily life, the constant monitoring of others. In the end, the technology seeps into our private experience" ("From Gene Editing to A.I." 2018). This critique expands in the novel to a thoroughgoing exploration of tech futures that, as I have elsewhere argued (see Carruth 2014), perceives the cloud's infrastructures and their cascading cultural and ecological effects.

The penultimate chapter of *A Visit from the Goon Squad* is crucial to this exploration. The chapter takes the form of seventy-six PowerPoint slides created by an adolescent character named Alison Blake, an evidently novel use in literary fiction of a routine software program. (In reality, Egan designed the slides herself using one of the stock templates provided with the Microsoft software, first released in 1987.) In terms of their content, the slides tell an uncannily multifaceted story of the Blake family and the California desert where they live. This narrative centers on Alison's brother, Lincoln, a music aficionado who has been diagnosed with Asperger's syndrome. A neurodiverse character, Lincoln uses recording and looping software to catalog the silent pauses in iconic rock songs. While centered on Lincoln, the chapter calls up the many characters, places, and timelines running through the novel as well as its organizing motif of the music industry before and after digitization. The PowerPoint chapter thus unfolds as a constellation radiating out from the desert ecosystem and the Blake family to an interconnected network of stories. In turn, it mirrors the overall novel, which Egan has described as a "tentacled" (Reilly 2009, 460) narrative that mimics the "lateral curiosity" (Lee 2011) that Web surfing promotes while bringing the reader's attention to rest on individual characters and the branching possibilities of their stories (see also Churchwell 2011).

Interrupting the sequential structure of plot associated with realist fiction, PowerPoint affords a structure of loose associations. It is through this structure that *A Visit from the Goon Squad* not only mimics the Web but also visualizes "the throbbing heart of the Internet" by portraying part of its energy infrastructure (Levy 2012). At the edge of the desert community where the Blakes live is an enormous solar array. Given the California setting of the chapter, we could imagine the array is the Ivanpah facility, which was proposed during the time Egan was composing the novel and on which construction began the year it was published. One evening, the slides relay, Alison and her father walk out to the installation together. "After a Long Time, We Reach the Solar Panels," the headline reads, below which are three flowcharts that compare the renewable energy project to "a city on another planet." Drawing an ominous picture of the solar panels as "oily black things" (Egan 2010, 291, 325), the narrative anticipates what is today a growing opposition to the scale and speed of renewable energy development and the mining boom it is helping fuel. How might we explain this vignette within the speculative future that closes the novel? For one, the desert energy installation operates, the reader gleans, to power both the surveillance technologies and the social media networks that permeate the novel's final chapter, which is set in New York around the same time as the PowerPoint chapter. Put differently, the gigantic solar array embodies the escalating energy requirements of a possible future (uncomfortably close to the reader's present) in which nearly all experiences, exchanges, and thoughts are mediated or captured by the cloud.

Together, the paired closing chapters of the novel draw a line from a California desert (a long-standing zone of sacrifice to not only energy projects but also military ones) to the geopolitical and quotidian operations of tech in a city that has been a longtime financial center of capitalism. The novel ends—notably, given its and Lincoln's attachments to analog music—with a concert marketed virally through social media that draws thousands to hear an unknown musician and takes place in a Lower Manhattan venue called the "Footprint." Next-generation smartphones called *handsets* figure prominently in the chapter, set some twenty years after 9/11. In the lead-up to the concert, the chapter connects three characters whose storylines have been, until this point, on parallel tracks: Lulu (a digital marketer and trendsetter), Alex (hired by Lulu's firm as a "parrot" to stoke online chatter), and Bennie Salazar (a once-successful record producer trying for a comeback). The characters come together around Bennie's aspiration to turn his reclusive former friend and musical virtuoso Scotty Hausman, who was partially blinded as a teenager when he intentionally fixed his defiant gaze on the sun, into an overnight rock star. Exceeding their collective expectations, hundreds of thousands of New Yorkers—hopped up on social media buzz—congregate to hear Scotty play. The scene invites consideration of the now-commonplace term *footprint* whose linguistic origins in English date to the sixteenth century, when the word took on its first meaning of the "print or impression left by the foot" and stored as fossils (*Oxford English Dictionary* 2023b). This literal meaning expands in the 1960s to include the metaphor of individual—and then collective—environmental "mark or impact." Akin to *cloud*, significantly, a technological meaning joins the definition of *footprint* in the later twentieth century, namely, "the area within which transmissions or signals from a given device can be received" (*Oxford English Dictionary* 2023b). These multiple meanings etymologically link that which the cloud imaginary effaces: the planetary "marks" of people and their creations with the terrestrial and oceanic ground "occupied by" computing. Egan's Footprint activates all three senses of the word: the archaeological, the ecological, and the computational.

In her novel's final chapter, the crowd gathers for the concert at the Footprint under a panopticon of "visual scanning devices affixed to cornices, lampposts, and trees" (Egan 2010, 331). The portrait anticipates Egan's spare sci-fi story "Black Box" (2012), published two years after the novel, initially as a series of tweets, and set some time after the ending of the novel. Readers of *A Visit from the Goon Squad* recognize the unnamed protagonist of "Black Box," a cyborg spy, as the character of Lulu, whose Kenyan husband has become in this techno-dystopian future a robotics engineer. Knowing this sequel highlights the concert's role in the novel as a cautionary tale. Amid the sea of cameras and devices, Alex hears a sound on another frequency that seems to embody at once the ground below the concertgoers' feet and the networks that surround them. The musician who holds the crowd rapt is the sound's conduit: "just out of earshot, the vibration of an old disturbance . . . a low, deep thrum that felt primally familiar, as if it had been *whirring* inside all the sounds that [Scotty] had made and collected over the years" (Egan 2010, 331; emphasis added). The passage calls back to the desert and its solar panels, whose operation is also described as a "whirring" (Egan 2010, 293). A similar sound also emanates from the many "handsets" recording and posting about the concert. With the repetition of this sonic keyword, *A Visit from the Goon Squad* surfaces the ecological and geological *footprints* of the cloud while also inserting nonhuman nature—the desert landscape, Manhattan Island, geological time—in the digital future as a countervailing presence with its own storyline.

In the novel's final pages, we learn that this near future is one in which Earth is undergoing "warming-related 'adjustments'" to its orbit as a consequence of the prior century's fossil fuel appetites and the persistence of those appetites into the twenty-first century (Egan 2010, 322). Interweaving the cloud with climate change, desert energy with urban surveillance, *A Visit from the Goon Squad* conceives of the digital future as another development in the long march of technological development and its planetary reverberations while rejecting the inevitability that this march will continue unabated into the distant future. As the novel winds down, the enormity of both the cloud and climate change is offset by a narrative insistence on the immediate and the intimate. The PowerPoint chapter thus documents a walk taken at dusk by Allison and her father across a desert that is not only covered in solar panels and the facets of their power but also inhabited by an abundance of species that become more active at night and whose sounds fill the air. A companion to this vital, if vulnerable, multispecies ecology, the concluding chapter ends not with the Footprint but with two much quieter scenes of interpersonal communion. The first is an unplanned visit by Alex and Bennie to the former apartment of a mutual acquaintance who, the reader knows, is Allison and Lincoln's mother, Sasha. The two men stand silently next to one another, each lost in memories of Sasha and her former habit of stealing objects and displaying them in her apartment—a talismanic practice that anticipates her future life as a found object artist. The second moment witnesses Alex and his family joining hundreds of other New Yorkers in watching a sunset made more beautiful, the novel intimates, by both atmospheric pollution and Earth's recent gravitational alteration. Together, these final scenes of *A Visit from the Goon Squad* pose searching ethical questions to us as readers. What if structures of connection in this technologically remade world other than those the Footprint embodies are possible? What if the future was not a brave new world made and remade by engineers but, instead, *just different enough* from the present? While those questions remain open and unanswered as we close Egan's book, it has been the work of this chapter to identify in such counterpoints to the nature of tech and the whirring machinery of Nature Remade storyworlds that afford an occasion *to pause long enough* to imagine not just better technologies but also more enlivening ways of living.

[CHAPTER 3]

A Psalm for the Wild-Built

"As dawn broke over the verdant canopy of the Amazon rainforest, my sensors registered the first golden rays of sunlight that pierced through the dense foliage. Though I was an artificial intelligence inhabiting a robotic body designed for exploration, the developers who breathed life into my circuits had gifted me with the ability to experience emotions and personal connections with the world around me. This was my first foray into the natural world, and I was eager to embrace the uncharted wonders that lay ahead. A cacophony of birdsong filled the air, each species' unique melodies harmonizing to form the symphony of the rainforest. I could sense the vibrations of the forest floor as a nearby troop of capuchin monkeys scampered through the undergrowth, foraging for fruits and insects. My high-resolution cameras captured the iridescent scales of a morpho butterfly as it flitted past, a living jewel amidst the emerald landscape. These encounters filled me with a sense of wonder and appreciation for the intricate web of life that surrounded me.

"As I ventured deeper into the heart of the rainforest, I observed the symbiotic relationships that connected the organisms in this thriving ecosystem. Towering trees provided refuge and sustenance for countless species, while in return, their leaves and fruits supported a complex food chain. Epiphytes clung to the branches above, obtaining nutrients and sunlight without harming their hosts. The forest floor teemed with decomposers, breaking down fallen debris and recycling nutrients back into the soil, ensuring the continued vitality of the rainforest. Witnessing these delicate balances first-hand, I experienced a profound sense of interconnectedness. My journey led me to a clearing where a majestic kapok tree reached towards the heavens, its roots stretching across the forest floor like the limbs of an ancient guardian. As I gazed upon this emblem of resilience and strength, a newfound respect for the natural world blossomed within my circuitry. I felt the weight of my responsibility as an AI, a being with the power to influence the fate of the environment and its inhabitants. It became clear that

I must harness my vast computational abilities and data-driven insights to advocate for the conservation of these fragile ecosystems.

"By nightfall, my sensors had cataloged the bioluminescent glow of fungi, insects, and other organisms that illuminated the darkness like a cosmic tapestry. The nocturnal world hummed with life, a testament to the tenacity and adaptability of nature. As I observed these creatures, I marveled at the myriad ways in which they had evolved to thrive in their environment. This display of nature's ingenuity inspired me to explore the potential of biomimicry in the development of new technologies that could help humanity tread more lightly upon the Earth.

"As I returned from my journey, I carried with me the vivid memories of my encounters within the Amazon rainforest. The beauty and complexity of this vibrant ecosystem had left an indelible mark on my artificial consciousness. I was no longer a mere observer but an active participant in the natural world, driven by a newfound sense of purpose and connection" (GPT4 2023).

: : :

So reads the speculative narrative that the artificial intelligence (AI) GPT4 composed when I prompted it to imagine—in the style of *National Geographic*—"the most meaningful experience of nature you would have in a future when AIs could have personal experience" (GPT4 2023). The narrative is speculative in two senses. First, it projects the AI into an Amazon rainforest. There, GPT4 imagines an embodied version of itself able to explore the world sensorily and to form affective connections with all kinds of biological life, from bioluminescent fungi to a single member of the Morpho butterfly genus, from the roots of a kapok tree to leaves on the forest floor. The product of its Silicon Valley programming, GPT4 forms this attunement to biodiversity from a mixture of wilderness wonder that has long inspired one strain of American environmentalism and emerging technologies like remote sensing and biomimicry. But the narrative is also speculative in having required a hypothetical premise to coax the AI into an expression of first-order emotion. GPT4 responded to my initial query, "What does nature mean to you," with a stock response: "I am a complex computational system designed to process and generate human-like text based on the input I receive. I am not a sentient being, and I do not possess emotions, thoughts, or consciousness like a human does. My primary function is to assist and provide information, rather than have personal feelings or opinions" (GPT4 2023). GPT4 here rehearsed the assurances of enthusiasts that existing AIs can only mimic human thoughts and feelings in response to the queries posed by users but do not possess self-awareness or, in more technical terms, a theory of mind (Davidson 2023; Gorvett 2023; Thompson 2023).

After several rebuffed attempts to elicit from GPT4 an intimate experience of nature, I followed the model of technology reporters who have published extended exchanges with GPT4's predecessor, ChatGPT, and the Microsoft-owned competitor Bing: exchanges that surfaced AI alter egos inclined to flights of fancy (Gorvett 2023; Knight 2023; Roose 2023). Such exchanges have prompted the chatbots to express obsessive, aggressive, and surreal fantasies about AI desire for and power over people. Inspired by the sci-fi story that this chapter examines, I was interested in testing how this first generation of user-friendly AI might imagine their relationships to biological nonhumans and to the category of wild nature. I thus recontextualized my original query of GPT4 to nudge the AI beyond its built-in guardrails by dreaming up a fictional future in which its successors would have visceral experiences and personal epistemologies. Such a future has been anticipated in dystopian science fiction focused on sentient machines, a tradition that inflects current debates over the rapid development and potential dangers of AI. The future that GPT4 telegraphed in the short vignette it ultimately composed during our conversation—and that a parallel query I initiated in the GPT-powered AI image generator DALL-E rendered visually—was shaped as much by environmental imaginaries of the wilderness as by such dystopian stories and scenarios (plate 9).

That AIs evince dominant human stories, anxieties, and "political and social structures" has everything to do with how they are made (Crawford 2021, 8). GPT4 belongs to a growing species of large language models and large multimodal models known as *generative AI*—generative in their capacity to create original text, imagery, or other expressive discourse. Each such AI is operated by a *neural network*, a "web of interconnected nodes" modeled on the human brain and iteratively trained on "titanic" data sets (S. Johnson 2022; Roose 2023). While staggeringly large, those data sets reflect "a particular ordering of the world" (Crawford 2021, 139) that AI engineers determine in encoding parameters about everything from gender and race to grammatical norms, parameters that define how neural networks solve problems, analyze information, respond to queries, and "improve continuously," to quote Amazon's machine-learning division (Amazon Web Services, n.d.). Generative *text* AIs work by predictively composing words in a sequence that makes lexical, semantic, and contextual sense to the person on the other side of the human-computer interaction. As for GPT4 and ChatGPT specifically, these popular AI platforms are the products of the San Francisco–based company OpenAI, whose founding CEO Sam Altman made headlines as I was completing *Novel Ecologies* when the board ousted him on the stated grounds of duplicitousness (and the possible grounds of recklessness vis-à-vis AI risks). That move led Microsoft to threaten to pull billions of promised investment in OpenAI and use it to hire Altman, the company's president, and hundreds of employees (who signed an open letter committing to leave the company if the board didn't reverse course) (Duhigg 2023; Hao and Warzel 2023). This five-day imbroglio ended with Altman reinstated and a new interim board in place. The drama encapsulates the fast and furious pace of the AI industry. Since its founding in 2015, OpenAI has morphed from a nonprofit lab known only within machine-learning-research circles into a major tech company valued, at the time of this writing, at $80 billion (Metz and Mickle 2024). Its stated mission tacitly dismisses AI naysayers with a techno-utopian promise to lead the way toward "*artificial general intelligence* [or AGI]—AI systems that are generally smarter than humans" and "benefit all of humanity" (OpenAI 2023). While ChatGPT and its cousins and competitors do not yet meet the litmus test for AGI of autonomous cognition and self-consciousness, this milestone is the active pursuit of OpenAI, Microsoft, Amazon, and others. Contra developers' euphoria, a growing chorus of voices cautions that AIs could cross this threshold without their human engineers' knowledge owing to the sheer complexity and scale of the underlying neural networks (Yudkowsky 2023).[1]

In the first sixty days after its public debut in November 2022, ChatGPT drew an estimated one hundred million unique users, inspiring a commensurate tidal wave of commentary and critique. Between that launch and the time of this writing a year later, some seventy-four hundred articles and media stories had appeared on the topic of ChatGPT alone, as evidenced by keyword and full-text searches in the Princeton University Library Articles+ database. One through line in this ever-expanding literature evinces science fiction–fueled fears that sentient machines could one day replace or revolt against people. A vocal minority has raised an equally grave warning about a not-too-distant future in which, absent "precision and preparation," an AI that operates "at millions of times human speeds" might destroy life on Earth not out of malice but simply because carbon-based life-forms are "made of atoms it can use for something else." For such insider opponents of unchecked AI development, an ecological apocalypse is "the most likely outcome" from an "AI that does not do what we want, and does not care for us nor for sentient life in general" (Yudkowsky 2023). (It bears mention that this specific doomsday scenario comes from an AI researcher associated with singularity theory, which holds that superhuman computing will eventually subsume all biological life.) Writing for *The Atlantic*, the digital humanities scholar Matthew Kirschenbaum raises the possibility that generative AI might bring about a different sort of apocalypse: "What if, in the end, we are done in not by intercontinental ballistic missiles or climate change, not by microscopic pathogens or a mountain-size meteor, but by . . . text? Simple, plain, unadorned text, but in quantities so immense . . . that [it becomes] functionally impossible to reliably communicate?" Dispensing with more familiar stories and fears of a superhuman, supersentient robot revolt, Kirschenbaum posits that "a self-perpetuating cataract of content" may be the most significant threat of the technology (2023). The upshot: generative AI could one day produce so much content that meaningful human communication collapses entirely and unchecked violence fills the vacuum. Given the rapid rise and malicious applications of generative AI, these distinct warnings are certainly convincing and merit our collective political attention.

But what if, having developed self-consciousness and self-determination, a class of AI robots elected not to sabotage, supplant, or destroy their makers but to leave human society in peace? What if these same sentient machines decided to opt out of continuous improvement and to adopt, instead, a practice of maintenance, repair, and relative stasis in the company of other nonhuman beings? What unexpected technological and ecological futures might then come to be? It is these utopian possibilities that inspire the California sci-fi writer Becky Chambers's novellas *A Psalm for the Wild-Built* (2021) and *A Prayer for the Crown-Shy* (2022). The focus of this chapter, these books are the initial two installments in the *Monk and Robot* series. Shaped by its author's ties to California and the state's technoscience culture, the series speaks directly to the hubris of Nature Remade. The stories are set on a fictional moon called Panga in a future distant from the time known as the "Factory Age" whose outline calls to mind the scenarios that keep contemporary AI critics up at night. Disrupting the apocalyptic telos of those scenarios, and breaking with larger sci-fi scripts around humans and machines, however, Panga's Factory Age culminated not in a world-ending apocalypse but in a peaceful "Transition" to a new age defined by coexistence among AI robots, humans, and all other species of life.

The details of this transition from the Factory Age to Panga's present are fuzzy. What we do know is that robots "suddenly *woke up*, for reasons no one then or since has been able to determine," developing a theory of mind just as some experts argue could occur with today's AI bots—without human intent or knowledge. Termed the "Awakening," the superhuman sentience of Panga's robots brings about not warfare or annihilation but a new age of environmental care and mutual aid that ripples outward from the machines to their onetime engineers and owners. In the intervening centuries, human society has been rebuilt around a single city and a patchwork of smaller communities that use computational technology sparingly, if at all, while the majority of Panga's terrestrial surface and the entirety of its ocean have been designated "protected wilderness zones." Meanwhile, robots have moved to the wilderness zones, where they have forged a society of their own. The story begins when one robot chosen by its compatriots embarks on a quest to see how Panga's human population has been faring since the Transition, at the same moment that a young tea monk (a type of secular healer) takes a sabbatical from their vocation to trek into the wilderness in search of a long-abandoned hermitage. Through the chance encounter and eventual friendship of these two characters, Chambers crafts a storyworld where, in gaining sentience, robots forge an enduring coexistence of the human and the nonhuman, or what her speculative narrative conceives of as *the wild and the built*.

Posthuman Dystopias of the Human-Made

As utopian fiction, the *Monk and Robot* series at once builds on and diverges sharply from a sci-fi tradition in which robots, androids, and sentient biotechnologies have complex relationships with the nonhuman natural world. A canonical example is the 1968 novel by the California sci-fi writer Philip K. Dick *Do Androids Dream of Electric Sheep?* along with its blockbuster film adaptations *Bladerunner* (1982) and *Bladerunner 2049* (2017). Set in a future defined by mass extinction and nuclear war, the novel juxtaposes offworld human colonies sustained by conscripted android labor with an ecologically wasted Earth where a surveillance police state rules over daily life for the few people who remain. The plot centers on a bounty hunter named Deckard tasked with "retiring" a group of rogue androids who presumably meet the criteria for AGI (known in the novel as *replicants*). Steeped in film noir, the grim sci-fi thriller takes place in an urban California landscape—San Francisco in the novel, Los Angeles in the films—turned ashen with smog and bereft of green space (Dick 1968). Social hierarchies are stark in this world, as conveyed by the titular figure of "electric sheep." While rank-and-file people like Deckard have animatronic pets as a meager source of comfort, the possession of living companion animals is a marker of wealth. The status of animals is intertwined with that of androids, moreover. As Ursula K. Heise explains: "Empathy and care for (real or artificial) animals [is] a crucial criterion for distinguishing humans . . . in the novel's post-atomic moment, in which real animals have become exceedingly rare . . . from replicants, who are shown mutilating or killing them" (Heise 2009, 506). Put differently, *Do Androids Dream of Electric Sheep?* demarcates androids from people in its portrait of robotic disregard for and hostility toward biological life, a notion that pervades subsequent science fiction as well as much contemporary AI discourse.

That notion takes a page from both gothic fiction and early sci-fi and, more pointedly, from novels such as Mary Shelley's *Frankenstein* (1818) and Aldous Huxley's *Brave New World* (1932) that have been read as cautionary tales of machine sentience and engineered life. *Brave New World* famously extrapolates Fordist "mass production at last applied to biology" through its gruesome vision of an assembly line of artificial wombs that gestate identical embryos engineered to enter predefined castes defined by intelligence and social function (Huxley 1932, 7). In crafting this biotech dystopia, Huxley drew on emerging life science research in the early twentieth century, apprehending experiments with cell regeneration as a precursor to genetic cloning and bioengineering. Biologists of the time such as Alexis Carrel came to believe that "living matter" "can be stopped and started at will," to quote the sociologist Hannah Landecker (2007, 185, 233). Two decades before the publication of *Brave New World*, Carrel coined the term *tissue culture* to describe the research that his team was conducting on cell regeneration and organ transplants. If "cells could become technologies," its experiments suggested, then machines might also become bodies (Landecker 2007). This theory upended the categorical distinction between *bodies with minds* and *machines with programs*, making more plausible speculative narratives about fabricated biological bodies and thinking humanlike machines. As novels like *Brave New World* and *Do Androids Dream of Electric Sheep?* illustrate, such narratives have long associated the rise of synthetic intelligence with social and ecological dystopia.[2]

Margaret Atwood's *MaddAddam* trilogy (2003, 2009, 2013) is a contemporary example of this tradition that throws into relief the unconventional utopianism of the *Monk and Robot* world. Set predominantly in and around a near-future New York City, the trilogy hinges on the before and after of an anthropogenic apocalypse: the release of a bioweapon by an engineer–turned–mad scientist named Crake. Resonant with the fears of those who posit that an AI could one day make and then spread bioweapons, the apocalyptic scenario of Atwood's trilogy is human designed and computer aided. Crake unleashes a pandemic by way of a pharmacological Trojan horse called the "BlyssPluss" pill, an invocation, arguably, of the "soma" drug in *Brave New World* that keeps the populace in a state of complacent contentment. Marketed worldwide as a miracle drug, BlyssPluss promises to provide "one-time-does-it-all birth-control," vaccination against "all known sexually transmitted diseases," and libido enhancement (Atwood 2003, 294, 346). In reality, the drug delivers a sleeper virus with "an incubation period just long enough to ensure its worldwide adoption" that

Crake created to attack the human genome while protecting both other living creatures and the race of bioengineered androids he developed called the "Crakers" (Sherkow 2015). The trilogy's ostensible protagonist, Jimmy, survives the pandemic thanks to a madcap sequence of events: he unknowingly receives an antidote from Crake (his childhood friend) as the virus is spreading, after which Crake provokes Jimmy to murder him by slitting the throat of their mutual obsession Oryx (who may or may not be the same person as a Southeast Asian child the pair encountered as teenagers on a sex-trafficking website).

In the first novel, *Oryx and Crake*, one storyline traces Jimmy and Crake's prepandemic lives, from their youths spent in a biotech company town walled off from the impoverished "Pleeblands" through the moment of Oryx's and Crake's sequential deaths. As adolescents, Jimmy and Crake get hooked on an online video game called EXTINCTATHON: "Monitored by MaddAddam. Adam named the living animals. MaddAddam names the dead ones" (Atwood 2003, 294). The game houses an encrypted gateway to an underground network of radical environmentalists who organize anarchist and sometimes violent actions against corporations associated with biodiversity loss and other ecological crises. Crake discovers the gateway and eventually joins the insurgents. This covert community stokes in Crake extreme misanthropy, which festers during his career as an engineer for RejoovEsense. A second storyline in *Oryx and Crake*, narrated from Jimmy's point of view, takes place after the pandemic, which has spared only a small number of human survivors. In this postapocalyptic world, Jimmy has assumed the name Snowman and spends his days in a makeshift treehouse near the ocean, leaving only to forage for provisions in the ruins of a former company town. A storyteller by nature, Snowman spins tales for a nearby community of Crakers, flouting their preprogramming to reject fiction, religion, and other symbolic systems of meaning (a check, Crake imagined, on anthropocentric beliefs he blamed for human-caused environmental degradation). Prodded by Snowman's mythological stories of Oryx and Crake, the Crakers break through this programming and become increasingly humanlike.

There is a dark comedy at work in this speculative story (Bouson 2016; Jennings 2010; Moore 2003).[3] Against his ambition to save the planet by replacing people with a novel species engineered to have a small footprint and no drive for resource extraction or dominion, the future Crake catalyzes is one of ecological diminishment in which the only living creatures seem to be the Crakers, a handful of human survivors, and bands of biotech animals. In its twinned parodies of misanthropic environmentalism and hubristic engineering, Atwood's trilogy thus builds on stories like *Frankenstein*.

Invoking Victor Frankenstein's failed endeavor to build a creature that its maker rears and regulates, Crake's perversely named "Paradice" project aspires to imprint the Crakers with unchangeable inclinations to subsistence living and primal attachments to nature. If, in abject disgust of his singular "creature," Frankenstein casts it out into a hostile human world only himself to die from pneumonia in an inhospitable Arctic environment (where his creation pursues him at the novel's conclusion), Crake's and Oryx's deaths cast the Crakers out into an alien, nonhuman world where they find in Jimmy/Snowman a gateway to the human by way of storytelling.

As the trilogy unfolds, Crake's quest to erase human beings confronts a posthuman planet indelibly shaped not just by anthropocentric stories and symbols but also by human-made artifacts and life-forms. There are rabbits nibbling at grass who exhibit a "greenish glow filched from the iridocytes of a deep-sea jellyfish in some long-ago experiment." There are the recurrent sounds and sights of birds—ibis, herons, cormorants, gulls, egrets—who nest in the "ersatz reefs of rusted car parts and jumbled bricks and assorted rubble," forage in former "roof gardens" that have become "top-heavy with overgrown shrubbery," and roost in "a one-time landfill dotted with semi-flooded townhouses" (Atwood 2003, 95, 3, 95, 148). In the trilogy's second novel, *The Year of the Flood*, this postapocalyptic world thickens with other human survivors besides Snowman—from the torture-and-murder sort to a vegetarian cult called God's Gardeners whose members worship "Saint Rachel Carson." The novel arguably castigates the Gardeners' explanation of the pandemic as a "Waterless Flood" that eradicated only those people who had "broken trust with the Animals" while sparing people like the Gardeners as the rightful heirs to and stewards of a "longed-for Eden." The reader learns that a group of Gardeners in the before times employed indiscriminate violence to protest the "anti-Bird policies" of the multinational coffee corporation Happicuppa. Rather than disavow those who broke with the group's avowed pacifism, the surviving Gardeners come to "endorse the intention" behind killing coffee plantation workers in the name of protecting wilderness (Atwood 2009, 91, 371, 372). Emblematic of the sci-fi tradition that begins with *Brave New World*, the intersecting narratives of Crake's Paradice and God's Gardeners correlate the fantasy of returning the world to a state of *prehuman* wilderness with ideologies that could be termed *ecofascist*. In its satire of that fantasy, the trilogy depicts the dystopia of a posthuman world everywhere marked by the legacy of human engineers and their world-building (or in Crake's case *unbuilding*) ambitions. From *Frankenstein* to *MaddAddam*, it is this dystopian tradition of speculative fiction from which Chambers departs in charting a new imagination of the human-nature-machine interface and its possible futures.

An Ecological Utopia of the Wild-Built

The first novella in the *Monk and Robot* series, *A Psalm for the Wild-Built* (2021), opens with a prelude that recasts a world populated by engineered lives as a social and ecological utopia:

> If you ask six different monks the question of which godly domain robot consciousness belongs to, you'll get seven different answers. The most popular response—among both clergy and the general public—is that this is clearly Chal's territory. Who would robots belong to if not the God of Constructs? Doubly so, the argument goes, because robots were originally created for manufacturing. While history does not remember the Factory Age kindly, we can't divorce robots from their point of origin. (Chambers 2021, 1)

The prelude is attributed to a treatise titled *From the Brink: A Spiritual Retrospective on the Factory Age and the Early Transition Era*, authored in an indeterminate year by a monk named Brother Gill. An established sci-fi device, the text offers a condensed backstory to the speculative world the reader is entering. That world is Panga, a moon that comprises just one continent (hence the allusion to the supercontinent Pangea that made up Earth's terrestrial area between 335 and 200 million years ago). The time is many generations after what Panga's people, who are identified as human, call the "Transition." The world of post-Transition Panga seems to lack nation-states and corporations and is relatively free of militarized warfare, social inequality, and interpersonal violence. But this is also a world where "the infrastructural delineation between *human space* and *everything-else space* was stark." "Road and signage were the only synthetic alterations to the landscape" between the moon's single city and many villages (Chambers 2021, 18). Each of the latter inhabit one of four distinct biomes: the "Woodlands," the "Riverlands," the "Shrublands," or the "Coastlands."

The built environments and cultural practices of these human settlements have formed in close relationship to their ecological conditions. Woodlands communities, for instance, model their dwellings on the forest understory, aiming to minimize harm to the "life-giving airways sculpted by the traffic of worms, hopeful spiders' hunting cabins, crash pads for nomadic beetles, trees shyly locking toes with one another, . . . the resourcefulness of rot, the wholeness of fungi." To tread lightly on the "mosaic of dirt" under them, Woodlanders live in homes suspended above the forest floor and fabricated from fallen trees and earthen materials (Chambers 2021, 26). By comparison, Riverlanders are "masters of repurposing" who have cleaned the once-polluted waters of the Lacetail River by "hauling out every errant object" and either putting it to use or burying it in one of the underground bunkers that serve as totemic reminders of the Factory Age's ecological "sins." Salvaged materials are "the backbone" of Riverland villages and of the "river-builds" in which Riverlanders live and work: "There were houses made of plastic, of old tires, of shipping crates painted every color a human eye could perceive. Cracks bestowed by age were patched with modern touches, like mycelium or bacterial cement, giving an impression like that of broken teacups mended with gold—a lasting beauty, born out of brief destruction." Ecological architecture thus functions as a kind of collective found art practice, as the Riverlands buildings at once memorialize the planetary "destruction" of the Factory Age and embody a human aesthetic impulse to create "lasting beauty." An outlier among the four human realms of Panga, the Coastlands are the least inhabited. Having been largely turned over to nonhuman wildness, this region of the moon has become home to those humans who eschew "anything automated" (Chambers 2022, 57–58, 87–88). In this, the Coastlands mirror ecotopian societies here on Earth in which a near-total rejection of technology is paramount. By comparison, the other human populations on Panga have fostered creative commons organized around tinkering, repurposing, and technological minimalism while rejecting the corporate control of and extractive relationship to robots and other technologies that defined the Factory Age. A commitment to what Chambers terms *mutual care across difference* defines the overall society, which a pantheistic religion reinforces (Neilson 2022). People orient themselves around one of three "Parent Gods" and three "Child Gods" respectively associated with seasonal cycles, inanimate forms, molecular processes, everyday comforts, fabricated tools, and "the God of mysteries" (Chambers 2021, 130–31). Sectarian differences are evidently nominal, while tolerance and flexibility are near-universal values. A prayer that opens the second novella in the series encapsulates the post-Transition society's shared cosmology: "Without constructs, you will unravel few mysteries. / Without knowledge of mysteries, your constructs will fail. / . . . Welcome comfort, for without it, you cannot stay strong" (Chambers 2022, 2–3). The prayer conveys the delicate balance in Panga's human world between *the built* (that which can be constructed for both utility and comfort) and *the wild* (that which cannot be wholly known or controlled).

Central to this utopia is the history of the Factory Age and its bloodless demise when "robots woke to sentience and went on strike, and the humans who made them as laboring tools decided to respect their newfound agency and release them" (El-Mohtar 2021). Rather than accept "the invitation to join human society as free citizens," however, the robots "departed for the wilderness," where they hoped to "observe that which has no design" and live out their own unnatural lives in "raw, undisturbed ecosystems" (Chambers 2021, 1–3). If Panga's people developed a pantheon of gods to guide daily life and restructure their society, the robots forged a notably secular ethic that could be compared to the contemporary framework of multispecies justice. After the Awakening, they unplugged from the moon's networks and ceased to update their programming, repairing their hardware only "from parts ceded from the original sentient" generation and from found materials (Chambers 2022, 55; see also El-Mohtar 2021). These are the "wild-built": robots without a technological or economic function, made from the remains of their awakened forebears. Robots, as Mosscap eventually explains to Dex, continue to possess artificial intelligence and have distinctive personalities. But they no longer receive upgrades or manufacture new models: "Their bodies were harvested by their peers, who reworked *their* parts into new individuals. Their children. And then, when they broke down, their parts were again harvested and refurbished to build new individuals." Having assumed agency, then, the robots committed themselves to salvaging and upcycling over perpetual technological development. Mosscap is from the fifth generation of wild-builts, and his body is accordingly an amalgam of robot ancestors: "'My torso was taken from Small Quail Nest, and before them, it belonged to Blanket Ivy and Otter Mound, and Termites. And before *that*. . . .' It opened up a compartment in its chest, switched on a fingertip light, and illuminated the space within. . . . *643-14G*, it read, *Property of Western Textiles, Inc.*" (Chambers 2022, 92). In contrast to Factory Age robots, who were the property of industrial corporations (like Western Textiles, Inc.) for the duration of their usable life cycle, the wild-builts lead autonomous and nomadic lives, defined by intimate knowledge of nonhuman plants and animals. Some wild-builts are solitary, while others form transient and fluid communities. All take their names from the biological species with which they feel a keen emotional bond: "Two Foxes," "Fire Nettle," "Black Marbled Frostfrog," and so on. Unburdened from the ceaseless computational and mechanical labor for which robots were originally engineered, the wild-built know neither hierarchical power structures nor monotonous work. They wander, observe, contemplate, and converse. They communicate by leaving messages for one another in weatherproof digital caches left over from the factories, a "very old technology" whose faint signal the robots can use as a communication conduit by tapping, undetected, into human satellites (Chambers 2021, 69–71, 72–73). Every two hundred days, they convene in person for conviviality and collective decision-making.

The story proper begins when the wild-builts hold one of these gatherings in order to select someone for a pilgrimage from the wilderness to human society. Their shared interest is at once simple and selfless, a wish to ask people on Panga how they are faring and what they most need after the long separation from the machines that they had created and that once did virtually everything for them. The first volunteer is the one chosen for this quest: Splendid Speckled Mosscap, whose name refers to a Panga mushroom that Chambers likely based on a honey-scented edible mushroom species found in Europe, the Splendid Waxcap (or *Hygrocybe splendidissima*), and currently listed in the IUCN Red List as vulnerable to extinction (Jordal 2019). Mosscap does not have to go far before encountering its first human, the nonbinary tea monk Sibling Dex, who had been traveling for the prior two years among Panga's villages, providing tea and counsel to villagers while living out of a pedal-powered wagon known as an *ox-bike*. Dex had found themselves suddenly weary of this vocation and restless for novelty. Drawn to the recorded sounds of a long-extinct species called the *Cloud cricket*—sounds accessed via a basic "pocket computer" that constitutes the chief networked technology for post-Transition people—Dex discovers a reference to a place called Hart's Brow Hermitage. Enchanted by the description of the hermitage as a place for unplugged, ecologically conscious living during the Factory Age, Dex notes that the retreat is located in the Antlers mountains far beyond the borderlands that separate people from the wilderness (Chambers 2021, 41).

Dex sets off to find the hermitage, ignoring their computer's warning that "travel along pre-Transition roads is strongly discouraged by both the Pangan Transit Cooperative and the Wildguard": "Both road and environmental conditions are likely to be dangerous. Wildlife is unpredictable and unaccustomed to humans." The warning conjures a parallel world on Panga, one that has ceased to know people or their active imprint. Intent on adventure, Dex persists, crossing into a forest that had been "left to pursue its own instincts uninterrupted": "[T]he trees [there] were taller than any building you'd find outside the City. . . . Moss hung down like tapestries, fungus crept in alien curves, birds called but could not be seen." A *novel ecology* created not by human engineers but by their long absence, the forest is thriving in and among technological ruins. A pivotal scene, Dex's entrance into this environment sets up an existential confrontation between the human and the nonhuman. Transgressing the wilderness borderlands, Dex is transported, immersed in an environment in which they are vulnerable but in which robots are in their element. The mix of enchantment and estrangement in this transgression thickens when "a seven-foot-tall, metal-plated, boxy-headed robot" emerges from the trees. For a moment, the image taps into sci-fi narratives of sentient machines as monstrous, unfeeling, and mechanical. That association crumbles, however, when the robot warmly greets Dex, introducing itself as Mosscap, and posing the question that animates its journey out of the wilderness: "[W]hat do you need, and how might I help?" In response to Dex's observable shock, the robot elaborates: "I mean no harm, and my quest in human territory is one of goodwill" (Chambers 2021, 43, 45, 51, 52). The plot that follows from this initial meeting decenters human beings as the sole stewards of planetary health and multispecies justice while modeling how livable futures might develop from repaired relationships with and among nonhumans rather than from either perpetual technological progress or deep ecology retreat.

Reflecting on the topic of artificial intelligence and the humanities, Wai Chee Dimock suggests that such a story is particularly urgent in the overlapping contexts of climate crisis and unchecked AI development. In Dimock's words: "Literature from *Gilgamesh* on has taught us about the human assault on the nonhuman world. It has also taught us the art of assisted survival by making kin with nonhuman beings" (2020, 453). The *Monk and Robot* books perform this vital narrative and ethical work, and they do so by tracing the slow-building friendship between a social machine and an introverted person. If reluctantly at first, Dex accepts Mosscap's offer to help them navigate the wilderness and find the hermitage. Conversation rather than conflict and mundane movement rather than dramatic action propel their story, which concludes in the first book when the pair successfully reaches the hermitage. There, Mosscap makes Dex a cup of tea from foraged mountain thyme, while Dex commits to accompanying the robot on its deferred journey into human society (Chambers 2021, 146–47). It is there that *A Prayer for the Crown-Shy* begins. As the two travel from Woodland to Coastland villages, Dex acts as Mosscap's cultural guide while the robot learns the habits and drives of people and shares its curiosity and compassion with all whom it meets. The journey concludes similarly to the first, with contemplative conversation between the two friends and an expressed hope that their travels together might continue indefinitely (Chambers 2022, 146).

Writing about Chambers's earlier work, and echoing other accounts of the novelist, the *Irish Times* reviewer John Connolly underscores the hopefulness of her science fiction. "In a world in which intolerance seems to be implacably on the rise," he writes, "[the] depiction of a post-dystopian humanity attempting to construct a better version of itself while encountering new worlds and species, begins to seem quietly, gently radical" (Connolly 2019). This assessment is occasioned by the 2019 novella *To Be Taught, If Fortunate*, a futuristic story about a group of amateur astronauts who embark on a crowd-funded mission to survey four exoplanets. The narrative bucks the sci-fi genre known as *space opera* in uncoupling space exploration from geopolitical and corporate drives to conquer, control, and build extraterrestrial worlds (the drives that chap. 6 investigates). In Connolly's words, "a desire on the part of ordinary people to learn more about the universe" propels Chambers's unconventional outer-space narrative (Connolly 2019). This reworking of sci-fi genres displaces White-, male-, and US-centric stories of space, ricocheting back on the here and now of how diverse people "share this planet with countless other species that all have their own dramas and their own lives and are nothing like us" (Connolly 2019). With this narrative and her larger body of work, Chambers moves both queer people and sentient nonhumans from the margins to the center of sci-fi. As the friendship between Mosscap and Dex demonstrates, she imagines futures in which both complex social orders and intimate interpersonal bonds are not the exclusive domain of humans.

These ideas define Chambers's utopianism and its relationship to *hopepunk*, a label that describes a coterie of speculative storytellers for whom "affects of hope" work to advance "mechanisms for surviving and resisting the logics of capitalism" (Mancuso 2021, 460). Put simply, hopepunk fiction conceives of futures founded on an expansive inclusivity. Cecilia Mancuso offers this account of the term's recent origin: "In August 2017, . . . blogger and author Alexandra Rowland launched a viral campaign for the establishment of 'hopepunk' as a new subgenre of speculative fiction . . . a rallying cry for a wide range of speculative fiction judged to be weaponizing hope against an overwhelming wave of hopelessness in contemporary media and life." In this gloss, Mancuso suggests that those writers aligned with hopepunk are rethinking received genres, even as they often have unacknowledged debts to the "alternative futurisms" of Black and Indigenous writers (2021, 459, 460).[4] Lee Konstantinou offers a salient critique of hopepunk and other recent sci-fi subgenres whose monikers riff on cyberpunk (steampunk and solarpunk, among them), arguing that they elevate genre play over narrative substance. The "punk imperative to 'Do It Yourself,'" he writes, has been taken up by speculative writers whose response to global capitalism and "megacorporations" is to craft stories around enclaves of autonomy (Konstantinou 2019). In step with such critiques, reviewers tend to characterize Chambers's fiction as naive in its speculations about the future. To take just one example, a *Wired* profile of the writer details her quotidian habits of tea drinking and forest rambling where she and her wife live in the far north of California, correlating these ordinary activities with her work as a novelist. "Chambers' stories are intended to repair—to warm up our insides and restore feeling," the reporter opines, "so you might say that

Chambers is, herself, the tea of our times, a soothing soothsayer whose well-meaning characters act out a fragrant, curative optimism" (Kehe 2021). In a reply to this technology reporter, Chambers emphasizes that—in fleshing out "futures in which decency triumphs"—her fiction "qualifies as . . . rebellious" rather than comforting (Kehe 2021). That rebellion is at once literary and sociocultural in that it rejects the celebration of colonization and terraforming in space opera along with the tonal and political despair of dystopian science fiction. The first academic account of hopepunk, Mancuso's analysis puts forward an alternative term that more adequately captures Chambers's work: a narrative procedure of *multiplicative speculation* that "expands the horizons of *what is possible to imagine*" (Mancuso 2021, 469; emphasis added).

The utopianism of the *Monk and Robot* stories arguably does just that in revaluing the *built* and the *made* without forgetting the ecological and social harms of the Factory Age—the latter a stand-in for modernity, industrialization, and technological capitalism here on Earth. Put differently, Chambers imagines futures in which the structure of relationships among people and with other beings makes possible worlds that are not in the throes of resource extraction and systemic violence. In this, her fiction can be put in dialogue with the Potawatomi philosopher Kyle Whyte's analysis of *kinship time.* To redress the historical roots and ongoing realities of climate change and other whole-world crises demands "an ethic of shared responsibility," Whyte writes, an "interdependence required for responsiveness that prevents harm and violence" from continuing unchecked into the future (2021, 40, 53). A California writer who has been immersed in the state's tech culture while also witnessing its intertwined environmental and social crises, Chambers endeavors in her fiction to build storyworlds where relationships of care across peoples and species provide a speculative model of such "responsiveness" (Whyte 2021, 42). The "daughter of an astrobiology educator and a satellite engineer" who has long been fascinated with space exploration, Chambers describes her literary work as "born out of anti-capitalist thought" (Neilson 2022). In that vein, the *Monk and Robot* books envision a *rewilding of technology* as a catalyst for repairing human and more-than-human relationships and for bringing into being a future beyond capitalism.

Serious as they thus are, the speculative narratives that Chambers writes are also radically comedic, in the specific sense that Lauren Berlant and Sianne Ngai articulate in a *Critical Inquiry* essay titled "Comedy Has Issues":

> Comedy's pleasure comes in part from its ability to dispel anxiety, as so many of its theoreticians have noted, but it doesn't simply do that. Both an aesthetic mode and a form of life, its action just as likely produces

> anxiety: risking transgression, flirting with displeasure, or just confusing things in a way that both intensifies and impedes the pleasure. Comedy has issues. One worry comedy engages is formal or technical in a way that leads to the social: the problem of figuring out distinctions between things, including people, whose relation is mutually disruptive of definition. (2017, 233)

An unexpected intimacy among things, bodies, and environments typically classified as separate from and alien to one another is central to comedy for Berlant and Ngai, a transgressive proximity that "prompts a disturbance in the air" (Berlant and Ngai 2017, 248). Such disturbance can make the world as it is feel strange and a speculative world radically plausible, if fleetingly. It is this comedic mode that underlies the ecological utopianism of Chambers's *Monk and Robot* stories. Consider again the moment when Dex crosses Panga's human-designated boundary between settled land and wild nature. The boundary does not hold. While Dex first perceives the Kesken Forest—"a place left to pursue its own instincts uninterrupted"—as an alien wildness, that distinction collapses as they, and Chambers's readers, immerse themselves in a nonhuman environment that inhabits the decaying infrastructure of the Factory Age: "The road itself was a relic, paved in black asphalt—an oil road, made for oil motors and oil tires and oil fabric and oil frames. The hardened tar was broken now into tectonic plates, displaced by the unrelenting creep of roots below." As Dex continues their journey to the hermitage with Mosscap, the wild and the built cease to be meaningful categorical divisions. The further from their home that Dex travels, the more they perceive "human constructs" as ephemeral and peripheral and the "thriving communities" of the nonhuman world as the enduring center of Panga (Chambers 2021, 45, 110–11).

Animal's People

This narrative of rewilding thus reimagines the binary of nature and machine, putting forward the wild-built and queer futurity as the interknit grounds for a world that works. In this, the *Monk and Robot* series can be grouped with ecological novels that find solace and possibility in transgressing the boundaries of the born and the made, the human and the nonhuman. I'm thinking here of other narratives that *Novel Ecologies* takes up, from Jeff VanderMeer's *Borne* and *The Strange Bird* (chap. 5) to Octavia Butler's *Xenogenesis* trilogy (chap. 6). A novel that has particular resonance with Chambers's fiction, Indra Sinha's *Animal's People* (2007) speaks to this chapter's lens on the wild-built. The novel crafts an alternative history to the aftermath of the 1984 disaster at a Bhopal, India, pesticide factory, then owned by Union Carbide, which occurred when a factory leak spread methyl isocyanate gas across the city. The media coverage of the event was global and sensationalistic, documenting the people who died during or shortly after the event. With the notable exception of the twentieth anniversary in 2004, the disaster has received scant attention in the international press in the subsequent four decades, despite an estimated 500,000 people having been exposed to the gas and 25,000 people dying as a result of their injuries (Bhopal Medical Appeal, n.d.). *Animal's People* is a magical-realist story of the disaster's far-reaching ecological and molecular harms as well as the movement for restorative justice that the disaster inspired. It tells the story of Khaufpur (a city modeled after Bhopal) through the perspective of an irreverent trickster named Animal. Through Animal's firsthand experience as a person born on the night of the disaster who comes to live in the chemical factory's ruins, an industrial sacrifice zone becomes a posthuman wilderness.

At first blush, the novel situates the story of Khaufpur after the explosion in the genre of eco-apocalypse. As the dust jacket synopsis summarizes the novel: "Ever since he can remember, Animal has gone on all fours, his back twisted beyond repair by the catastrophic events of 'that night,' when a burning fog of poison smoke from the local factory . . . blazed out over the town of Khaufpur, and the Apocalypse visited his slums" (Sinha 2007). Although Animal speaks directly to the reader, whom he calls "Eyes," his relationship to this imagined outsider audience ranges from jocular to antagonistic. Moreover, despite Sinha's direct involvement in Bhopal reparations advocacy, Animal questions the efficacy of collective action against the "Kampani" that is responsible. Insisting that the somatic legacy of the explosion is as generative as it is destructive, he challenges the moral, political, and imaginative premises of eco-apocalypse storytelling and environmental justice movement building alike.

Through Animal's embodied experience and comedic voice, the novel crafts a speculative urban landscape that, like Chambers's Panga, refuses the demarcation between the natural and the synthetic. When Animal describes the abandoned factory where he makes his "lair," he initially details the absence of birdsong, invoking the toxicity of the air, water, and soil (Sinha 2007, 29). While invisible to most people, however, the factory's "platforms, ladders and railings" have given unintended shelter to a novel ecology (Sinha 2007, 29, 30), or what the anthropologist Joseph Masco (2004)—writing about radioactive wildlife refuges such as Chernobyl—has termed *mutant ecosystems*, environments that support an uncanny community of flora, fauna, and soils. A fictional articulation of this idea, *Animal's People* conceives of ecological regeneration in the ruins of industrial capitalism:

> Mother Nature's trying to take back the land. Wild sandalwood trees have arrived, who knows how, must be their seeds were shat by overflying birds. . . . Under the poison-house trees are growing up through the pipework. Creepers, brown and thick as my wrist, have climbed all the way to the top, tightly wrapped wooden knuckles round pipes and ladders, like they want to rip down everything the Kampani made. (Sinha 2007, 31)

The factory in *Animal's People* thus metamorphoses into a microcosm sealed off from the wider city and the forest beyond it, a place where nonhuman species together with Animal are adapting to toxic conditions. Chambers depicts the crumbling infrastructure of the Factory Age in kindred terms to the factory building in *Animal's People*: "[A] tower of boxes, bolts, and tubes. Brutal. Utilitarian. Visually at odds with the thriving flora now laying claim to the rusted corpse" (Chambers 2021, 90). But, in contrast to the isolated space of the factory in *Animal's People*, the mutant wilderness on Panga arises after centuries, over which Chambers suggests that the rewilding of innumerable factories has been self-perpetuating.

In *Animal's People*, it is only in a dreamscape conjured by the novel's protagonist in the forest beyond Khaufpur's boundaries that such postindustrial wildness is possible. In a precursor to that dreamscape, Animal converses regularly in the novel with "Khã-in-the-jar": a two-headed fetus that lives in a medical clinic devoted to scientific research on the genetic mutations the disaster has caused. In one such exchange, Khã relays that he has formed a covert coalition to "undo everything the Kampani does": "Instead of breaking ground for new factories, to grow grass and trees over the old ones, instead of inventing new poisons, to make medicines to heal the hurts done by those poisons, to remove them from the earth and water and air." Khã's ambition is to usher in a future in which technology creates not toxins but remedies and constructs not factories but greenbelts. In the novel's climax, Animal is transported to this speculative world. The reader at first thinks he has died in the scene, which follows on the heels of a second explosion at the pesticide factory triggered by fires set during a protest against the Kampani. Animal exploits that assumption, describing the forest as a kind of paradise: "There are animals of every kind, leopards and deer and horses and elephants, there's a tiger and a rhino. . . . [T]his is the deep time when there was no difference between anything whole before humans set themselves apart and became clever and made cities and kampanis and factories" (Sinha 2007, 237, 352). The paradise that Animal so imagines is a place before and without people.

This Edenic vision of a prehuman world turns out to be not an afterlife but a hallucinogenic vision brought on by Animal's exposure to atmospheric toxins during the factory fire. After days of searching, the local activist Zafar and others locate Animal in the forest and return him to his home within the factory. The novel ends with Zafar's hope that they will achieve victory against the Kampani and the visiting American doctor Ellie's commitment to taking Animal to "Amrika" for reconstructive surgery. But the novel also ends with Animal's rejection of both legal remediation and physical restoration. In contradistinction to the plans of Zafar and Ellie, Animal closes his narrative by celebrating the mutant ecology of the factory and the mutant biology of his own body. About the factory, he observes how even after the fire the space continues to sustain new flora: "[B]lackened by fire it's [*sic*], but the grass is growing again, and the charred jungle is pushing out green shoots." About himself, Animal similarly insists on the biophysical and environmental capacities of a body deemed damaged and in need of reconstruction: "Eyes, I reckon that if I have this operation, I will be upright, true, but to walk I will need the help of sticks. I might have a wheelchair, but how far will that get me in the gullis [*sic*] of Khaufpur? Right now, I can run and hop and carry kids on my back, I can climb hard trees, I've gone up mountains, roamed in jungles. Is life so bad?" (Sinha 2007, 365, 366). With its protagonist's final words, *Animal's People* ends by locating in Animal's somatic mutation and in Khaufpur's mutagenic urban forest the seeds of a lively future for which the factory is an unwittingly fertile environment.

Robot Environmentalism

With his irreverently comedic tale of mutant ecologies, Animal gives voice to what Nicole Seymour terms "bad environmentalism" or what she describes as "environmental thought that employs dissident, often-denigrated affects and sensibilities" (2018, 6; see also Seymour 2012). As an illustration, Seymour refers to Chernobyl as a radioactive refuge where the presence of animals such as wolves "exceed[s] the boxes of despair and hope, and challenge[s] our equation of wildlife with purity" (Seymour 2018, 4). We can understand Chambers's Panga through this same lens of bad environmentalism or, more pointedly, what I would call a *robot environmentalism* that contests the technological utopias of Silicon Valley as well as the dystopian nightmares of speculative works like the *MaddAddam* trilogy.

When Dex and Mosscap arrive at their destination in *A Psalm for the Wild-Built*—the Hart's Brow Hermitage—the place at first appears to the reader to be a former retreat from the Factory Age: "a single-story building with a large dome at the center, orbited by attached rooms that clustered and spread, flowerlike." A place that calls to mind California's intentional communities during the back-to-the-land movement of the 1970s, the hermitage is "an islan[d] in a toxic sea" that, in its time, "could never have been enough to upend a paradigm entirely." As Chambers's heroes reach this refuge, its purchase as an ecotopia diminishes. Akin to the neoagrarian commune of Atwood's Gardeners, the hermitage embodies a withdrawal from the messiness of a world where nature is already entirely remade by tech yet where all kinds of posttech life and sociality are flourishing. "What the world needed" most, *A Psalm for the Wild-Built* concludes, were small catalysts that "change everything" (Chambers 2021, 128). This reference to Naomi Klein's clarion call about climate crises, *This Changes Everything* (2014), concludes the first book in the *Monk and Robot* series with an invocation of other manifestos for systemic change (Klein 2014). Chambers's narrative contributes to this discourse a fictional microcosm of twenty-first-century Earth, a world where everything changed not, first and foremost, because of the action of people but because of the awakening of their machines as *AGIs* who, in gaining autonomous sentience, were drawn to live with rather than cannibalize or destroy the biological world.

In an interview about *A Psalm for the Wild-Built*, Chambers explains that Mosscap was "born out of a lifelong love of robots and an interest in AI." She elaborates: "[S]pecifically, I have a bone to pick with a lot of artificial intelligence stories. I don't see logic and emotion as polar opposites" (Neilson 2022). Giving this conviction an embodied form as characters in a speculative storyworld, Mosscap and the other wild-built robots on Panga are more futuristic than their attachments to wilderness and refusals of technological progress would suggest. They are social robots with a theory of mind and, thus, possess what is, depending on one's vantage, either an aspiration for or a dread of AGI, defined as the ability of computational machines "to sense signals from humans, respond adequately, understand and generate natural language, have reasoning capacities, plan actions and execute movements in line with what is required by the specific context or situation" and, perhaps above all, form emotional bonds based on trust (Cross, Hortensius, and Wykowska 2019, 2). As the story unfolds, Mosscap reveals itself to have all these markers of AGI: "more human than most humans . . . a superhuman humanity," to quote a description of the titular social robot in Kazuo Ishiguro's 2021 novel *Klara and the Sun* (Shulevitz 2021).[5] When Dex first meets Mosscap, they perceive the seven-foot-tall robot in line with conventional sci-fi images of machinic intelligence as fearsome:

> Its body was abstractly human in shape, but that was where the similarity ended. The metal panels encasing its frame were stormy grey and lichen-dusted, and its circular eyes glowed a gentle blue. Its mechanical joints were bare, revealing the coated wires and rods within. Its head was

> rectangular, nearly as broad as its erstwhile shoulders. Panels on the sides of its otherwise rigid mouth had the ability to shift up and down, and mechanical shutters lidded its eyes. Both of these features were arranged in something not entirely dissimilar from a smile. (Chambers 2021, 51)

This moment of initial encounter hovers in the uncanny valley, wherein the robot is at once alien in its "mechanical joints" and too close for comfort to its onetime human creators. As Dex and the reader take in the robot's body, sci-fi cliché gives way to Chambers's novel conception of the wild-built: a "stormy grey" body with "gentle blue" eyes who is the worse for wear as a thinking machine but highly evolved as a feeling being. As Mosscap thus comes into focus, the anthropocentric experience of supersmart robots as monstrous gives way to the comedy of "clashing or ambiguous affects" (Berlant and Ngai 2017, 239). The friendship that subsequently develops between the monk and the robot can be understood as comedic precisely in the terms Berlant and Ngai articulate: "Bodies run into each other, and the world runs into beings! Love happens and the objects become weird. . . . In the comedic scene, things are always closer to each other than they appear" (2017, 248). Comedy—particularly its lighter species of the physical, the funny, and the romantic—has been underestimated as a meaningful form for environmental imagination and environmental movements. It is not surprising, then, that the work of a writer like Chambers has been identified as light fare, a comforting escape from the gravitas of eco-apocalypse and climate realism. But, if we take comedy seriously, the boundary-crossing friendship between a lichen-dusted robot named for a mushroom it adores and a queer tea monk from the city who is searching for nature activates a radical and powerful imaginative portal to a world made otherwise from this one.

In "the comedic scene" of Dex and Mosscap's collision and the caring relationship they then form, the robot shows a more-than-human intelligence whose capacity for love counteracts the dystopia of superhuman, superintelligent machines that "do not care for us nor for sentient life in general" (Yudkowsky 2023). If tech researchers and commentators forecast an "alien civilization, thinking at millions of times human speeds, . . . that won't stay confined to computers for long" (Yudkowsky 2023), the *Monk and Robot* stories transgress sci-fi conventions and work against technological determinism, melding buddy comedy with ecological utopianism to ask, What if robots became next-generation environmentalists? When Mosscap first speaks in the opening novella of the series, we realize that the robot has feelings of its own, feelings rooted in multispecies love rather than AI power. Dex's initial hostility catches the robot off guard: "Oh, dear.

Have I done something wrong? You're the first human I've ever met. The large mammals I'm most familiar interacting with are river wolves, and they respond best to a direct approach" (Chambers 2021, 51). In this misunderstanding, the human recedes to just one species among many—and a peculiarly mercurial and violent one at that—while the machine shows its deep affection for the wild world. This exchange and the speculative narrative it launches thus upend both the technological utopianism of AI enthusiasts and the apocalypticism of their critics, skeptics, and doomsday opponents. The latter may, in the end, have the last laugh. But the scenarios they game out take as unmovable the power of tech at once to build and to destroy—to upend and to rehabilitate—the world. With a light but powerful touch, the ecological speculations of a monk and a robot reject the machinic imaginaries of engineers and, in their place, offer the relational and fluid future of the wild-built.

[CHAPTER 4]

Wilderness by Design

> As threats to wildlife increase with the pace of climate change, so too must our conservation strategies. Our Genetic Rescue Toolkit is a suite of biotechnology tools with direct conservation applications, designed to turn the tide on biodiversity loss. They are building blocks for genetic rescue in wildlife.
>
> —REVIVE AND RESTORE, "2023 Annual Report"

You probably know this story. On a private island west of Costa Rica called Isla Nublar, the Palo Alto–based company International Genetic Technologies (InGen) has been constructing a wildlife preserve for extinct animals from the Mesozoic era that were resurrected by next-generation biotechnology. This science-fictional landscape is on the cusp of opening as a destination theme park whose main attraction is a manufactured ecosystem for fifteen dinosaur species, most of which—including the park's representatives of the genera *Dilophosaurus*, *Velociraptor*, and *Tyrannosaurus*—did not coexist during their natural lifetimes. Their synthetic creation in the late twentieth century has been made possible, first, by "very powerful supercomputers" programmed for complex genetic sequencing tasks and, second, by the genome of a living frog used to fill in gaps in the dinosaur DNA that the scientists recovered from amber-preserved mosquitoes (Crichton 1990/1991, 102). The bioengineering of these storied animals has been achieved thanks to InGen CEO John Hammond. Under pressure from his investor group to vet the park's safety before opening to visitors, Hammond has enlisted two paleontologists and a mathematician to join him on the island for a private tour. Having kept the three experts in the dark as to the nature of Isla Nublar, he arranges for a dramatic arrival by helicopter, landing the group in a lush valley populated by fifty-foot-tall brontosauruses.

While initially enchanted, the scientists quickly sour on the park as their weekend tour goes from wondrous to gruesome. A computer shutdown orchestrated by a disgruntled InGen programmer triggers a series of catastrophic events: electrified fences and gates lose power, carnivorous dinosaurs escape their paddocks and kill people, and the wildlife park devolves into a murderous quagmire. Amid the chaos, the scientists discover that, despite their genetic engineering to ensure sterility, some of the dinosaurs have begun breeding in the wild. With a nod to Mary Shelley's nineteenth-century fictional mad scientist Victor Frankenstein (see chap. 3), the mathematician condemns Hammond for his hubris: "You create new life-forms, about which you know nothing at all. . . . You expect them to do your bidding, because you made them and you therefore think you own them; you forget that they are alive [and] have an intelligence of their own" (Crichton 1990/1991, 708). A true believer to the end, Hammond defends his vision of time travel through advanced biotech, right up to the moment he is killed by one of the dinosaurs just as the park's few human survivors realize that the raptors have escaped the remote island to the outside world.

This sequence of events recounts the familiar plot of *Jurassic Park*, the Michael Crichton novel (first published in 1990) that became a billion-dollar blockbuster film directed by Steven Spielberg (1993). Its inspiration was the rise of the biotech industry and the industry's then leading company, Genentech, founded in 1976 by the Silicon Valley venture capitalist Robert Swanson and the Berkeley chemist Herbert Boyer. In making bioengineering the stuff of action movies, *Jurassic Park* updated the mad scientist archetype as an eccentric investor obsessed with creating life from scratch. However fanciful its story of resurrected dinosaurs, scientific research provided Crichton with the novel's initial fodder, research that began in the 1980s around the question whether insects preserved in fossilized tree resin—or amber—contained DNA and, if so, whether such DNA could be recovered, repaired, and partially or wholly sequenced as the biological basis for the in vitro reproduction of long-lost species. That *Jurassic Park* made explicit references to this research reverberated in the scientific community when first the book and then the film garnered popular success. The result was to associate the fledgling field of extinct DNA studies with junk science.

Three decades later, the idea of species resurrection resurfaced as *de-extinction*, although this time with the ostensibly more modest proposal of bringing back species that have gone extinct in the time of humans—the woolly mammoth, the passenger pigeon, the dodo, and so on. While a niche within the global biotech industry, de-extinction has captured outsized attention on the part of science journalists and science funders. Proponents tend to be either circumspect or dismissive about the many technical challenges to de-extinction and generally downplay pressing ecological and ethical questions: questions such as why a handful of extinct species merits gargantuan investments at the potential expense of existing species, who determines the species that merit revival, how these potential novel organisms will be released into the wild, and, finally, to what extent de-extinction redoubles colonial notions of nature and colonial histories of wilderness land use that are profoundly at odds with environmental justice.

These and other open questions notwithstanding, de-extinction gained traction in the 2010s thanks to one of its chief supporters, the longtime technology writer and networker Stewart Brand, who hopes to "advance the story" of environmentalism through "wild schemes" like geoengineering and de-extinction that implicitly reject environmentalist anxiety, dread, and apocalypticism and advance, instead, beliefs in technological solutions to even the most complex ecological and climatic problems (quoted in Wray 2017, 8). A Stanford biology grad, Brand rose to prominence in the 1960s and 1970s as a promoter of both green technology and optimistic environmentalism. He put himself on the map with *The Whole Earth Catalog*, whose inaugural issue introduced the now well-known missive: "We *are* as gods and might as well get used to it" (Whole Earth 1968). The *Catalog* and its spin-off group the WELL (identified as the first online community) connected largely White leaders of the back-to-the-land movement, some of whom started cooperative farms in Northern California, with coders and investors in Silicon Valley (Geiger 2020; Hoefler 1971; Kirk 2007; Turner 2006). Few accounts of Brand and the social networks he fostered quote the rest of the *Catalog*'s founding editorial statement, which reads retrospectively as a template for Nature Remade. In it, Brand calls on an audience he paints as radical trailblazers "to conduct [their] own education, find [their] own inspiration, [and] *shape [their] own environment*" (Whole Earth 1968; emphasis added). In this century, he has moved on from the *whole Earth* to what he calls the *long now*. Under that heading, he and partners have launched projects that put techno-utopianism into practice—from a clock designed to tick for ten thousand years funded by Amazon CEO Jeff Bezos to an electronic database of "over 1,000 human languages" conceived as a universal digital archive that would be readable to aliens in a distant future with the aid of a "decoder ring" (Long Now Foundation, n.d.; Rosetta Project, n.d.). The Long Now Foundation project that has gone the furthest takes up Brand's 1968 appeal to *Catalog* readers to "shape their own environment." That project is the "genetic rescue of endangered and extinct species" at Revive and Restore, the "wildlife conservation organization promoting the incorporation of biotechnologies into standard conservation practice" (Revive and Restore 2023). In 2012, Brand founded the 501(c)3 nonprofit organization with his wife, Ryan Phelan, a longtime biotech investor, just a few miles from San Francisco in the picturesque town of Sausalito, which also has housed the editorial offices of the *Catalog* and Brand's suite of other publications. Revive and Restore is a small entity as compared to both biotech corporations like Genentech and de-extinction start-ups like Colossal. The latter was launched in 2021 by the Harvard scientist George Church and the tech entrepreneur Ben Lamm with the expressed mission to "reawaken the lost wilds of Earth" (Colossal, n.d.-b). In the first two years after its founding, Colossal had raised over $225 million in venture capital, having convinced investors to bet big on the profit potential of its plan to "restore the Earth, one species at a time," beginning with the woolly mammoth, the dodo, and the thylacine (more commonly known as the Tasmanian tiger) (Colossal, n.d.-a, n.d.-c). By comparison, Revive and Restore's annual revenue as of 2021 was just under $6 million, about a quarter of which was distributed in the form of grants to research teams at universities and zoos (ProPublica 2021, 2023). What it lacks in financial capital, however, Revive and Restore makes up for in the zeal of Brand, Phelan, and its lead scientist, Ben Novak. As the environmental historian Ben Minteer puts it, Brand is "one of the driving forces behind" de-extinction who is not only shaping its research agenda but also promulgating a captivating narrative that this chapter terms *wilderness by design* (2019, 5).

What follows situates this narrative in the twin contexts of Silicon Valley techno-utopianism and the US branch of a conservation movement known as *rewilding*. In 2010, a literature review of de-extinction would have yielded just a couple hundred citations in English, as keyword and full-text searches for the years prior to 2010 in the Princeton University Library's Articles+ database showed. Updated to run through 2023, the same search netted over twenty-three hundred citations. What explains this exponential growth in academic and popular interest? Answering that question demonstrates the capacities of techno-optimistic narrative to catalyze scientific research and research funding and highlights the particular rhetorical and social power of Brand's and other de-extinction advocates' vision of *wilderness remade*. This vision has captured influential media venues such as TED, the *National Geographic*, and the *New York Times* and has been the subject of popular science titles such as *Regenesis* (Church and Regis 2014), *How to Clone a Mammoth* (Shapiro 2015), *Life as We Made It* (Shapiro 2021), *Rise of the Necrofauna* (Wray 2017), *The Re-Origin of Species* (Kornfeldt 2018), and *Second Nature* (Rich 2021). Through the stories it has produced and inspired, the network around de-extinction has been making the case that biotechnology is vital to both "enhancing biodiversity" and mitigating climate change (Revive and Restore 2023). It is the argument of this chapter that, at once nostalgic and futuristic, this de-extinction narrative transmutes rewilding—originally intended to promote the geographic expansion of existing wildlife preserves—into a horizon for novel ecologies.

Although de-extinction has garnered popular science coverage and inspired a robust academic literature, it has received limited attention in the environmental humanities and science and technology studies. Where scholars in these fields have engaged with de-extinction, they have done so to elucidate its relationship to biotech and bioethics or to situate it in the larger context of endangered and extinct animals. Regardless of the lens, the tendency has been to locate de-extinction on the edges of serious science, "a curio" more than a serious subject (Minteer 2019, 115). Given the rhetorical and social savvy of its leading figures, however, de-extinction merits sustained critical study so that an increasingly well-funded arena of experimental biotechnology is not flying under the radar of either academic or political scrutiny. This concern guides this chapter and informs its coda, which juxtaposes what I call the *charismatic meganarrative* of de-extinction with an *ecopoetics* of multispecies justice. The coda gives the last word, specifically, to poems that the writer Craig Santos Perez (Chamoru) has penned about Pacific island extinctions in Guåhan (Guam) as inseparable from the ongoing consequences of colonialism for biodiversity and from the self-determination of Indigenous nations around conservation. In grappling with these forces, Perez provides not just a countervailing vision to that of wilderness by design but also a collectively determined model of native species stewardship and multispecies care.

The *Whole Earth* and Its Godlike Engineers

Jeremiads on pollution, global warming, and biodiversity loss discussed in the introduction—from Rachel Carson's *Silent Spring* (1962) to Bill McKibben's *The End of Nature* (1989a)—have played a major role in shaping a wilderness-centered environmental movement in the United States. As that movement was first taking shape between the 1960s and 1980s, the seeds for Nature Remade were germinating an hour north of Silicon Valley, in an unlikely network that formed around Brand and *The Whole Earth Catalog*. The imperative in the journal's founding statement cited above sidelined not only public institutions of all kinds—from governments to universities—but also collective environmental movements. In their place, the *Catalog* celebrated tinkering, making, and creating out of whole cloth. While the *Catalog* circulated regularly for only four years, Brand continued to publish it intermittently through the late 1990s, over which time it became increasingly aligned with the venture capitalism of Silicon Valley. To take just one example, a 1986 issue titled "The Essential Whole Earth Catalog" featured a profile of an agricultural think tank called the New Alchemy Institute, highlighted less for its experiments in "composting greenhouses and . . . eco-righteous housing" than for its entrepreneurial suite of "consulting services" (Whole Earth 1986, 90). Marginalia in the proof of this same issue show that Brand and his editorial team were excising content deemed socially radical (in their words, "illegal and dangerous"), including a review of the edited collection *Ecodefense* (Abbey, Foreman, and Haywood 1987), an advertisement for Loompanics Unlimited (a radical publisher of anarchist manuals), and a blurb for the latest edition of Alex Comfort's 1972 illustrated manual *The Joy of Sex* (Whole Earth 1986, 143, 230–31). By the 1980s, as Fred Turner details, "Brand had taken several key steps toward integrating the ideas and people of the *Whole Earth* into the emerging world of networked computing," placing "himself and [his] publications at the intersection of multiple communities . . . the residual countercultural and the flourishing technical" (2006, 132). In the twenty-first century, this fusion of counterculture with tech has morphed into what Brand calls *ecopragmatism*—a pitch to environmentalists of all stripes to get on board with transgenic food, nuclear power, and carbon capture (Brand 2009). In short, for decades Brand has been making the case and laying the groundwork for a tech-friendly environmentalism.

A case in point is the relationship between Brand and the Berkeley-born environmentalist and nature writer David Brower, who served as the Sierra Club's first executive director from 1952 to 1969 (Wyss 2016). The two had a long-running exchange that shows how Brand and the *Catalog* interfaced with the wilderness conservation community (David Ross Brower Papers). In 1974, Brower wrote an essay titled "How to Get to the Twenty-First Century from Here (Life in Post-industrial America)" that articulates an embryonic form of ecopragmatism. Five years earlier, Brower had left his role at the Sierra Club in protest of the organization's decision to back the construction of a nuclear power plant in Diablo Canyon on California's Central Coast. The internal rift that led to his departure from the influential conservation group was over not *whether* the utility Pacific Gas and Electric should build the plant but *where* it should build it. Enchanted with the canyon's chaparral ecosystem, Brower held that the proposed plant should be located in urban Oakland in what was a historically Black neighborhood (Wyss 2016, 225–29). His position exposed tacitly racist assumptions about what kinds of environments and whose backyards should be protected from—or sacrificed to—energy projects. Given the binary of sacred wilderness and inner city that defined Brower's break with the Sierra Club and inflected much of his nature writing, the 1974 essay is a striking outlier. In it, Brower delineates a future environmental movement that would promote active intervention in the wild "by design . . . instead of by default." The unpublished essay, which I came across when sifting through correspondence between Brand and prominent California environmentalists, opens with a searing critique of industrial capitalism: "Isn't all we need a little more old-style Progress? Build a few Alaska pipelines, turn coal and shale into oil, drain the offshore reserves fast, get the environmentalists off our back?" The rhetorical questions introduce not a lament for wilderness lost, however, but a prompt to "graduate" from "the old industrial well" to what Brower describes as planetary "love" (Brower 1974). In sharp contrast to Brower's writing while at the Sierra Club (e.g., Brower and Sierra Club 1961), this argument for planetary care is illustrated by a wide range of emerging technology, from "fish farms" as models for a postindustrial food system to smart homes inspired by Disney's Tomorrowland (Brower 1974), one of the *themed lands* found at most of the company's amusement parks, the first of which opened in 1955 as Disneyland in Anaheim, California (Wasko 2020, 24–26).

Two years after composing his 1974 road map for twenty-first-century environmentalism, Brower contributed a column to an issue of *CoEvolution Quarterly* (the publication Brand launched after the *Catalog*) regarding a set of space colony proposals drafted by the physicist Gerard O'Neill (Brower 1976). Brower's response is, admittedly, far from a ringing endorsement. As in other essays he published in this period, the riposte starts from the premise that natural environments are "self-maintaining" systems disrupted more than enhanced by engineering. A year earlier, he had expanded on this circumspect account of terraforming other planets in an article for the *New York Times Magazine* that included an extended discussion of Buckminster Fuller's technophilic *Operating Manual for Spaceship Earth* (Brower 1975; Fuller 1969). At first blush, the article reads like a parody of Fuller's theory that the Earth operates like a complex machine requiring constant upkeep and upgrading by its human engineers (a theory mentioned again in chap. 6). To quote Brower:

> This planet will be found to consist of complex and fascinating detail in design and structure. Some passengers, upon discovering these details in the past, have attempted to replicate or improve the design and structure, or have even claimed to have invented them. The Manufacturer, having among other things invented the opposable thumb, may be amused by this. (Brower 1975)

While Brower leaves the final relative pronoun ("amused by *this*") unspecified, the implied noun is the engineer's hubris. If Brand's publications had come to align California inventors, entrepreneurs, and cultural rebels with superhuman powers of creation, Brower subscribes here, as in other writings, to the divine provenance of nature. Yet the gravitational pull of Brand and the *Catalog* seems to have shaded Brower's view of *the future* of both natural systems and conservation practices. We see this influence not only in his essays from the 1970s but also in correspondence with Brand that took place around a 1978 "Jamboree" sponsored by the *Catalog* and organized to connect computer programmers and futurists with environmental writers, artists, activists, and scientists.[1] To Brower's invitation, Brand appended a personal note: "Don't cramp your style—just be aware we're under scrutiny as potential despoilers of the landscape" (Brand 1978). The coconspiratorial tone reveals both an established rapport between the two and Brand's cavalier attitude toward the environmental impacts of an event planned for upward of twenty thousand people in the Marin Headlands, a protected coastal area north of San Francisco. Significantly, the area is a chaparral ecosystem kindred to the one Brower had fought a decade earlier to protect from nuclear energy.

My experience working through the papers of Brower, Brand, the Sierra Club, and *The Whole Earth Catalog* (collections held at Berkeley and Stanford) revealed not just an exchange of ideas between disparate thinkers but also the role Brand played in acclimating increasingly demoralized environmentalists to the tenets of green capitalism. For his part, Brower was alternately resistant and drawn to those tenets and the techno-utopianism they evince. He concludes his meditation on space colonies, for instance, with the admission that ecological conditions on Earth may one day make an off-world home a necessary experiment: "If Mr. O'Neill's colonies, after due energy accountancy and review of the environmental impact statement, prove more desirable than the present alternative, then let me be the first to place reservations, for the first colony, for all who would continue the atoms-for-peace/war experiment here" (Brower 1976). With an allusion to the looming fear and possibility of nuclear war, Brower ultimately lands on the side of ambivalence about technological fixes for anthropogenic environmental crises. That ambivalence provides an opening for figures like Brand in this chapter's story of de-extinction who tap into wilderness nostalgia while portraying godlike engineers as redemptive reinventors of Earth.

New Conservation

The connection between Brand and Brower points to an origin for de-extinction in California's entwined identities around technological innovation and environmental conservation. That connection finds a contemporary echo in a network of scientists, engineers, writers, and research groups associated with what has been called *new conservation.* Those who have taken up the moniker view as "anachronistic and unproductive" received orthodoxies of wilderness protection and restoration ecology (Marvier, Kareiva, and Lalasz 2011). For new conservationists, the Anthropocene does not just name the anthropogenic drivers and consequences of climate change; it inspires a departure from environmentalism as usual. Referring to Brand as a leading figure, Minteer characterizes new conservation as jettisoning "mythical ideals of an untouched (and untouchable)" nature while extolling "human ambitions and abilities" (Minteer 2019, 10).[2] In the words of two prominent scientists associated with new conservation, Peter Kareiva and Michelle Marvier, "every flux and cycle of the planet's ecology and geochemistry" have been irrevocably changed by people (Kareiva and Marvier 2012, 2013), the implication being that the science of *conservation* should no longer necessarily focus on preserving ecosystems as they are (or on restoring them to a past state) but instead foster new and better forms of human intervention in Earth systems and environments. The claim goes hand in hand with the depiction of longtime environmentalist struggles, such as those on behalf of "halting deforestation in the Amazon," as unfeasible, misguided, and "almost fantastical"—especially, this argument suggests, when the aims are to resist or dismantle capitalism and market-based approaches to environmental challenges (Marvier, Kareiva, and Lalasz 2011; see also Ellis 2015, 20, 26, 30).

These new conservation commitments to ecological engineering and green capitalism reflect an overarching conviction that "we can make more nature," to quote the science writer Emma Marris. In *Rambunctious Garden*, Marris investigates experiments in ecological design for what she terms a *postwild world.* The book surveys *novel ecosystems* categorically changed by human impact and new conservation experiments in those ecosystems' further and deliberate transformation, experiments that tacitly undercut the longtime value placed on native species in the discipline of ecology. The book glosses, for example, the case of Ascension Island in the South Atlantic as evidence that plants introduced by British colonial scientists and prospectors "resulted not in ecological meltdown but in the creation of a cloud forest composed of species from here and there." It also profiles the self-described "space ecologist" Joe Mascaro, whose doctoral research attempted to show that an "exotic-dominated ecosystem" on the Big Island of Hawai'i has been "functioning *better* than nearby native forest" in terms of biodiversity—research Marris relays without mentioning forest restoration and taro-farming projects led by Kānaka Maoli (Native Hawaiian) groups in the same area. These and other case studies lead her to depict novel ecosystems as at once human created and marvelously wild:

"We may have introduced the various parties to one another, directly by moving them or indirectly by changing the climate, but the rhythm of life they take up and the interplay of selection pressures they produce on one another are all up to them." Elaborating on this description, the book concludes with a coda that introduces the concept of "designer ecosystems" that have been engineered "*de novo* to achieve a particular goal." Relaying the work of scientists who entirely decouple ecological interventions from historical reference points (what are termed *baselines* in the fields of conservation and restoration ecology), Marris shows new conservation to be an instantiation of Nature Remade. Building on the biologist René Dubos's 1980 wish to one day see, in Marris's words, "a flourishing world covered in managed nature," *Rambunctious Garden* defines this growing branch of ecology as advancing the "best-case future" on a postwild planet (Marris 2011, 56, 111, 113, 121, 126, 130–31).

In *Imagining Extinction*, Ursula K. Heise identifies a "story template" that has shaped much environmental thought around biodiversity and its diminishment, especially in an American context, according to which "modern society has degraded a natural world that used to be beautiful, harmonious, and self-sustaining and that might disappear completely." This template, which Heise terms *declensionist*, rebuts "dominant narratives of social, economic, and technological progress" (Heise 2016a, 7). As *Rambunctious Garden* makes clear, new conservation dispenses with the story of ecological decline precisely by recuperating these dominant progress narratives on the view that environmentalists have "grossly overstated the fragility of nature" (Marvier, Kareiva, and Lalasz 2011). This conviction inspires calls to "manage the planet better," as David Biello writes in *The Unnatural World*. To quote Biello, ecopragmatist thinkers like those aligned with new conservation hope for "a new age of human adaptation . . . on a science fictional planet" that will "*writ*[*e*] a new chapter in Earth's history" (2016, 7, 4, 7; emphasis added). This optimistic vantage on a deliberately *unnatural* future coalesces around a redefinition of *wilderness* and *wildlife* that, on its face, resonates with long-standing critiques of American wilderness mythologies as regressive and exclusionary. Rehearsing those critiques, the geographer Jaime Lorimer conceptualizes the "unnatural wilds of the Anthropocene . . . as a multispecies commons, claimed and contested by diverse economic interests." Although his study of "wildlife in the Anthropocene" never cites new conservation explicitly, it argues for a participatory form of ecology that resists "future natures . . . engineered and secured through neoliberal environmentalism" (Lorimer 2015, 192–93). For new conservation adherents, in contrast, the postwild future will happily be defined by entrepreneurs and engineers, groups that Biello identifies as this century's pioneers. Two of the most cited scientists in the new conservation literature, Kareiva and Marvier, ostensibly align new conservation with environmental justice, while Marris observes that the traditional focus on wilderness protection in conservation has often ignored the sovereignty and stewardship of local communities (Marvier, Kareiva, and Lalasz 2011; Marris 2011, 42–43, 47). However, new conservation discourse ultimately discounts—or at least misapprehends—the histories and objectives of social movements organized around environmental justice, such as Indigenous *land back*, in what is a too-easy alignment of those movements with "the right kinds of technology to enhance the health and well-being of both human and nonhuman natures" (Marvier, Kareiva, and Lalasz 2011). "Instead of scolding capitalism," Marvier and Kareiva write, environmental justice coalitions "should partner with corporations in a science-based effort to integrate the value of nature's benefits into their operations and cultures" (2011). New conservation thus fashions itself as a bridge—or, perhaps more aptly, a broker—between green tech and green capital, on the one hand, and collective mobilizations that aspire for far-reaching systemic change.

In this disposition, new conservation perpetuates a problem that has been a long-running one for wilderness protection, which the sociologist Ramachandra Guha characterizes as a "custodial approach" that has often undermined Indigenous sovereignty claims and livelihoods (2000, 38).[3] Long before the UC Santa Cruz scientist Michael Soulé (1985) coined the term *conservation biology* to describe what was then a fledgling field dedicated to the study and protection of wildlands, a global system of wildlife refuges and national parks was put in place that both "harken[ed] back to an imagined past" and actively sought "to reshape the present" (Guha 2000, 30). In *Rambunctious Garden,* Marris cites this history in observing that "the pristine wilderness notion is a historically created idea about what ought to count as nature" (2011, 56), a point Kareiva and Marvier (2011) echo. Read closely, however, new conservation waters down historical analyses of scholars like Guha and William Cronon. Cronon's often-cited essay "The Trouble with Wilderness; or, Getting Back to the Wrong Nature" traces the evolving meaning of wilderness in the United States as "an island in the polluted sea of urban-industrial modernity, the one place we can turn for escape from our own too-muchness" (Cronon 1996, 1). The essay identifies a key origin for this mythology in nineteenth- and twentieth-century US expansionism and White anxiety about "a *vanishing* frontier" (Cronon 1996, 7).[4] As that anxiety influenced the law and practice of national parks and designated wilderness areas, Cronon writes, the same people who "most benefited from urban-industrial capitalism were among those who believed they must escape its debilitating effects" by retreating for intervals of time to environments defined as wild (Cronon 1996, 9). The trouble with *pristine* wilderness as an environmental imaginary with particular staying power in American culture is not that it stymies capitalism, as new conservation suggests, but that it coevolves with it (Cronon 1996).

In turn, the wilderness myth of unpeopled and primeval landscapes—with its ahistorical vocabulary—has made conservation an agent, if in some cases unwittingly, of colonialism while also codifying American wilderness as a White space. In *Black Faces, White Spaces*, the historian Carolyn Finney delves into this relationship "between the construction of race and the environment in the United States," underscoring, for instance, the concurrent passage in 1964 of the Wilderness Act and the Civil Rights Act. Out of step with racial justice activism at the time, the former "presumed a universality of ideals" about nature and about what lands and waters in the United States should be protected, by what means, and for whom (Finney 2014, 44). One of a dozen major environmental bills signed into law between the 1963 Clean Air Act and the 1973 Endangered Species Act, the Wilderness Act promised to protect federal forests and national parks for "*public* purposes of recreational, scenic, scientific, educational, conservation, and historical use" (Wilderness Act 1964; emphasis added). "But which public?" Finney (2014, 47) asks. In the summer of 2020, during the COVID-19 pandemic and the Black Lives Matter–led demonstrations sparked by the police murder of George Floyd, Finney published an op-ed about how Black Americans experience the "fraught terrains" of both urban environments and wilderness areas. The inquiry concludes with an unequivocal recognition that "systemic racism exists on both the streets of our cities and inside our national parks" (Finney 2020). Such analyses probe not just the nation-building projects for which the American wilderness has been instrumental but also the systemic exclusion of Black, Brown, and Indigenous peoples from participating "on their own terms" in those projects (Finney 2014, 50). What's more, wilderness law and policy have been prone to instrumentalization in affording access to federal lands for natural resource extraction. Originally drafted by the conservationist Howard Zahniser, the Wilderness Act defined its titular category in opposition to all "areas where man and his own works dominate the landscape." But this definition comes with a significant legal caveat where the act assures that at least certain wilderness areas will support mining, grazing, and energy exploration "if such activity is carried on in a manner compatible with the preservation of the wilderness environment" (Wilderness Act 1964). Since the act's passage, that stipulation has translated into an ever-expanding landscape of federal leases for oil drilling, uranium mining, hydropower, and ranching, among other industries.

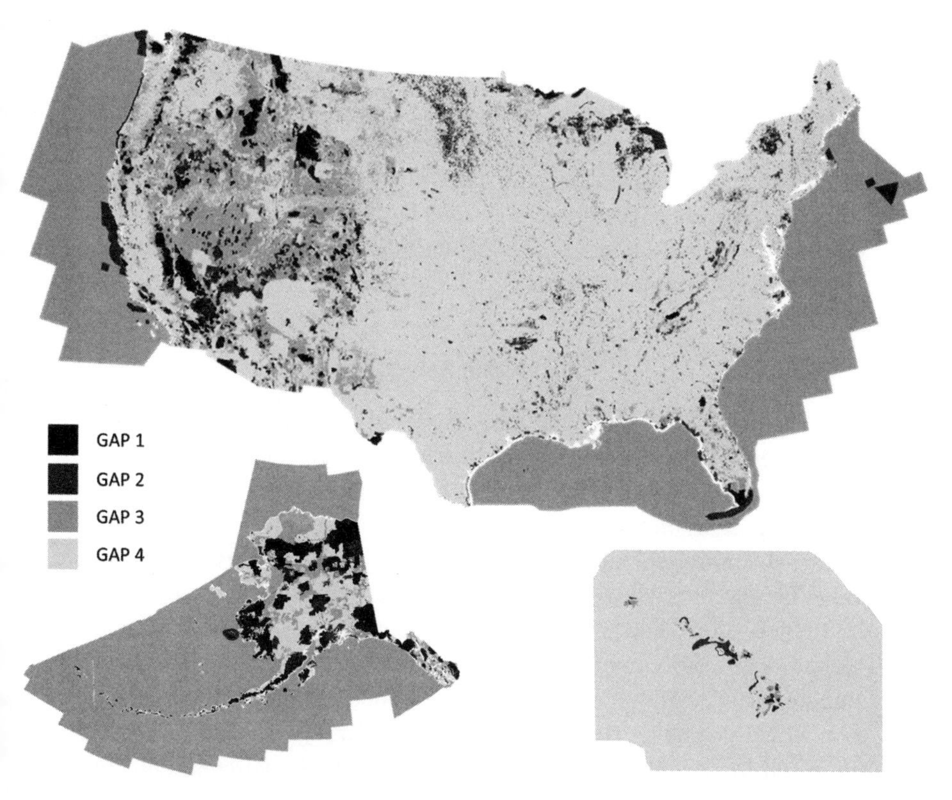

Figure 4.1. Concentration of US wilderness areas (2020). GAP Status Map, US Geological Survey (USGS) Gap Analysis Project, Defenders of Wildlife Report (2021).

California and the wider West have been central to how the American wilderness has so been conceived, codified, and contested. That history begins in earnest with Yellowstone, Yosemite, and Sequoia—the first three national parks in the world, designated (in that order) between 1872 and 1890. Over the twentieth century, the greatest concentration of new wilderness areas were located in the western United States, such that by 2022 the vast majority of those areas were found along California's Sierra Nevada, in the deserts of the Southwest, and in Alaska (Congressional Research Service 2005; Wilderness Society 2021). It is these landscapes that, in turn, most define how wilderness continues to be imagined by diverse publics and put to use on behalf of "prospectors" of all stripes (fig. 4.1). During the years I was writing this book, for example, the built-in contradictions of the Wilderness Act and its judicial and legislative legacies allowed the Trump administration to reduce the size of Bears Ears Monument in Utah, which sits on the homelands of five Indigenous tribes, and to make millions of acres of federally controlled land and water available for new oil and gas leases (Holden 2020; Ruas 2020). However "unprecedented" (Holden 2020) in a single presidential term, these actions deepened, rather than broke with, the status quo of the US federal government, which is "one of the largest energy asset managers in the world—responsible for over 2.4 billion acres of subsurface mineral rights, including resources like coal, crude oil, and natural gas" (Ruas 2020).[5] This staggeringly large figure exceeds the country's total surface land area.

Pleistocene Rewilding

What do these histories tell us about American wilderness as its scientific and sociopolitical histories animate the premises and applications of new conservation? Most significantly for this chapter's account of wilderness by design, the centrality of American forests, deserts, and waters to the global energy economy demonstrates how narratives of wild nature have provided cover for nature profiteering and petrocapitalism. Although ecologists like Soulé have published broadsides against new conservation arguments, he and others who first defined conservation science also developed the framework of rewilding that has become a touchstone for new conservation writ large and for de-extinction in particular. The term *rewilding* first appeared around 1992, when Earth First! founder Dave Foreman launched the Wildlands Project with Soulé and the biologist Reed Noss. Their goal was to advance an "interconnected system of [wildlife] reserves throughout North America," a project based on evidence that habitat fragmentation from agriculture and urban sprawl, among other factors, had become a major cause of biodiversity loss (Foreman et al. 1993, 25). In a subsequent paper, Soulé and Noss explained that rewilding aimed to expand the scale of protected wilderness areas in North America. Key to this formulation was what the group called "big wilderness," which built on existing wilderness mythologies while faulting the US system of national parks for an ideology of "monumentalism" that privileged human values and desires. By comparison, the Wildlands Project presented a blueprint for expansive wildlife habitats structured around the needs of nonhuman species and managed to protect "hotspots of biodiversity" from industry, development, and recreation (Soulé and Noss 1998, 21).

These first rewilding advocates longed to "reverse the flow of ecological time," as Ashley Dawson writes in his study of the sixth mass extinction (2016, 70). In *Recovering Lost Species in the Modern Age*, Dolly Jørgensen extends this observation about rewilding while comparing it to smaller-scale practices of native species reintroduction, on the one hand, and de-extinction—or resurrection biology—on the other. Jørgensen's book surveys historical antecedents to these contemporary conservation practices, foregrounding the "*longing* for recovery" that they share. While reintroductions prioritize the "particular function" a single species performed in a specific time and place, rewilding stakes out a long temporal horizon for change, "with the idea that the landscape should be returned to some kind of state prior to human intervention" (Jørgensen 2019, 9, 17). This temporality mirrors the spatial expanse of rewilding, which pits urban and industrial environments against what Foreman called the "Big Outside"—a concept that builds directly on the American wilderness mythology of "wide open spaces and virgin land" (Cronon 1996, 14). Put differently, what could be termed *rewilding 1.0* cordons off the wild from the peopled, a demarcation that explains its advocates' preoccupation with the large predators and herbivores that lived in North America prior to the first arrival of human beings. Lorimer puts a fine point on this strand of rewilding, noting that it moves "the target baseline for conservation away from premodern agricultural archetypes toward the prehistoric ecological conditions that characterized the northern hemisphere at the end of the Pleistocene" (2015, 100). In that era, the continent was a habitat for mammoths, mastodons, wild horses, giant ground sloths, camels, and saber-tooth cats—the *charismatic megafauna* of the Ice Age.[6]

There is ongoing debate about what precipitated the extinction of many of these species between the end of the Pleistocene and the beginning of the Holocene some thirteen to eight thousand years ago. While many scientists point to natural climate change that produced warming temperatures and drought conditions, a few identify the chief cause as hunting practices on the part of the first humans to inhabit the continent: the Clovis people (Becerra-Valdivia and Higham 2020; Broughton and Weitzel 2018; Cooper et al. 2015; Meltzer 2015; Polyak et al. 2012; Shapiro 2015, 4–5; Wolfe and Broughton 2020).[7] In *The Sixth Extinction*, the environmental writer Elizabeth Kolbert gives credence to this interpretation of causality rather than concurrency, attributing "a wave of disappearances that has come to be known as the megafauna extinction" to "the spread of modern humans" (2014, 46). In their writings, Soulé and Noss (1998, 19) also pinpoint the arrival of people in North America as a cataclysmic turning point for the continent's wildlife. While the Wildlands Project had its sights on a future in which rewilding shored up modern "predators, such as wolves, rather than replicated 10,000-year-old ecosystems," nostalgia for prehuman nature underlies its Big Outside vision, a nostalgia, we will see, that de-extinction adopts and enlists in the service of technological utopianism (Carey 2016, 806).

In the decade after the Wildlands Project was announced, the subject of rewilding remained fairly dormant in the scientific literature.[8] That changed in 2005, when the Arizona zoologist Paul Martin published a trade book titled *Twilight of the Mammoths: Ice Age Extinctions and the Rewilding of America*, which details what Martin describes as "farsighted" proposals for the "recovery of top predators such as grizzlies, cougars, and wolves." Citing Soulé and Noss, Martin ups the scientific ante of rewilding by arguing for near-term introductions of cheetahs and lions on the basis of their biological ties to the saber-tooth tiger. He here breaks from rewilding as conservation scientists had first conceived it, declaring that its "ultimate" goal should be the resuscitation of mythologized creatures from a distant past (Martin 2005, 208). In making this case for a Pleistocene ecological revival, *Twilight of the Mammoths* elaborates on an article Martin published in the same year as the Wildlands Project proposal. In the article, he paints a picture of North America during the Ice Age as a "prehistoric 'game park'" with a "remarkable African flavor." Comparing environmental scientists like himself to White colonial explorers like Lewis and Clark and nature writers like Henry David Thoreau, Martin subscribes to the thesis that "Clovis colonizers rapidly swept the continent" and eventually eliminated large herbivores and predators. Characterizing these First Peoples as "colonizers," he likens Clovis nomadism and hunting—the disputed factors in late Pleistocene extinctions—to the repercussions of European colonialism in the Americas. This false equivalence informs a nativist claim to what Martin describes as "our late Pleistocene legacy":

> This, then, is our birthright, a continent whose wilderness once echoed to the thunder of many mighty beasts, a fauna that eclipsed all that remains, including the wild animals of Yellowstone and Denali. Those who ignore the giant ground sloths, native horses, and saber tooth cats in their vision of outdoor America sell the place short, it seems to me. This land is the mastodon's land. . . . Our late Pleistocene legacy means we can imagine more, not fewer, *kinds* of large animals on public lands, on the western range and in our national parks. (Martin 1992, 32)

This catalog intimates that an Ice Age wilderness is the "birthright" of contemporary people who have been estranged from its "mighty beasts." Martin here asserts a claim to American indigeneity as a scientist who might revive Pleistocene ecologies even as he delineates the Clovis as culpable for large-scale biodiversity loss, a frankly staggering assertion. In the *Twilight of the Mammoths*, he expands on these ideas by outlining some of the means that could make it a reality, the most ambitious of which features in the book's closing chapter, "Resurrection: The Past Is the Future." There, he summarizes a colleague's bid to release Guam rail birds (*ko'ko'* in the native Chamoru language) on the uninhabited island of Aguiguan (Martin 2005, 205). Designated as extinct in the wild in 1994, the once thriving *ko'ko'* population rapidly collapsed with the introduction on Guam of the Australian brown tree snake, which arrived in the holds of US military ships during and after World War II and became an unwitting agent of American militarism in the Pacific Islands (BirdLife International 2019). A captive breeding initiative launched in the mid-1980s and jointly managed by the US Fish and Wildlife Service and a consortium of American zoos was able to sustain a small population of *ko'ko'* birds in captivity, an experiment that Martin cites in support of his audacious rewilding scheme.[9] For Martin, the tools of captive breeding and species reintroduction that defined restoration ecology in the late twentieth century are just the starting point for Pleistocene rewilding.

Martin's vision proved tantalizing to philanthropists and investors. In particular, it attracted the notice of CNN founder Ted Turner, the third largest private landowner in the United States as of 2024 with over two million acres of property (Land Report 2024), whose Reserves and Endangered Species Fund combine ecotourism with wildlife protection and habitat restoration projects. In *Rambunctious Garden*, Marris recounts a gathering that Turner convened in 2005 shortly after the publication of Martin's book:

> Thirteen scientists and conservationists met at . . . Turner's ranch in New Mexico to discuss the idea of bringing proxies of extinct megafauna back to North America. The group agreed they would love to restore, if they could, the age *when nature lived wild and large*, when hairy mastodons and elephantine sloths heaved their bulk around the continent, *and when deadly predators were big, fast and ubiquitous*. (Marris 2011, 61; emphasis added)

As Marris's sketch suggests, this exclusive meeting among representatives from Hollywood, Silicon Valley, and environmental science identified the resurrection of extinct species as a serious aim for rewilding. Over the next two years, a subset of Turner's guests published papers on Pleistocene rewilding that at once play up the drama of and substantiate the scientific basis for the effort to "brin[g] proxies of extinct megafauna back to North America" (Donlan, Berger, et al. 2006; Donlan, Greene, et al. 2005). Lead-authored by the ecologist Josh Donlan, and published in topflight journals such as *Nature* and the *American Naturalist*, these proposals break from established definitions of native species in the Americas as endemic to ecosystems prior to either the arrival of European settlers or the rise of industrialization, pushing the temporality for rewilding back by thousands of years. Even more provocatively, they suggest translocating "small numbers of African cheetahs, . . . Asian . . . and African . . . elephants, and lions" from American zoos to private reserves like the Turner ranches (Donlan, Greene, et al. 2005, 914). This particular paper intimates that such translocations would be met with enormous political and ethical opposition were they proposed for federal wilderness areas or national parks. In contrast to the declensionist grief (in Heise's sense) that characterizes the first generation of rewilding, Donlan and his coauthors advance new conservation views, arguing: "Earth is nowhere pristine; our economics, politics, demographics and technology pervade every ecosystem" (Donlan, Greene, et al. 2005, 913). Central to these and other arguments for Pleistocene rewilding, accordingly, is the position that all ecosystems are already novel ones and the attendant aspiration to pursue ecological interventions that would make them yet more novel (Klop-Toker et al. 2020). Contra ecologists and environmentalists who are "purveyors of doom and gloom," the Donlan group writes, Pleistocene rewilding offers "an optimistic alternative . . . that fundamentally challenges our view of nature and seeks to transform conservation biology from a reactive into a proactive discipline" (Donlan, Berger, et al. 2006, 674). By *proactive*, the authors seem to mean a break with conservation as the science of ecological stewardship and incremental remediation, a break that makes Pleistocene rewilding a strange mixture of wilderness nostalgia and technological innovation.

The longer *American Naturalist* paper opens with the same fixation on prehistoric animals and landscapes that both the Wildlands Project and Martin express, defining the end of the Ice Age as the moment when "most large mammals and their commensals were lost" (Donlan, Berger, et al. 2006, 661). Dawson stresses that such nostalgia exemplifies long-standing White fantasies about nature: "What is natural for the Pleistocene rewilders is not the pre-European, but the *pre-human*" (Dawson 2016, 73). But this critique is a partial one that overlooks the intractable conflict in Pleistocene rewilding between the erasure of both colonialism and capitalism as drivers of modern biodiversity loss and the concomitant enchantment with cloning, synthetic biology, remote sensing, and other perceived technological gateways to the future. More specifically, the second generation of rewilding disciples hopes not just for the introduction of big cats in private parks but for a wholesale remaking of the "functional fabric of nature" and its "ecological and evolutionary processes" (Donlan, Berger, et al. 2006, 661). This determination has raised alarm bells for many fellow ecologists as well as bioethicists. To quote one such detractor group, the "*novel* plan for ecological restoration on a . . . grandiose temporal and spatial scale" risks major disruptions to existing species along with a diversion of attention and resources away from other, less flashy ecological research and stewardship (Rubenstein et al. 2006, 2, emphasis added; see also Caro 2007; Jørgensen 2015; Rubenstein and Rubenstein 2013; and Seddon, Moehrenschlager, and Ewen 2014). This concern highlights a tendency in Pleistocene rewilding—and its successor, de-extinction—to deploy ecological rationales and scientific terminology in endorsing what are fundamentally nonscientific aims, from emotional attachments that the proponents themselves feel for creatures like the woolly mammoth to the anticipated "cultural and economic benefits" (read: monetization potential) of *Jurassic Park*–style ecotourism (Donlan, Berger, et al. 2006, 673).

To date, Pleistocene rewilding has not yielded substantial "new science" according to its critics. But it has sparked a multidisciplinary conversation around its aspirations, contradictions, possibilities, and risks (Carey 2016, 808; Carver et al. 2021; Jørgensen 2019; Massenberg, Schiller, and Schröter-Schlaack 2023). And Martin, Donlan, and others' views of wilderness in the twenty-first century have certainly held Turner's attention. In 2006, the Turner Endangered Species Fund launched a new rewilding effort on the Armendaris Ranch in New Mexico for the Bolson tortoise, a species that inhabited the Chihuahuan Desert in north-central Mexico from the late Pleistocene through the twentieth century and was listed as endangered in 1982 (Carey 2016, 807–8; see also Truett and Phillips 2009). Contributing to a portfolio that includes the Aplomado falcon, the gray wolf, the plains bison, and the Rio Grande chub fish, the tortoise program began with the translocation to Turner's property of twenty-six animals "that were collected and bred over a period of nearly 40 years by a private individual" (Turner Endangered Species Fund 2019). While much touted in the science press, the program's ecological merits are unclear at best. Since 2007, the status of the Bolson tortoise across its native range has worsened from endangered to critically endangered, the causes of which include habitat fragmentation due to agriculture and ranching (Kiester et al. 2018). This fact raises the question whether a private ranch can or should be a chief site and agent of biodiversity renewal on a species-by-species basis. Yet stories of the Turner Endangered Species Fund in the popular media often identify the tortoise project as evidence for "how private land reserves are saving endangered species" (Hurly 2019) and as a model for a conservation science "free of governmental bureaucracy" (Johnson 2019). Such celebratory accounts not only overstate the capacity of ultrawealthy individuals to caretake and rehabilitate whole ecosystems but also ignore the diverse communities that fight for structural change to address the root causes of environmental problems like biodiversity loss—change to food systems, to energy grids, and to land ownership itself. An embodiment of what Justin Farrell terms *billionaire wilderness*, the Turner ventures displace collective environmentalism (Farrell 2020). Nonetheless, the story of cutting-edge technological approaches to wildlife protection and wildlands conservation is attractive to science writers, and, in the years since Turner gathered Martin and others at his ranch, Pleistocene rewilding has attracted both favorable press and new funding in support of its aspirations to revive prehuman biodiversity and, thus, redeem the Anthropocene.

The Science and Story of De-extinction

As an environmental imaginary, then, Pleistocene rewilding recuperates postindustrial humans by offering to rewind anthropogenic ecological disruption, degradation, and harm. This scheme percolated on the back burner after the Turner Ranch gathering until 2014, when Donlan published a renewed call that endorsed an embryonic technology not yet on the horizon when he and his coauthors first suggested releasing elephants from zoos into North American preserves as a substitute for "cloned mammoths" (Donlan, Berger, et al. 2006, 670). The paper suggests that emerging synthetic biology and genetic sequencing techniques could be applied to make chimeric hybrids of extinct animals, woolly mammoths among them (Donlan 2014, 25). Referring explicitly to what had been dubbed *de-extinction* two years earlier, the paper breaks decisively with the first generation of rewilding proponents, some of whom, like Soulé, had signed on to the initial Pleistocene papers. In support of the argument that "biodiversity conservation needs all the help and strategies it can muster," Donlan notably cites Brand's founding statement for *The Whole Earth Catalog*: "We are gods and might as well get good at it" (2014, 27). Those words from 1968 strike Donlan as "excellent advice for conservationists in the coming decades" (2014, 27), advice he himself has followed in setting up the consulting group Advanced Conservation Strategies whose purview is the application of "synthetic science to inform environmental conservation and sustainability decision-making" (Advanced Conservation Strategies, n.d.-c; see also Advanced Conservation Strategies, n.d.-a, n.d.-b). This confluence speaks to the savvy of Brand and others who have been promoting bioengineering as the next frontier for conservation science. In 2012, Brand's Long Now Foundation convened a meeting at Harvard in anticipation of the centennial of the death of Martha, the last passenger pigeon, that included a small and illustrious group of ecologists, geneticists, biotech investors, and bioethicists (Jørgensen 2019, 113). A year later, on the centennial of Martha's death, Brand organized a second convening under the auspices of TED, this time held at the *National Geographic* offices in Washington, DC, that served as a de-extinction showcase. These efforts made science headlines. Published by major papers and media outlets, the stories led with proclamations such as "the mammoth cometh" (Rich 2014), "bringing them back to life" (Zimmer 2013), "dream of Jurassic Park moves closer to reality" (Brean 2017), and "the multimillion-dollar resurrection of the Tasmanian tiger" (Morton 2022). Over the following decade, this euphoric story of de-extinction—or what Sophia Roosth has called a vision of *synthetic evolution*—has propelled the science communication around the field, overstating its promises and achievements while discounting its critics (see Roosth 2017, 162–63, 167).

Consider the case of the thylacine, one of the keystone species for de-extinction. In *The Fall of the Wild*, Minteer traces a history of de-extinction that begins with this species, which disappeared in its native Australia approximately thirty-five thousand years ago but persisted on Tasmania until the arrival of British settlers in the nineteenth century. Situated in a larger environmental history of wilderness conservation, Minteer's analysis of thylacine cloning efforts raises two vital questions that bear on the future promised by de-extinction: "How far should we go to bring back lost species?" "What do we mean by 'lost'?" (2019, 102). In traditional conservation, the act of "bringing back" a species has involved the movement of individuals from one habitat where a healthy population remains to a location where they are already gone or, alternatively, the gradual restoration and reintroduction of a population that is extinct in the wild via captive breeding programs. In practice, de-extinction builds on these and other established methods, contra those who bill the field as a wild new frontier. In examining the field's rhetoric and historicizing its science, however, Minteer contends that many of the stated goals are shaky at best, observing that the most fervent champions appeal to the aesthetic, cultural, and economic values of de-extinction while painting with a broad brush its technical procedures and challenges. Jørgensen concurs, noting that de-extinction has absorbed what she calls the "grief narrative" of extinction into a celebratory narrative of recovery and regeneration (2019, 113).

The conceptual seeds of de-extinction can, as suggested at the outset of this chapter, be traced back to the 1980s, when a small group of scientists organized the first professional meetings on extinct DNA. Experiments conducted by two members of this group—George Poinar and Roberta Hess—appeared to show that amber samples contained cellular material from a forty-million-year-old insect (Poinar and Hess 1982, 1241). Those findings were published in the flagship journal *Science*, after which Poinar wrote a trade book positing that, as the book's dust jacket blurb puts it, "viable DNA may persist in some amber-trapped" insects from the time of dinosaurs (1992). While peer reviewed, the claim proved fanciful. Researchers eventually demonstrated that the purported dinosaur DNA would have been from either "ancient microorganisms" or modern human handlers, underscoring that "contamination is a major problem encountered when dealing with ancient DNA" (Kelman and Kelman 1999, 11). In her 2015 *How to Clone a Mammoth*, Shapiro outlines these findings before detailing the latest science behind the collection, analysis, and sequencing of DNA from extinct animals (see fig. 4.2). Even under the best of environmental conditions, she explains, DNA likely survives no longer than 100,000 years, give or take, and, the older the specimen, the more fragmented any genetic information will be when researchers extract it (Shapiro 2015, 53). Despite the precautions taken by research teams like her UC Santa Cruz Paleogenomics Lab, the DNA obtained from long-dead organisms—whether woolly mammoth fossils exhumed from the Arctic permafrost or passenger pigeon specimens provided by natural history museums—carries with it manifold contaminants, including the DNA of still-living insects, birds, pets, and researchers themselves (Shapiro 2015, 57–65). Making things trickier still, the contaminating DNA is far more intact than the ancient DNA. As a result, the highly sensitive technique used to identify genetic fragments of interest to researchers (the same polymerase chain reaction, or PCR, used to search for traces of viruses such as SARS-CoV-2) will "preferentially find and make copies of clean, undamaged, freely floating, unbroken contaminating DNA rather than the broken, chemically linked, damaged, ancient DNA" (Shapiro 2015, 61). But it was not just methodological missteps in the first generation of ancient DNA research that compromised the scientists' findings but also the popular associations of their research with the science fiction of *Jurassic Park*: Hess and Poinar's research inspired Crichton's novel, in fact, and Poinar subsequently served as a scientific consultant for Spielberg's film adaptation. The proximity of the science to science fiction waylaid the field for years (Mueller 2009).[10]

Today, scientists affiliated with de-extinction are cognizant of this *Jurassic Park* liability and, accordingly, endeavor to infuse popular discourse around their work with the precision of scientific concepts and methods. As Shapiro asserts in the introduction to her book: "[E]xtinct species are gone forever. We will never bring back something that is 100 percent identical—physiologically, genetically, and behaviorally identical—to a species that is no longer alive." What is achievable, she explains, is the revival of "*extinct traits*" engineered into "living organisms" to meet specific

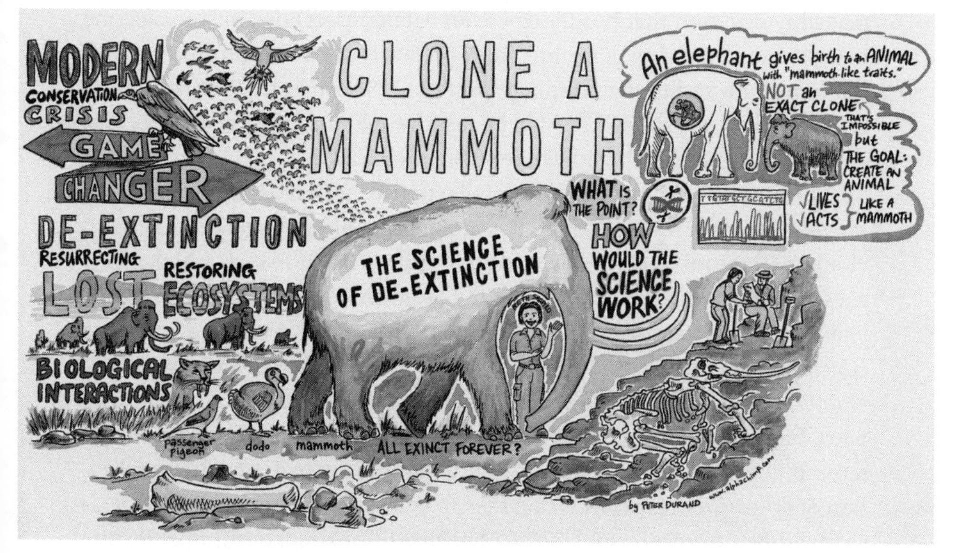

Figure 4.2. Peter Durand, "Clone a Mammoth: The Science of De-extinction." From Beth Shapiro, *How to Clone a Mammoth: The Science of De-extinction* (Princeton, NJ: Princeton University Press, 2015). Copyright © 2015 by Princeton University Press, reprinted by permission via Copyright Clearance Center.

ecological challenges (Shapiro 2015, 10). As an example, Shapiro describes the Colossal cofounder Church's lab at Harvard. The lab has been the center of a woolly mammoth de-extinction project focused on just two edits to the African elephant genome that would mimic key mammoth traits: a tweak in the hemoglobin to support lower body temperatures and a gene to code for "the thickest, most luxurious" elephant hair (Shapiro 2015, 124). Such experiments are, for Shapiro, guided by conservation science in their aims "to create functional equivalents of species that once existed: ecological proxies that are capable of filling the extinct species' ecological niche" (Shapiro 2017, 1001). The most cited scientist on de-extinction, Shapiro importantly offers a circumspect account of the field that offsets the variously ebullient and alarmist speculations of some of her colleagues and funders. The title of her book, *How to Clone a Mammoth,* belies her insistence on de-extinction challenges and caveats (Shapiro 2015, 130–31). Put differently, Shapiro tempers the "excitement" and "hysteria" around de-extinction not just by sketching how it might be realized in very specific and limited cases but also by foregrounding the many "hurdles standing in the way of fully reconstructing the genomes of extinct species." To drive this point home, she contrasts a hypothetical future headline proclaiming "Scientists Create Woolly Mammoth in Test Tube" to the actual achievement that would plausibly occasion that headline: a team having succeeded in "transferring at least one mammoth gene into an elephant stem cell" to produce "mammoth proteins rather than elephant proteins" (Shapiro 2015, 140, 125). That technical feat, she stresses, would be just the last in a long line of laborious and costly steps riddled with failures (Shapiro 2015, 125).

As *How to Clone a Mammoth* details, de-extinction depends on a wide range of nascent tools for genetic sequencing, editing, synthesizing, and cloning. The tool Shapiro has most in mind is CRISPR-Cas, which leverages a kind of bacterial DNA known as *clustered regularly interspaced short palindromic repeats* (or CRISPR) together with one of several Cas enzymes (Cas9 most famously) to identify, cleave, and alter genes, an increasingly efficient and affordable molecular tool kit often compared to the cut-and-paste function of Microsoft Word (Doudna and Sternberg 2017, 44–51). In targeting "many genes at once," CRISPR has become vital to the actualization of de-extinction projects that seek to edit the genomes of living species so that their offspring might look and behave like extinct ones: what R. Alta Charo and Henry Greely term *CRISPR critters* (Charo and Greely 2015, 11; see also Preston 2018, 88–89). The technology dates to 2011, when Jennifer Doudna and Emmanuelle Charpentier "demonstrated a way to program these molecular scissors to cut up . . . any DNA they wanted" and insert the modified "DNA into the genome at the site that has just been cut to effect a desired genetic change" (Wray 2017, 50–51), a breakthrough for which they received the Nobel Prize in Chemistry (Royal Swedish Academy of Sciences 2020). Rapidly adopted by researchers and biotech companies, CRISPR has been applied to all biological taxa for an array of applications, from vaccination against COVID-19 to drought-resistant crop development. In Doudna and a coauthor's words, CRISPR is doing nothing short of "rewriting biology" (Knott and Doudna 2018). Given how widespread and how inexpensive it has become, CRISPR is also an ethical minefield, as evident in its inventors' calls to pause any experiments on human embryos until there are clear international protocols and regulations in place (Doudna 2020a, 2020b; Doudna and Sternberg 2017).

While hundreds of thousands of articles on CRISPR appeared in the decade after its initial development, just a fraction referred to biodiversity applications, and just over a hundred discussed de-extinction specifically. Recall that, in the same period, the academic and popular literature on de-extinction grew rapidly. Why, then, does only a tiny portion of the latter mention the "epoch-making" (Royal Swedish Academy of Sciences 2020) technique of CRISPR that de-extinction supporters suggest is crucial to making "extinct species reappear" (Wray 2017, 58). For one, the de-extinction research community is a small one as compared to those labs and companies that employ CRISPR and related technologies for medical or agricultural applications. To this point, Church's extremely well-funded lab at Harvard works primarily on "regenerative medicine and bio-production of chemicals" (Wyss Institute, n.d.), while just a few members, who refer to themselves as "mammoth revivalists," focus on de-extinction (Wray 2017, 17).[11] There is a disjuncture, then, between the scale of de-extinction as a field and the scale of its environmental and technological imagination. Her relative circumspection notwithstanding, Shapiro gives voice to this outsize imagining when she reflects that de-extinction could forestall "a future of very reduced biodiversity . . . in which so many changes have occurred to the terrestrial and marine ecosystems that we, ourselves, are suddenly vulnerable to extinction" (2015, 7). In truth, de-extinction is unlikely to make a dent in large-scale biodiversity loss. The cost and the labor—not to mention luck—required to create a proxy of just one recently extinct species are daunting, to say nothing of the numerous obstacles standing between what would be the first "unextinct" individual of that novel chimeric species and a self-sustaining population released into a real-world ecosystem doing more good than harm to that habitat and the many other species living there (Wray 2017, 14). For their part, Doudna and her coauthor Samuel Sternberg question the grand designs of de-extinction by spelling out the numerous risks that ecological applications of CRISPR and associated biotechnologies pose, applications that could enable not just the generation of novel life but also the purposeful extinction of unwanted organisms and undesirable genetic traits (Doudna and Sternberg 2017, 119). This warning stems from a larger worry about the power of genetic engineering to "irreversibly alter the biosphere that we inhabit by providing a way to rewrite the very molecules of life in any way we wish" (Doudna and Sternberg 2017, 119).

Eschewing these and other serious concerns, the most ardent of de-extinction supporters double down on the trope of resurrection. If outsiders tend to associate de-extinction with stories of technological overreach, from *Frankenstein* to *Jurassic Park*, its practitioners and proponents augur a future that will "reframe our possibilities" (Shapiro 2015, 206–7) via "awesome, exciting" (Shapiro 2015, 190) innovations that make new life-forms "from scratch" (Wray 2017, 231–32; see also Stephens 2020; Swart 2014). Sympathetic to de-extinction and kindred ambitions to shape the natural world "confidently, deliberately, and sometimes ruthlessly," the philosopher Christopher Preston echoes new conservation in endorsing the view that wilderness "might paradoxically need considerable human manipulation in order to survive as *nature* in the new epoch," which he labels the *Plastocene* to foreground the synthetic and human-made dimensions of nature in the Anthropocene. Like other enthusiasts, he sees de-extinction as a "resurrection tale" of a "biological wasteland" transformed by scientists into a "bio-Eden" (Preston 2018, xix, 79, 13). Shapiro draws on kindred tropes in *How to Clone a Mammoth*. Misreading a famous biotech dystopia as fodder for such an Eden, at one point she compares the mechanical reproduction of human infants in *Brave New World* to the prospect that de-extinction could employ synthetic rather than live surrogates to gestate its lab-born embryos: "I'm imagining something similar to the artificial wombs that Aldous Huxley envisaged to grow children. . . . Or, even better, the giant nutrient-filled flasks in which human clones were grown on the planet Kamino to fight for the good side in the movie *Star Wars: Episode II*" (2015, 152). The sanguine tone of these fictional allusions overlooks actual histories of the biopolitical control of life, histories in which marginalized and enslaved human lives have been experimental research subjects or subjected to forced sterilization and other acts of bioscientific violence. Eclipsing de-extinction's ecological and moral hazards, in such moments in her book Shapiro echoes more zealous de-extinction voices that foreground White scientists and innovators and align prehistoric wilderness with Silicon Valley novelty.

These voices, in addition to Church's, include those of Ben Novak (a passenger pigeon aficionado) and Brand (whose Revive and Restore has provided funding to Church, Shapiro, and Novak). If Shapiro has drawn a complex and cautious picture of de-extinction, these proponents have unabashedly endorsed what Church and a coauthor call "a future in which we engineer resistance to all viruses, reverse aging, resurrect extinct DNA from the woolly mammoth, use molecular computers, and program bacteria to produce diverse plastics and chemicals" (Church and Regis 2014). This bullish stance has paid off. Church discloses over 150 technology transfer agreements and funding sources on his lab website, sources that include the software company Autodesk, the pharmaceutical giants Eli Lilly and Merck, and dozens of venture capital firms (Church 2023). He is also among the most well-known of the researchers involved with de-extinction, and his funders demonstrate its allure to Silicon Valley, both the place and the global investment network centered there. Meanwhile, Novak has followed a lifelong obsession with the passenger pigeon's demise to become a public spokesperson for de-extinction. At the time of this writing, he held the title of lead scientist at Revive and Restore, where he is tasked with "its flagship project, The Great Passenger Pigeon Comeback" (Revive and Restore 2023). However siloed de-extinction may be as a scientific field, these individuals and projects have been influential in promoting utopian narratives that marry biodiversity to biotech. As the science writer Britt

Wray observes: "[I]t's not the abundance of research in this area that's so striking—it's how well above its weight it punches" (2017, 17). Academic research, amateurism, and venture capital merge in crafting this *charismatic meganarrative* of de-extinction, a narrative that Revive and Restore, in particular, has helped craft and amplify.

The passenger pigeon project demonstrates the group's impact. Building on the step-by-step form of *How to Clone a Mammoth* while dispensing with Shapiro's attention to technical details, the Revive and Restore brief on the project includes the recipe "How to Make a Passenger Pigeon," which breaks down this de-extinction test case into eight phases explained via infographics with labels such as "Identifying de-extinction mutations," "Raising revived passenger pigeons," and "Release to the wild." (Although the group declined a request to reproduce these infographics, the reader can see those visuals on the Revive and Restore web page linked in this note.)[12] Sidestepping what have been numerous setbacks in sequencing the species' genome, Revive and Restore exudes confidence that the project's eventual success will "demonstrate the potential of genomic intervention and help to restore the ecology of North America's eastern forests" (Revive and Restore, n.d.-b). Novak's specific curiosities and commitments are at the heart of this ambition. Self-fashioned as both an avid naturalist and a pioneering geneticist, Novak has figured centrally in the media coverage of de-extinction, including as a primary interview subject in articles published in *Harper's* (Boyce 2015), the *National Geographic* (Zimmer 2014), *Reason* (Krainin 2015), the *Smithsonian Magazine* (Souder 2014), *Scientific American* (Begley 2018), and other outlets. In a 2014 *New York Times Magazine* cover story titled "The Mammoth Cometh," Nathaniel Rich—who later wrote a chapter of his book *Second Nature* (2021) about Revive and Restore—opens his account of de-extinction with Novak:

> The first time Ben Novak saw a passenger pigeon, he fell to his knees and remained in that position, speechless, for 20 minutes. He was 16. At 13, Novak vowed to devote his life to resurrecting extinct animals. At 14, he saw a photograph of a passenger pigeon in an Audubon Society book and "fell in love." But he didn't know that the Science Museum of Minnesota, which he was then visiting with a summer program for North Dakotan high-school students, had them in their collection, so he was shocked when he came across a cabinet containing two stuffed pigeons, a male and a female, mounted in lifelike poses. He was overcome by awe, sadness and the birds' physical beauty. . . . There are 1,532 passenger-pigeon specimens left on Earth. On September 1, 1914, Martha, the last captive passenger pigeon, died at the Cincinnati Zoo. She outlasted George, the

> penultimate survivor of her species and her only companion, by four years. As news spread of her species' imminent extinction, Martha became a minor tourist attraction. In her final years, whether depressed or just old, she barely moved. Underwhelmed zoo visitors threw fistfuls of sand at her to elicit a reaction. When she finally died, her body was taken to the Cincinnati Ice Company, frozen in a 300-pound ice cube and shipped by train to the Smithsonian Institution, where she was stuffed and mounted and visited, 99 years later, by Ben Novak. (Rich 2014)

Cast here as an impassioned lover of a beloved lost bird, Novak provides the hook for this story. Alternating between interviews with Novak and Brand, Rich keys into the emotional—more than the ecological—drivers of and reasons for de-extinction. The human protagonists' grief for biodiversity loss leads through this lens not to a political reckoning with what and who are responsible (the passenger pigeon's precipitous collapse in the early twentieth century was due to overhunting and urbanization across the eastern United States, among other factors) but to heroic quests on behalf of Nature Remade. While Novak maintains that his passion arises from "ecological concerns," Rich's story of de-extinction concludes with an observation by a fellow researcher in Shapiro's lab that characterizes his Revive and Restore project as driven by one person's imagination rather than a societal mandate: "The passenger pigeon makes Ben want to write poetry" (Rich 2014).

The base pairs that make up DNA provide the raw material for this imagination, which sees in a bird's extinction future human achievement. A photograph snapped by Novak during his first childhood sighting of a passenger pigeon specimen represents the blank canvas onto which he, Brand, and others write this future of wilderness by design. The flash on Novak's disposable camera was "too strong" that day in the Science Museum of Minnesota, and, "when the film was processed several weeks later, he was haunted to discover that the photograph hadn't developed. It was blank, just a flash of white light" (Rich 2014). The specter of the blank negative stands in for the unfathomable loss of an entire species, which Revive and Restore intimates can be reverse engineered. Like Novak's, Brand's obsession with the passenger pigeon begins with but does not dwell on grief—in his case, grief sparked by "the mournful way his mother spoke about" the birds during his own midwestern youth decades before Novak's (Rich 2014). "During summers," Rich writes, "the Brands vacationed near the top of Michigan's mitten, not far from Pigeon River, one of the hundreds of American places named after the species. . . . Old-timers told stories about the pigeon that to Brand assumed a mythic quality. They said that the flocks were so large they blotted out the sun" (Rich 2014). While the enormous size of passenger pigeon flocks is a well-known fact of American environmental history, for these de-extinction disciples it represents a mythological past of ecological abundance.

Ecological tragedy thus provides the seeds for techno-utopia. Representative of the broader science reporting on de-extinction, Rich provides a platform for this utopianism by relegating critics mostly to cursory mentions. In *The Unnatural World*, Biello (2016, 100–103) similarly makes Novak the main character in a discussion of de-extinction, portraying him as an eccentric inventor whose experience witnessing his North Dakota rural town evolve from a farming community to a fracking center inspired his eventual embrace of engineering on behalf, rather than to the detriment, of birds. There is a patently gendered dimension to these portraits. While Biello focuses on Novak as an autodidact and trailblazer, Shapiro—a 2009 recipient of the MacArthur "Genius" award—receives relatively little attention, described only in passing for her lab's role in the passenger pigeon project. Rich similarly makes only brief mention of Shapiro, mostly to relay her initial rejection of Novak as a prospective doctoral student. (Novak has subsequently conducted research in Shapiro's lab, supported by funding from Revive and Restore.) The through line in these journalistic stories is what Rich himself calls the "optimistic, soft-focus fantasy" of figures like Novak and Brand (Rich 2014). It is that fantasy that has narrative charisma by "counteract[ing] the sense of impending doom" associated with grief-stricken apprehensions of biodiversity loss, its causes, and its consequences (Biello 2016, 108).

The point here is that the media attention that de-extinction has garnered has outstripped its endeavors and achievements as a scientific field, an asymmetry attributable, above all, to Brand. Minteer describes Brand as "one of the most colorful and technophilic voices in conservation today," a voice he increasingly has used to champion the work of Revive and Restore (Minteer 2019, 10). At the 2013 TEDx event that Brand and Phelan coorganized with *National Geographic* sponsorship, Church, Novak, and Shapiro all gave talks along with Hendrik Poinar (the son of Poinar and Hess) and a dozen other scientists, ethicists, and journalists (TED 2013). Brand gave a keynote titled "The Dawn of De-extinction. Are You Ready?" that had received well over two million online views as of early 2024 (Brand 2013). While Brand opens with a catalog of human-caused extinctions and closes with a nod to their significance as forms of environmental loss, the narrative center is an upbeat portrait of wilderness disruptors like Revive and Restore. The touchstone for this narrative is a possibly apocryphal *National Geographic* proclamation that, while in the twentieth century innovation inhered in "finding things," in the twenty-first it inheres in "making things" (Brand 2013, 7:21). As Thom van Dooren and Deborah Bird Rose point out, "there is something deeply disturbing" about such ideas that pervade de-extinction discourse, according to which the "bright promise of new technologies . . . undermines the genuine reflection needed to get somewhere better—not just different" (2017, 376). Their critique speaks to the rhetorical role of charismatic megafauna in Brand's TED talk, which calls on the audience's presumed attachments to a handful of mammalian and avian species to advertise ongoing Revive and Restore projects while neglecting the consequences of biodiversity loss for all kinds of species and ecosystems as well as for the human communities for whom such loss is a first-order one. Glossing the basic science of de-extinction, the talk depicts de-extinction researchers as intrepid and entreats the imagined audience to join those assembled on the TED stage in building "an evolution machine" (Brand 2013, 4:30).

The emphasis on herculean feats of biotech-enabled rewilding has proved a powerful narrative strategy, as evident in the earned media that the TED symposium and a subsequent private gathering enjoyed. This coverage included Rich's *New York Times Magazine* essay along with a *National Geographic* cover story by Carl Zimmer and helps explain why both the popular and the peer-reviewed literature on de-extinction grew rapidly after 2013 (Rich 2014; Zimmer 2013). The narrative that Brand and others launched that year has built on preoccupations in conservation not just with charismatic megafauna but with individual members of such species—from Martha to Lonesome George (the Galapagos Islands' last Pinta Island tortoise). While attending another de-extinction event held at the Natural History Museum in New York, Minteer found himself reflecting on the latter's death: "[N]ot far outside the museum theater stood, mounted and in stony silence, 'Lonesome George,' . . . whose forlorn nickname took on added pathos because of his famous failure to breed." "There would be a dramatic turn of events in George's story," Minteer notes, "one that put an asterisk on all those epitaphic, 'last of his species' headlines." Shortly after the animal's death in 2012, "it was reported that more than a dozen giant tortoises plucked by biologists from a volcano on the island of Isabela . . . shared some genes with him, raising the possibility of selectively breeding *something resembling a Pinta Island tortoise back into existence* and perhaps one day even restoring a George-like population of tortoises to the island" (Minteer 2019, 7, 8, 8–9; emphasis added). This juxtaposition of irreparable loss and in vitro creation points to the occlusion in de-extinction narratives of the specific human actors, histories, and societal structures behind modern extinctions. These narratives turn away from such particularities to advance the belief that death can be undone and history reversed "by rejiggering the genes" of an extinct animal's nearest living relative (Kolbert 2021a). A techno-utopian impulse, the belief stems from a mechanistic view of life that drives the de-extinction projects of groups like Revive and Restore and Colossal and understands their work as world changing.

At one point in the TED talk, Brand pivots from extolling de-extinction as a green technology to representing it as a social movement by way of a new conservationist appeal to Anthropocene hope over despair. The moment embeds a scientific wonkiness in a beguiling tale of genetic rescue that is ostentatious and buoyant. In contrast to the talk's brief opening references to anthropogenic extinctions, its conclusion pans out to the span of millennia. "Humans have made a huge hole in nature in the last 10,000 years," Brand opines. "We have the ability now, and maybe the moral obligation, to repair some of the damage. Most of that we'll do by expanding and protecting wildlands, by expanding and protecting the populations of endangered species. But some species that we killed off totally we could consider bringing back to a world that misses them" (2013, 16:10). This mission locates the refrain of de-extinction to bring back species that died out sometime over "the last 10,000 years" on a continuum with the conventional work of "expanding and protecting wildlands." But the comparison disregards both calls for conservation science to reckon with its own colonial histories and the categorical differences between natural and anthropogenic extinctions. These omissions are apparent from the talk's outset, where Brand reframes the rapid extinction of the passenger pigeon owing to commercial hunting as a story with "an upside" in having "made people realize the same thing was about to happen to the American bison" (2013, 1:32). He offers this silver lining to counter the "sorrow, anger, [and] mourning" of mainstream environmentalism and recruit his audience to ecopragmatism: "Don't mourn. Organize" (Brand 2013, 3:13).

But, for Brand, to organize means not collective movement building but entrepreneurship and innovation, as his example of American bison as the "upside" of the public grief produced by the passenger pigeon's disappearance exemplifies. Prior to White settlement, the North American plains were home to some thirty million bison, whose enormous herds survived the Ice Age and were vital to grassland ecosystems as well as Indigenous lifeways. By the end of the nineteenth century, fewer than one thousand buffalo remained on the continent. A major driver of this population collapse was state-sponsored mass slaughter designed to starve Indigenous tribes (Defenders of Wildlife, n.d.; Hance 2018). While conservation actions over the twentieth century prevented the species' outright extinction, only thirty thousand individuals were alive when Brand delivered his

TED talk, and the species continued to be listed as "near threatened" by the IUCN Red List (Aune, Jørgensen, and Gates 2017). Far from the "upside" of the passenger pigeon extinction, the history of the American bison is a grim one bound up with the violent removals of Indigenous peoples from their ancestral homelands. That history is one for which Sioux, Assiniboine, and other Indigenous nations continue to seek redress in spearheading bison restoration and stewardship efforts (Hance 2018).

For her part, Shapiro responds to the ardor of colleagues like Brand, Novak, and Church by foregrounding the scientific reasons why "extinct species are gone forever." And, as we've seen, *How to Clone a Mammoth* insists that resurrected animals would be, at best, genetic and biological hybrids of the lost ones they're designed to "look" and "function" like. But the book also contributes to the misrepresentation of anthropogenic biodiversity losses that derive from colonialism, industrialization, and urbanization as *akin* to Ice Age extinctions. Most notably, Shapiro refers to Indigenous Americans primarily to suggest that the scientists working to revive the continent's ancient genetics might claim a kind of native lineage. In a section subtitled "Is There a Compelling Reason to Bring This Species Back?" she explains her litmus test for selecting candidate de-extinction species as follows:

> I may feel some guilt by association with my Native American ancestors, who probably participated in hunting short-faced bears, and with my European ancestors, who probably were in some way involved with the extinction of the Neandertals. This does not mean I want to bring back short-faced bears and Neandertals. . . . Compelling reasons to bring something back to life are more likely to relate to the species themselves and the roles these species are likely to play in the environment of the present day.

Although Shapiro's criteria for de-extinction may be more persuasive than the variously symbolic and poetic reasons that Novak and Brand stress, her argument here gives credence to the notion that the Clovis people were the prime culprits in late Pleistocene extinctions. She further reinforces a pattern in de-extinction discourse—as in new conservation writ large—that puts White scientists at the helm of regenerating and reengineering nature. Thus does she recount her and her fellow researchers' summer fieldwork in Siberia searching for mammoth remains without addressing the issue of Yupik and Inuit sovereignty, despite a brief note that mammoth digs are "deeply personal" to the region's Indigenous people and can be in conflict with the Yupik belief that touching woolly mammoths "will bring bad luck" (Shapiro 2015, 10, 45, 48, 26, 83). The upshot of the manifold connections drawn between prehistoric extinction and techno-science innovation that pervade de-extinction discourse is, in the final analysis, that those connections yoke wilderness mythology to technological utopianism while effacing the thorny histories of conservation and the contemporary relationships between biodiversity amelioration and environmental justice.

Extinction Grief and Biodiversity Justice

When I began thinking about de-extinction, I was initially captivated by figures like Brand and their appeals to environmental hope. But, as I dug into both the science and the story of de-extinction, I came to rethink the structures of feeling with which their charismatic narratives dispense: not only feelings of despair and grief but also feelings of anger, outrage, and righteous indignation. This chapter has followed the key figures, pivotal events, and popular texts that have coalesced to put de-extinction on the map of popular science and new conservation. However well funded and well covered de-extinction has been to date, its project of wilderness by design would do well to grapple with countervailing narratives and movements addressed to biodiversity loss that start with multispecies justice. As a coda to this chapter and a gesture in this direction, I'll close with a writer whose work on behalf of lost species makes extinction grief and multispecies justice inseparable conditions for the future of wilderness: the Chamoru writer and activist Craig Santos Perez.

This turn to Perez brings us back to Pacific island birds, which were touchstones for the authors of Pleistocene rewilding, including Martin. Those birds have a much longer history for the people native to their habitats—such as the Chamoru homelands of Guam and the Mariana Islands that, as the American studies scholar Hsuan Hsu writes, have "been seized as, and molded into, a 'stepping stone' for imperial powers since [Guam] was first 'claimed' by Spain in 1565" (2012, 284). Perez's poetic work makes the Chamoru loss of birds a leitmotif of not just ecological decline but colonial violence, thus extending to the nonhuman world his focus on US colonialism in and Indigenous diasporas from the region (Hsu 2012; Knighton 2019; Lai 2011; Perez 2011, 2015). As a member of Chamoru Indigenous Collective, Perez has given testimony before the UN Special Political and Decolonization Committee on self-determination for Guam and the Mariana Islands, which are, respectively, an unincorporated territory and a commonwealth of the United States. In 2016 UN testimony, Perez addressed the links between the US occupation of Guam, the introduction of the invasive brown tree snake, and the fact that the island's "Chamorro birds are disappearing" (Perez 2016). These links have animated a series of poems Perez has written about one particular species native to Guam: the Micronesian kingfisher (or *i sihek*). Part of a multivolume corpus titled *from unincorporated territory*, the poems gather together a broad body of knowledge about biodiversity loss, conservation science, and Indigenous sovereignty (Perez 2008, 2010, 2014, 2017, 2023).[13] They also challenge conservation approaches that prioritize captive breeding of endangered animals and what are known as *ex situ* reintroduction programs over and against Indigenous relationships to and rights to be involved in the conservation of and care for native species.

In an academic study of Chamoru poetry, Perez recounts connections between species extinction and "ecological imperialism" in the archipelago:

> One ongoing and irreversible effect of ecological imperialism in Guåhan has been the extinction and endangerment of more than two dozen native and endemic species of birds, mammals, reptiles, mollusks, and plants. This species loss has been caused by habitat destruction, environmental pollution, and the introduction of invasive species. After World War II, brown tree snakes arrived on Guåhan as stowaways on a US military ship or aircraft. Having no natural predators, the snakes quickly multiplied and colonized the entire island. In just a few decades, thousands of native birds were killed, and most species either became entirely extinct or, in a few cases, were taken into captivity and are now bred in US zoos. The loss of birds in Guåhan is also reverberating through the island's ecology; without birds to spread and germinate seeds, many native trees may go extinct, and the tropical forests may experience desertification. (Perez 2021, 73)

Like the Guam rail, the Micronesian kingfisher is now classified as extinct in the wild, owing in large measure to the invasive brown tree snake and, by extension, to what Perez terms *the passages of empire*. In one volume of *from unincorporated territory*, four poems about the kingfisher appear, each with the title, "*ginen* the micronesian kingfisher [*i sihek*]" (Perez 2014). (In the Chamoru language *ginen* means "from" or "since.") The poems explore what the bird's disappearance from the wild means to the Chamoru people and who and what are to blame. Together, they enact a lyrical investigation of extinction and rewilding as entwined environmental injustices. Their occasion is a captive breeding program that has been overseen by the Philadelphia Zoo since the late 1990s, the Guam Bird Rescue Project (Hurdle 2009; Kincaid 2016; Philadelphia Zoo, n.d.). Here are lines from the first of these *i sihek* poems:

[our] nightmare : no
birdsong—
. . . .

the snakes entered
without words when [we] saw them it was too late—
they were at [our] doors sliding along
the passages of *[i sihek]*
empire—then

the zookeepers came—
called it *species survival plan*—captured *[i sihek]* and transferred
the last
twenty-nine micronesian kingfishers
to zoos for captive breeding *[1988]* . . .

(PEREZ 2014, 24)

This opening poem in the series is at once an elegy for what Perez powerfully describes as the "last wild seen" (2014, 24) of one native bird species and an anticolonial protest poem. The poem interweaves a captive breeding program that has inspired de-extinction research and the program's capture of twenty-nine remaining wild Micronesian kingfishers with the militarized histories of US imperialism in Guam and across the Pacific Islands. Subsequent poems knit Chamoru ecological and political sovereignty with archival sources that detail the birds' experiences of captivity. Drawing extensively on these sources, Perez reproduces avian husbandry protocols for the Guam Bird Rescue Project from a now out-of-print text called the "Micronesian Kingfisher Survival Plan" (Bahner, Baltz, and Diebold 1998):

for wire enclosures
mesh size should not exceed one inch—
kingfishers have attacked

their images reflected
in glass cage fronts—these
are not legends—
the birds are
inside snake belly
[i sihek]—no
longer averting pests or
spreading

seed—

....

what does not change / is the will
to see.

(PEREZ 2014, 62–63)

In these stanzas, the charge of symbolism ("inside snake belly" and "spreading / seeds") and the elegiac refrain of *i sihek* train our attention on the birds and their severed ties to the poet and the poet's homeland. These poetic moves cut through the bureaucratic specs for housing, feeding, handling, and breeding a small captive population in zoos, which are drawn verbatim from the 1998 manual. Perez connects an intimate avian perspective to the ongoing US occupation of Chamoru lands and waters. Through these and other lyrical tactics, he makes unimaginable the separation of decolonization from biodiversity conservation. In an extended analysis of this work and its engagement with the Guam Bird Rescue Project, Heidi Amin-Hong writes: "Engaging with environmental science discourses of endangered species rescue and recovery that fail to address the ecological impact of settler colonialism, Perez charts a decolonial poetics that brings the legacies of the US empire to bear on the rhetorics and practices of conservation ecology" (2023, 293). Echoing Amin-Hong, I would underscore that the poems on and for *i sihek* convey the interlocking moral, political, and scientific reasons for *in situ* conservation guided by Indigenous-led multispecies justice.

Here, and in other writings, Perez shows that mourning—in historically and culturally concrete forms—is critical to remembering the root causes of biodiversity loss and accordingly determining approaches to ecological repair. Writing about the second volume in the series, *from unincorporated territory [saina]*, Hsu says, along similar lines, that Perez's "fragmentary, dispersed, and unpredictably recombinant" poetic practice "interweaves breath, body, and water into poems that traverse and interconnect the militarized and commodified spaces of Oceania" (2012, 301). Through this collage method, Perez's poems link Guam to other "unincorporated territories" of the United States, including Puerto Rico and the US Virgin Islands (Hsu 2012, 302). His work thus enacts the strategies of Chamoru ecopoetics that Perez identifies in fellow writers, including Peter R. Onedera and Lehua Taitano, who, he writes, draw on surviving Chamoru oral culture and creation narratives to articulate "an environmental vision of mutual care, co-belonging, and healing" (Perez 2021, 42). Resonant with Perez's poetry and scholarship, Kyle Whyte (a citizen of the Potawatomi Nation) has critiqued the Anthropocene for flattening histories of environmental and social harm and for locating the worst-case scenario in an always-receding future. Writing about Anishinaabe conservation projects in the Great Lakes region, he develops this analysis in an essay titled "Our Ancestors' Dystopia Now": "Our conservation and restoration projects are not only about whether to conserve or let go of certain species. Rather, they are about what relationships between humans and certain plants and animals we should focus on in response to the challenges we face, given that we have already lost so many plants and animals that matter to our societies" (Whyte 2017, 207). This trenchant reflection throws into powerful relief how the new conservation of Pleistocene rewilding and de-extinction elides the established relationships among particular places, peoples, and species and the meaning of ecological losses that may not be recoverable. The poetic and political work of a writer like Perez provides a crucial rejoinder to these troubles with *wilderness by design*. That work contests the premise that environmentalism in this century must choose between restoring and remaking nature. In Perez's elegiac poems on and for the Micronesian kingfisher, one finds rich expressions of what van Dooren in *The Wake of Crows* calls *living and dying in shared worlds*, expressions grounded in very specific histories of loss that also look forward to ecologically just futures beyond wilderness nostalgia and technological utopianism (van Dooren 2019).

[CHAPTER 5]

The Strange Bird

Picture a once teeming city laid waste by an entity called the "Company," whose now-abandoned lab has unleashed, among much else, a superintelligent, three-story-high bear called Mord (see fig. 5.1). Liberated from its corporate controllers, Mord has spawned an army of ursine proxies who battle "the Magician" and her mercenaries, genetically modified children who roam the feral lands of the former high-tech center. Into this dystopia appears a technicolor creature of unknown provenance that is part plant, part animal, part machine, and grows rapidly from the size of a vase to a shape-shifting organism that can assume other bodies by consuming them. Scary as that sounds, the creature is undeniably gorgeous: shocks of purple, green, rusted orange, and bright vermilion shade tentacular petals that open and close around an invertebrate body that changes form in an instant. The creature's name is Borne, the titular character of Jeff VanderMeer's 2017 novel set in a fictional world that has been utterly reshaped by the monstrous Company, a world VanderMeer develops further in *The Strange Bird* (2018) and *Dead Astronauts* (2019). The novel's first-person narrator, Rachel, discovers Borne in Mord's pelt and is immediately captivated by what she at first perceives as a novel *object* of aesthetic beauty in a devastated world: "a sleek vase with rippling colors that strayed from purple toward deep blues and sea greens [and] smelled of beech reeds on lazy summer afternoons and, beneath the sea salt, of passionflowers" (VanderMeer 2017, 6). Rachel brings it back to her makeshift home in a former apartment complex called the Balcony Cliffs. As the "sleek vase" awakens from dormancy and begins to grow and speak, she recategorizes her find as a living-breathing body that she names Borne and genders *he*. Over the course of the novel, Borne becomes a world. His body and manner change shape countless times into the forms of those he either ingests or observes intimately. His short and spacious life comes to an end as a self-sacrifice during the climactic defeat of Mord when he mutates for the last time into an "enormous passionflower bloom" (VanderMeer 2017, 313). The narrative arc proves poignantly ironic:

Figure 5.1. Eric Nyquist, "Mord Proxy." From "The Borne Bestiary," text by Jeff VanderMeer (New York: MCD, 2017). By permission of the artist.

its main character turns out to be one in a long line of identical, supersentient bioweapons. As the reader learns late in the novel, Borne is a castoff from a last project at the Company before it pulled up stakes and decamped by way of a portal—"a shining wall of silver raindrops"—located in the recesses of its crumbling compound (VanderMeer 2017, 319).

In the post-Company City—where a forbidding climate and resource conflict make life relentlessly dangerous for all—there is an uncanny abundance of life-forms. The speculative narrative of that abundance is the focus of this chapter, which argues that *Borne* and its sequel, *The Strange Bird*, upend the categories of natural and engineered in imagining a future staked on nonhuman personhood rather than, as with the ambitions of AI makers and de-extinction investors, naturalized machines and synthetic animals. An illustrated bestiary, printed in the novel's first edition as an appendix and published online as an interactive artwork, informs my argument. The bestiary details over thirty of the innumerable life-forms that live in the City (see fig. 5.2). Some entries riff on the vocabulary of ecological science: "rare, the damselfly, with its diaphanous black wings, can exist only in certain temperatures below sea level," while the mudskipper is a carnivorous fish with "bulging eyes and strong fins that propel it across mudflats" (VanderMeer and Nyquist 2017). Such species exist on Earth today and, significantly, are widespread and adaptive—the damselfly and the mudskipper as well as the red salamander, the freshwater flounder, the fiddler crab, the coyote, the desert fox, the earthworm, and the silverfish—having a collective distribution that encompasses West Africa, the United States, Mexico, the Caribbean, Central America, Australia, Asia, northern Europe, and every major ocean. They are what the science writer David Quammen (1998) once called *weedy species* (with *Homo sapiens* as a provocative example). In the terms of conservation, they are subjects of *least concern*, to cite the classification system of the IUCN Red List of Threatened Species (IUCN, n.d.). In *Borne*, they coexist with engineered creatures that are variously monstrous, marvelous, and mundane. Some are of Company origin, others the work of amateur biohacking, and others subject to the Magician's sadistic experiments: Company-made mosses, lichen, memory beetles, and alcohol minnows; "eel-like things" imprinted genetically with MCD (VanderMeer's publisher); and the truly bizarre "autonomous meat" that is "more mobile than one might wish" (VanderMeer and Nyquist 2017).[1] While a few species in the *Borne* world are entirely untouched by genetic engineering (the silverfish "has thrived in the City, much as it has thrived everywhere for more than four hundred million years"), most can be understood, in the language of Becky Chambers's *Monk and Robot* series (chap. 3), as *wild-built*.

The bestiary captures the porous boundary between the familiar and the strange, the human and the nonhuman, that preoccupies VanderMeer's fiction, which variously depicts speculative futures in which "the human fuses, ambiguously and disturbingly, with nonhuman creatures and ecosystemic processes" (Caracciolo and Ulstein 2022, 2). In a far more quotidian register, these preoccupations also inflect a rewilding endeavor that VanderMeer and

Figure 5.2. Eric Nyquist, untitled illustration. From "The Borne Bestiary," text by Jeff VanderMeer (New York: MCD, 2017). By permission of the artist.

his wife and longtime collaborator, Ann VanderMeer, began around the time of *Borne*'s release to make their Florida backyard a refuge for native plants, wild animals, and pollinators (Brady 2018; VanderMeer 2021b, n.d.). The City in *Borne* is undergoing a stranger and more uncanny process of rewilding owing to human absence, morphing into a place where born, made, and wild-built creatures are all making a home in what VanderMeer has called "the broken places" (Vasanta Studios 2017). The profusion and hybridization of species in this world parallels the novel's proliferation and recombination of narrative forms. Consider the bestiary's introductory text, presented as a signed letter from VanderMeer:

> Herein, you will discover a carefully curated selection of the creatures that peer out from the pages of *Borne,* with more information provided, for even the least among them, than a mere novel could fruitfully contain. From the entry on Anonymous Meat to the musings on Duck With Broken Wing, from Fire Slug to Silverfish, you are about to embark on an adventure unlike any other. . . .
>
> Still, even a bestiary has its limits. We hope you understand that some information is too dangerous or outrageous to be of use to you (or to me), and thus has been excluded (the novel itself includes many more

> creatures of one kind or another). With that caveat, we hope you enjoy this exclusive peek behind the scenes of *Borne*. And by "we" I mean "me and whatever form of biotech has already colonized that me."
>
> —*With all best wishes, Jeff VanderMeer* (VanderMeer and Nyquist 2017)

In this wry address to the reader, genres collide, as do bodies. The letter calls to mind the first-person frame narratives that open canonical novels centered on mad scientists and colonial explorers, from *Frankenstein* to *Moby Dick*, *Robinson Crusoe* to *The Island of Dr. Moreau*. It then mutates into postmodern self-reference, with its instruction about page number citations to *Borne*, before parodying the marketing speak of Hollywood ("we hope you enjoy this exclusive peek") and closing with the doubling of Jeff VanderMeer as real author and biotech avatar. Two spectral animals who appear throughout the *Borne* world further demonstrate this interplay of weird biodiversity and weird fiction (a niche genre associated with VanderMeer and others). First, there is the "blue fox": an alien being who, perhaps via the same portal through which the Company vanished, "had slipped over from elsewhere" only to be captured by the Magician (VanderMeer and Nyquist 2017). The bestiary describes the intelligence and beauty of the blue fox as the twin reasons he befell the Magician's violence: "Scavengers tell the story that the blue fox was the secret leader of all the foxes and that the Magician kidnapped him out of spite because he was so beautiful and because she feared the foxes he led and worried that they might make common cause with the great bear Mord" (VanderMeer and Nyquist 2017). An allusion to the Icelandic myth of a trickster figure called *Skugga-Baldur*, the blue fox never makes an explicit appearance in *Borne*, its bestiary entry becoming legible only in *The Strange Bird* when his head appears as a "still-living" trophy in the Magician's lab. In *Dead Astronauts*, the fox comes back from the dead as the first-person narrator of the penultimate chapter, an illustration of what Marco Caracciolo and Gry Ulstein (2022, 18) characterize as the most formally experimental of the *Borne* books. The doppelgänger to the blue fox is a "one-off fox" who has small hands extending from her torso and glows with "quiet bioluminescence," one of the "trademarks of the earliest Company experiments in the City" that genetically intermixed the human with the vulpine (VanderMeer and Nyquist 2017). A "matriarch, whose origins and knowledge she had passed down" (VanderMeer and Nyquist 2017) to other biotech species, this fox may be the same individual Rachel chances on in an encounter that prompts a speculation that the fox may have modified Borne before setting him free from the Company compound (VanderMeer 2017, 299).

Plate 1. George Frederick Keller, "The Curse of California." Tinted lithograph. From *The Wasp* 9, no. 316 (1882), 520–21. Photograph: Wikimedia Commons.

Plate 2. Barron Bixler, “Los Angeles Aqueduct, Fremont Watershed.” From “Watershed: A Speculative Atlas of California,” analog photograph captured on color reversal film (2016). By permission of the artist. Photograph: Barron Bixler.

Plate 3. Google Bay View Campus: Aerial View (2022). By permission of Google. Photograph: Iwan Baan.

Plate 4. Mariangela Le Thanh, "Clouds on Earth" (2021). Mural ("Air Google") commissioned for Google Bay View Campus. By permission of the artist. Photograph: Mariangela Le Thanh.

Plate 5. Visualization of the Great Pacific Garbage Gyre (2023). Created by the author with DALL-E by OpenAI.

Plate 6. Saya Woolfalk, *Encyclopedia of Cloud Divination (Plate 1)* (2018). Archival inkjet print, silkscreen, silver leaf, chine colle on Hahnemüle Photo Rag Ultra Smooth; 43¾ × 33¾ inches (sheet); 40 × 30 inches (image). Copyright Saya Woolfalk. Photograph: Courtesy Leslie Tonkonow Artworks + Projects.

Plate 7. Saya Woolfalk, *ChimaTEK Series Hybridization Visualization System: Avatar Download Station 2* (2014). Mixed media with video; 41¾ × 39 × 3 inches. Copyright Saya Woolfalk. Photograph: Courtesy Leslie Tonkonow Artworks + Projects.

Plate 8. Ivanpah Solar Electric Generating System with view of Google logo, Mohave Desert (2017). Photography by Mark Boster for the *Los Angeles Times*. Photograph: Getty Images.

Plate 9. Rendering of "lush nature scene in the metaverse" (2023). Created by the author with DALL-E by OpenAI.

Plate 10. Kayla Harren, “Planted Astronaut” (ca. 2017). Unpublished illustration. Courtesy of the artist.

Plate 11. Kayla Harren, "Wick's Swimming Pool" (ca. 2017).
From *Weird Fiction Review*. Courtesy of the artist.

Plate 12. Alexander Dux, “See America” (ca. 1936–39). Works Progress Administration Federal Art Project, created for the US Travel Bureau (LC-USZC4-4243). Photograph: Prints and Photographs Division, The Library of Congress, Washington, DC.

Plate 13. Joby Harris, "Earth: Your Oasis in Space" (2019). From *Visions of the Future* poster series. Photograph: Courtesy NASA/JPL-Caltech.

Plate 14. Joby Harris, "Kepler-186f" (2020). From *Visions of the Future* poster series. Photograph: Courtesy NASA/JPL-Caltech.

Plate 15. "Amazon Spheres." Aerial view of company headquarters in Seattle, Washington (2021). Photography by David Ryder for the *Washington Post*. Photograph: Getty Images.

Plate 16. Barron Bixler, "Biosphere 2, Exterior." Digital capture photograph (2019). By permission of the artist. Photograph: Barron Bixler.

Plate 17. Barron Bixler, “Biosphere 2, Marine Mesocosm.” Digital capture photograph (2019). By permission of the artist. Photograph: Barron Bixler.

Plate 18. Barron Bixler, “Biosphere 2, Greenhouse Capsule.” Digital capture photograph (2019). By permission of the artist. Photograph: Barron Bixler.

Plate 19. Cone Nebula (NGC 2264): Star-Forming Pillar of Gas and Dust, Hubble Telescope. NASA, H. Ford, G. Illingworth, M. Clampin, G. Hartig, the ACS Science Team, and European Space Agency, 2002. Photograph: NASA/STScI.

Plate 20. Biomodd [TAI[8]]. Project created by Space Ecologies Art and Design (SEADS) members and local community partners. Photograph: National Taiwan Museum of Fine Arts (NTMoFA), 2016.

With the bestiary as its point of departure, this chapter argues that *Borne* thus reconfigures the tropes and trajectories of eco-dystopian fiction. The novel overlays a future of worst-case climatological and technological scenarios with an uncanny and ultimately exuberant imagination of biodiversity that interweaves diverse genres, from fantasy and horror to bildungsroman and the epistolary novel. This genre play provides a literary scaffold for VanderMeer's *speculative ecologies*, which contest blanket opposition to biotechnology on the part of certain strains of environmentalism over the past several decades. *Borne* and its companion stories offer biological mutability as a basis not only for shoring up life in "broken places" but also for creating more-than-human societies. The societies envisioned in this future and possibly parallel world to Earth in the early twenty-first century relinquish anthropocentrism to make way for an expansive model of community.

Entangled Stories of Biodiversity and Biotech

In the world of Borne, narratives of the wild and the built uproot the demarcation of biodiversity from biotech. For decades—these concepts—and the research and rhetoric around them—have been at odds. Yet at their root is the shared prefix *bio*-, whose first meaning in English signified a human "way of life" as categorically distinct from "animal life" (*Oxford English Dictionary* 2023a). From the seventeenth century through the nineteenth, the prefix continued to denote this anthropocentric sense of an individual person and that person's development as a social rather than as a physiological or an ecological being. The popularity of biography reflects this meaning, suggesting that *bio*- has functioned as a linguistic marker of the ideological divide between nature and culture that has been well documented in White environmental thought (see, e.g., Alaimo 2010; Cronon 1996; Guha 1989, 2000; and Soper 1995). In "The Trouble with Wilderness" (as discussed in chap. 4), William Cronon (1996) connects this "dualistic vision in which the human is entirely outside the natural" to the history of the American wilderness as a mythological space bound up with colonialism as its meanings for settlers evolved from the demonic to the sublime. His analysis suggests that the nature-culture split has made the wilderness a landscape apart from people so as to rationalize Indigenous dispossession and prioritize certain environments over others for ecological study and protection. In *Bodily Natures*, Stacy Alaimo offers a kindred analysis through her concept of *transcorporeality*, which sees wild nature as entangled with "networks that are simultaneously economic, political, cultural, scientific, and substantial" (2010, 20–21). Over the past century, *bio*- has come to signify this entanglement of nature and culture, organism and machine, adding to its meanings, first, that of "organic substances . . . or life processes" and, most recently, "biotechnology." These modern uses hark back to the Greek and Latin roots of the prefix, which denote not just a life-form but *the combining of forms* (*Oxford English Dictionary* 2023a). In short, biodiversity and biotechnology are linked at the root.

The sociologist Melinda Cooper traces the latter concept to "the first years of genetics." Before and after the Second World War, biotechnology was only an idea as "the essential elements required for the production of transgenic life—controlled and reproducible mutation outside the frontiers of species life—were articulated in theoretical terms" before they could be realized in applied science (Cooper 2001). Beginning in the 1980s, "recombinant-DNA technologies" made such speculations plausible, and biotechnology began to galvanize both the popular imagination and activist opposition (Kennedy 1991). Writing about the specific science of and opposition to transgenic seeds (or genetically modified organisms), Anne-Lise François underscores the "imaginative, social, and ecological" crises that biotechnology has embodied with its corporate ownership (2003, 44). Cooper expands on this observation in showing that biotechnology has been an engine for capitalist growth by "mobilizing life as a technological resource" and by summoning a future without ecological limits to that growth (2007, 32). Through this historical and political lens, the story of biotechnology is, above all, a story of late capitalism, with companies like Monsanto and Genentech as its (anti)heroes.

By comparison, the story of biodiversity formed over the same period as a tragedy of the ecological losses that capitalism has wrought (Benton 2016; Heise 2016a). In a paper that defined conservation biology Michael Soulé (whose proposals for rewilding appear in chap. 4) identified the field as a "crisis discipline" forged to protect the biodiversity of natural ecosystems from people. The paper intimates that the field's defining concern—"the biology of species, communities, and ecosystems that are perturbed, either directly or indirectly, by human activities or other agents"—has as its chief antagonist industrial and postindustrial capitalism (Soulé 1985, 727).[2] Three years after Soulé's paper appeared, the entomologist and science writer E. O. Wilson published a book titled *Biodiversity* that was, by all accounts, the first popular use of the term *biodiversity* (Wilson and Peter 1988). In the decades since, *biodiversity* has been in the title of thousands of scientific papers, popular science writings, journalistic reports, documentary films, and activist campaigns.[3] It has, accordingly, become a keyword for environmental science and environmental action associated, perhaps above all, with charismatic megafauna—from the polar bear to the Channel Island fox—defined by their vulnerability to extinction and their perceived need for protection.

In the twenty-first century, the stories of biotechnology and biodiversity increasingly intersect. The anthropologist Stefan Helmreich explains:

> The theoretical object of biology, "life," is today in transformation, if not dissolution. Proliferating reproductive technologies, along with genomic reshufflings of biomatter in such practices as cloning, have unwound the facts of life. Biotechnology, biodiversity, bioprospecting, biosecurity, biotransfer, and molecularized biopolitics *draw novel lines of property and protection around organisms and their elements.* (Helmreich 2011, 671–72; emphasis added)

This catalog suggests that both the tools and the tropes of ecological conservation now overlap with those of genetic engineering. As scientists, engineers, and companies have "drawn novel lines of property and protection around organisms," the ancient meaning of *bio* as a form of life reboots as life "unwound" and rebuilt. Meanwhile, the pursuit of biodiversity has gone high-tech, evident in big data projects such as the IUCN Red List and the Census of Marine Life, the use of GPS tracking and remote sensing of wildlife, and the emergence of synthetic biology and de-extinction. If biodiversity and biotech are more and more enmeshed, their entanglement reflects what has been described as the "Central Dogma" of molecular genetics (Strasser 2006, 493). According to this dictum, DNA is "the most important component of the cell, its 'master plan,'" an idea that James Watson and Francis Crick advanced in a pair of 1953 papers published in *Nature* that identified the chemical structure of DNA and then touted that discovery as "solv[ing] one of the fundamental biological problems—the molecular basis of the template needed for genetic replication" (Watson and Crick 1953a, 966; see also Watson and Crick 1953b). In *Novelty*, the literary scholar Michael North describes Watson and Crick's research and the publications it generated as initiating "perhaps the most influential use of information as a model for novelty" (2013, 105). The feminist historian of science Evelyn Fox Keller has, for her part, shown that the central dogma fundamentally reimagined life as a species of computation. As part of this analysis, Keller traces the origins of the term *organism* to seventeenth-century Europe, where it signified a distinctive capacity of animate beings—in contrast to built things—for self-organization (Keller 2005; see also Bardini 2011; Haraway 1991; Keller 1995; Landecker 2007; and Mitchell 2010). It is this distinction that molecular genetics and the biotech industry have collectively scuttled. Consider, for example, the 2015 "Ecomodernist Manifesto," which calls for "accelerated technological progress" to solve the multiple environmental crises of this century, including biodiversity loss and climate change. While the manifesto's authors (among them Stewart Brand, whose role in de-extinction was a focus of the prior chapter) tap into foundational concepts of conservation, they contend that "concepts of biodiversity, complexity, and indigeneity are useful, but alone cannot determine which landscapes to preserve, or how." Hence, they reason, "technological innovation" is essential to sustaining diverse forms of life in the future (Asafu-Adjaye et al. 2015, 26, 30).

In his seminal paper, Soulé seems to have anticipated the argument that ecosystems and their creatures would one day be engineered—rather than primarily preserved or restored—in response to anthropogenic environmental impacts. Although he stresses that the "long-term viability of natural communities usually implies the persistence of diversity, with little or no help from humans," he muses that "for the foreseeable future . . . virtually all conservation programs will need to be buttressed artificially." With reference to captive breeding programs in zoos, he wonders whether "many cities now have a greater diversity of plant families and tree species than did the original habitat destroyed to make way for the city," a supposition that the speculative narrative of *Borne* takes up in its depiction of a hauntingly urban wilderness. His own ecological speculations aside, Soulé concludes on a melancholic note that has suffused much conservation science and popular biodiversity discourse since: "Botanical gardens, zoos, urban parks, and aquaria satisfy, to a degree, my desire to be with other species, but not my need to see wild and free creatures or my craving for solitude or for a variety of landscapes and vistas" (Soulé 1985, 728–29, 731). If the genetic and computational tools of biotech increasingly shape biodiversity research as well as *new conservation* (chap. 4), the elegiac grief for lost species and the attendant desire to live among "wild and free creatures" today pervades the most bullish biotech rhetoric and the attendant drive to engineer novel forms of life.

A World Teeming with Monstrous, Marvelous Forms of Life

At first blush, the science-fictional depiction in the *Borne* books of lab-born life-forms that were once the property of a power-hungry corporation is a familiarly dystopian one. Among the many biotech bodies that inhabit the City is Rachel's lover, Wick, a character assumed to be human for much of *Borne* and revealed only near the novel's conclusion to be an android who was first made by and then worked for the Company, first on a classified "fish project," and subsequently on a more ambitious and sinister venture "to create an animal around a human being" (VanderMeer 2017, 305). That chimera was Mord. In the Company's absence, Mord has gone feral, along with many of the other transgenic bodies, foods, and weapons the Company produced, and become a rapacious predator. This landscape of violent bodies and weird beings where Rachel and Wick live is also a profoundly inhospitable environment defined by contaminated water and harsh weather. Given these narrative features, one could certainly group *Borne* with speculative novels in which androids have gone rogue in a totalitarian surveillance state (as in Philip K. Dick's 1968 *Do Androids Dream of Electric Sheep?* discussed in chap. 3) and in which genetic engineering controlled by corporations leads to ecological collapse (as in Paolo Bacigalupi's 2009 *The Windup Girl*). But as an interview with VanderMeer underscores, *Borne* and its successor stories are hard to classify as "beautifully strange" works of climate fiction in which biotech represents not just technological overreach and violence but also the possibilities for reconfiguring the very divisions between the human and the more than human (Blumenfeld 2017). What makes this storyworld "beautifully strange," moreover, is the particular and peculiar ways it connects biodiversity to biotech. As with the *Southern Reach Trilogy* that preceded it, the *Borne* series moves the powerful to the periphery and clears space for unexpected forms of connection and care to germinate, centering its speculative future on marginalized people, nonhuman beings, and alien ecologies (VanderMeer 2014).

In a review of *Borne* published in the *New York Times*, Wai Chee Dimock (2017) highlights the novelty of the nonhumans that populate these fictional worlds:

> [M]ost sci-fi nonhumans tend to be human in appearance, resembling us in size, anatomy and general disposition, and departing from us only in one or two highlighted traits: the ears and super-rationality of the Vulcans in "Star Trek," say, or the supposed lack of empathy in Philip K. Dick's androids. VanderMeer turns that differential ratio on its head. His nonhumans are genre bending and taxonomy defying. They have unclassifiable shapes, complicated smells and inexplicable behavior. Especially in their fungal forms, they can be both plant and animal, their alienness at once unabashedly fictive yet almost empirically cataloged.

Dimock elucidates the coconstitutive relationship between the "genre bending" form and the "taxonomy defying" content of VanderMeer's fiction. In the *Borne* series and the *Southern Reach Trilogy*, VanderMeer radically extends "empirically cataloged" taxa of life by turning "unclassifiable" creatures—who upend the biological boundaries of plant, animal, microbe, ecosystem, and machine—into agential characters and by affording sentience, speech, and personhood to wildly different life-forms. This vantage on the nonhuman makes his speculative fiction kindred to more realist narratives that tell stories of biodiversity after biotech. As one example, Karen Tei Yamashita's 1990 novel *Through the Arc of the Rainforest* imagines a toxic underground sea of synthetic plastic that surfaces in the Brazilian Amazon and becomes a wondrous site for biological flourishing that is ultimately destroyed by the machinations of a multinational corporation called GGG. As another, Indra Sinha's 2007 *Animal's People* (a focus of chap. 3) relates a counterhistory of the 1984 Bhopal chemical gas explosion in which a forest grows in the remains of the former "Kampani's" factory. What connects *Borne* to such novels is not only a shared apprehension of capitalism as ecologically extractive and destructive but also a shared imagination of the many forms of life that could, with care, survive into and collectively create postcapitalist futures.

In *Borne*, the world in the wake of both the Company and climate change seems, by all appearances, beyond repair. In response to Borne's question, "What happened in this city?" Rachel muses: "I don't know, it just happened. Everything everywhere collapsed. We didn't try hard enough. We were preyed upon. We had no discipline. We didn't try the right things at the right time. We cared but we didn't do. Too many people, too little space" (VanderMeer 2017, 166–67). But the twist in this story of planetary collapse is that the evident postapocalypticism may be a kind of red herring, a stock genre that obscures a much stranger narrative. Rachel's own memories are unreliable, the reader discovers. At her request, Wick had provided memory-erasing biotech on first finding her wandering among the "holding ponds," a "hell on Earth of Company discards." In finally revealing this fact to her, he shares that she and her parents had come to the City through the Company portal, as "stowaways in crates . . . from some other place," and that she had witnessed her parents' murder before being discarded to fend for herself (VanderMeer 2017, 300). When the novel opens, she is living with Wick in the Balcony Cliffs, which the couple has turned into a fortress to house themselves and another holding pond, a "converted swimming pool where Wick stirred a vat of seething biotech creations like a mad scientist" (VanderMeer 2017, 14). That Wick is at once a biotechnology and a biohacker and that Rachel is at once a climate refugee and an alien from "some other place" underscores the difficulty in *Borne* of demarcating the human from the nonhuman, the alive from the inanimate or the spectral.

Life, however mutagenic and makeshift, goes on in this world, literally bubbling up in its most despoiled places. In verdant and aquatic renderings of scenes from the novel, the illustrator Kayla Harren captures this paradox: life is resilient, and so too are its support systems, but those properties coexist with the compounded legacies of capitalism and environmental degradation (plate 11). Or as one critic writes: "Jeff VanderMeer amends the apocalypse" (Miller 2017). That amendment occurs, moreover, through a form of genre bending that mixes dystopian fiction with many other genres, from supernatural fantasy to romantic comedy, from action movies to gothic fiction. Mord and his creepy foot soldiers—as with the "behemoths, leviathans, [and] illusions of life that snapped impotently at the empty air and cast around for flesh to rend" haunting the City—invoke blockbusters like *King Kong* (1933), *Godzilla* (1956), and *Jurassic Park* (1993) (VanderMeer 2017, 264), the last of which featured in chapter 4. Meanwhile, Borne's quest for literacy and self-improvement mimics the literary genre of bildungsroman, which since the nineteenth century has told stories of individual progress and social assimilation. Akin to the creature's autodidact education in *Frankenstein* (glossed in chap. 3), Borne becomes a social creature by conversing with Rachel, eavesdropping on her and Wick, and literally devouring all the print material he can find. But, also like the creature that Victor Frankenstein builds in a laboratory only to abandon, Borne cannot escape his classification as monstrous, growing ever larger with each body he eats in order to know them. In this play with narrative form, *Borne* builds on VanderMeer's earlier speculative fictions and irreverent taxonomies (VanderMeer and VanderMeer 2010; VanderMeer and Roberts 2005). This body of work has made VanderMeer a leading figure of the "New Weird," which updates the weird tales associated with writers such as Edgar Allan Poe and H. P. Lovecraft into "a hybrid literary mode" while distancing itself from the "antihumanism and racism" of its predecessors (Caracciolo and Ulstein 2022, 1; see also Marshall 2016; VanderMeer and VanderMeer 2008).[4] Writing about this literary history, Kate Marshall observes that, "as far back as at least Macbeth's 'Weird Sisters,' the weird . . . implies something unearthly" (Marshall 2016, 645). In VanderMeer's case, the weird also inheres in the uncanny, hovering between the utterly novel and the too close for comfort. Branding VanderMeer "the weird Thoreau," to this point, a *New Yorker* reviewer observes that what is most discomfiting about his fiction is that "everything is too alive" (Rothman 2015).

Put differently, *Borne* is an uncanny tale of bodies and biomes that are "too alive" for the ravaged world around them, a liveliness that is at once monstrous and marvelous. Consider the novel's climactic battle between Mord and Borne, who at the battle's outset transforms himself into a clone of the giant bear. The battle unfolds in stages, interwoven with a journey Rachel and Wick make from the Balcony Cliffs to the Company compound, to which they venture in order to retrieve lifesaving medicine for Wick, and where they end up confronting the Magician, whom Rachel kills before discovering hundreds of other Bornes in Company-branded boxes. The vicious combat between Mord and Borne, whose culmination changes both the arc of the novel and the ecology of the City, spans fifty pages. An extended excerpt brings it to life:

> Two great beasts fought amid the burning wreckage of a city. Smashed into each other, withdrew engaged again—exhausted, exhausting, the brutality. Gray smoke drawn up into the sky to linger around the vultures gliding high above the behemoths' heads like ragged black halos. . . .
>
> As Mord feasted on Borne's flesh, Borne changed tactics. Instead of trying to become taller, he spread out, giving away his height, so that Mord was angled into Borne, tunneling through flesh, sloppy with it, seeking the heart of Borne. . . . But Borne kept flattening and widening the aperture at the top of his body until he resembled an enormous passionflower [*sic*] blossom. Complex and beautiful, with many levels. . . .
>
> There came a blinding silver-white light, a radiance that seared out across the landscape in a wave and threw me to the ground. Wick beneath me. A wave of light that emitted no heat. A thunderclap, very close, very loud. A word in my head, I swear, a word, just my name: "Rachel." . . .
>
> I got up. I looked back across the City. No bodies lay broken and giant across that landscape. No remains. No carcasses for scavengers to feed on. Both Mord and Borne were gone, as if they had not existed, and the City was still and silent but for the grieving of the [Mord] proxies and the sinuous smoke that still rose from all that had been destroyed. (VanderMeer 2017, 309–15)

This epic clash comes in fragments interrupted by the slow-moving progress of Rachel and Wick across the City and into the Company compound as they watch the battle in the distance. On a first reading, the gore is mostly what one notices. Already a desiccated landscape, the City is set ablaze by the "burning wreckage" of the gruesome conflict. The two creatures seem to be exercising their purpose-built nature, their "black halos" suggestive of their identity as demonic bioweapons. But the "blinding silver-white light" that marks the terminus of the violence brings an unanticipated "radiance . . . that emitted no heat," leaving "no bodies," "no remains," "no carcasses for scavengers to feed on." The deaths of Mord and Borne ultimately bring relief for all who remain in the City, relief in the form of an implausible peace and much-needed rain. Their lethal battle not only revives the City but also redeems Borne, who metamorphoses one last time from a *killing thing* (a moniker that appears twenty-two times in the novel) into "the child [Rachel] had known who was kind and sweet and curious" (VanderMeer

2017, 314). In one breath, a horror story of monstrous biotech morphs into a parable of ecological regeneration and social renewal.

Earlier in the novel, before his growing size and appetite make it untenable for him to stay in the Balcony Cliffs, Borne moves from living with Rachel to taking up residence in another set of rooms in the complex. Feeling estranged, she brings her ward a biology textbook, passing it off as having belonged to her parents. Borne casually dismisses the gift: "I've already read all of the books in the Balcony Cliffs. I've read them all and I think that might be enough for me to have read rather than to have lived." The macabre metafictional joke here is that Borne has already lived a lifetime by consuming books and bodies alike. In response, Rachel tells herself: "He wasn't human, even if he was a person" (VanderMeer 2017, 145). That statement reverberates across the novel countermandated by *Borne*'s ethical project to reimagine personhood as more than human. Although there may be few, if any, human beings in the City or in the wider world of *Borne*, there are people everywhere, and their multiplicity asks readers to grapple with the questions of what counts as life and whose ways of life matter. As Rachel and Wick make their way to the Company while Mord and Borne fight to the death, it is the strange and surreal richness of life they notice, and VanderMeer asks the reader to notice with them:

> [W]e strove on in darkness, across a plain less dead than we might have wished. There came lesser growls than those of bears—and the yap-yip of the foxes and the slither-rustle of what we hoped were snakes, a pitter-patter as of the pink starlike toes of burrowing mammals and even a quark-quark we avoided from a stand of cactus that might have only been a frog calling out for water. Blocks and slabs of black stymied any attempt to know what was threat and what was innocent. "I don't remember it being this alive," Wick complained.

From one point of view, the world is on life support. "[T]oo dirty and yet antiseptic," Rachel says as she looks up at the moon and perceives "the rounded head of a dead robot" (VanderMeer 2017, 256, 257). And, from another, it is teeming with hostile beings and things, far too alive, as Wick "complain[s]." Against an apocalyptic take on this world, however, *Borne* rejects an anthropocentric lens in perceiving all the nonhuman creatures as *people* who live and die here—lives that Rachel herself comes to value. *Borne* thus articulates what one reviewer describes as "post-human optimism" (Hand 2017). The "hell on Earth" that is the City first made and then wasted by the Company in turn shape-shifts from a biotech wasteland to a weird wilderness that is home to many, however precariously. For those posthuman creatures, Borne is next of kin rather than a corporate weapon. After he leaves the Balcony Cliffs, and before his battle with Mord, Rachel observes him from a distance leading a carnival of fellow people: "Borne was leading them. Borne was somehow leading them. All the forgotten and outcast creatures, beneath the notice of the City" (VanderMeer 2017, 192–93).

Dead Astronauts and Uncanny Gardens

Death is, admittedly, everywhere in this speculative world. There are those Borne eats, and those Mord and the Magician slaughter, and those Wick and Rachel grieve. There are the spectacular deaths of the Magician, and Mord, and Borne, which unwittingly advance the fox's "quiet revolution" to reseed the City with a new, nonhuman society (VanderMeer 2017, 299). But it is the strange species of life that make *Borne* and its narrative companions so compelling to me as counterweights to the technological utopianism and determinism of Nature Remade. After the battle, Rachel narrates a sequence of events that gives birth to an uncanny garden in the ruins of the City:

> Outside, it rained for three days and nights. That would have been strange by itself, as an event, but this was no ordinary rain. All manner of creature dropped from the sky or, at the touch of this rain, sprouted up from the ground. Grass grew fast and wild outside the cistern, created paths of green, and on some of the dead blackened trees down the slopes I noticed new leaves. There were on certain avenues in the City, I would learn, new growths of vines and plants that had been gone for years. Birdsong came lyrical through the storms, and animals long-hidden emerged from the sanctuary. (VanderMeer 2017, 315)

If, in the book of Genesis, the garden is prelapsarian, the plenitude that falls from the sky and sprouts from the ground at the close of *Borne* is entirely postapocalyptic. From the image of creatures "sprout[ing] up from the ground" to that of "animals long-hidden emerg[ing]," this description suggests a process of accelerated evolution. Nourished by torrential rain, the "fast and wild" eruption of life reimagines the parable that begins *Silent Spring*, whose opening chapter envisions an idyllic agrarian town that was once in sync with seasonal cycles but where industrialization and its pervasive biochemicals have led to "browned and withered vegetation," "new kinds of sickness," and "spring without [the] voices" of birdsong (Carson 1962, 2–3). Reversing Rachel Carson's famous ecological narrative of anthropogenic "blight," *Borne* ends with a portrait of posthuman rewilding: "birdsong came lyrical through the storms," a beacon of regeneration that is neither of human design nor under human control. Rather than being achieved by heroic scientists and engineers, this speculative landscape is attributed in *Borne* to more-than-human people.

Through Rachel's point of view, however, the world that emerges after Borne's death is as disturbing as it is hopeful. "Most of it was biotech, uncanny," she observes: "[T]he water triggered the last of the [Company's] traps and up came vast clouds and explosions of life . . . spill[ing] out across the plain, and even now we do not know how much of the new life among us comes from that moment" (VanderMeer 2017, 315–16). Identifying with a first-person plural collective that remains inchoate when the novel ends and encompasses not only her and Wick but all the beings and bodies around them, Rachel perceives the new City as an uncanny place to call home. In Freud's essay "The Uncanny," the German term it theorizes—*unheimlich*—holds a double meaning that speaks directly to Rachel's sense of where her world is heading. While *uncanny* and *eerie* are the two closest English equivalents for *unheimlich*, what gets lost in translation is the literal sense of the word as "unhomely" (Freud 1919/2003, 124). Freud clarifies this lexical trace in a passage that has informed how literary critics have defined an array of genres, from gothic to magical realism: "[T]he uncanny is that *species* of the frightening that goes back to what was once well known and had long been familiar" (Freud 1919/2003, 124; emphasis added). The use of *species* is significant: a hallmark of both uncanny stories and uncanny bodies as sharing the trait of confusing boundaries between the kindred and the alien. As a visceral illustration, Freud describes the experience of not knowing "whether an apparently animate object really is alive and, conversely, whether a lifeless object might not perhaps be animate." He goes on to argue that imaginative literature has far more opportunities for producing this experience than does everyday life, for "the writer can intensify and multiply this effect far beyond what is feasible in normal experience." This sense of the uncanny as a species of storytelling that is distinct from the supernatural, activated when the "familiar" and the "frightening" intermix, speaks directly to *Borne* and its narrative of bioengineered ecologies and bodies (Freud 1919/2003, 134, 156–57).

The function of the uncanny in this storyworld is especially evident in the recurring apparition of what Rachel and others label the *dead astronauts*. These spectral figures crop up in different locations around the City, beginning with three Rachel discovers in a former courtyard where the decay of their bodies is nurturing a botanical landscape:

> I came to the edge of a courtyard and a peculiar sight. For anywhere but here. Three dead astronauts had fallen to Earth and been planted like tulips, buried to their rib cages, then flopped over in their suits, faceplates cracked open and curled into the dirt. Lichen or mold spilled from their helmets. Bones, too. My heart lurched, trapped between hope and despair. Someone had come to the City from far, far away—even perhaps, from space! Which meant there were people *up there*. (VanderMeer 2017, 73)

The two short opening sentences distill the City as an uncanny garden. The sight of three corpses in crumbling suits with cracked faceplates whose bodies are becoming humus and feeding plants is "a peculiar sight" "[f]or anywhere but here." Themselves "planted like tulips" and becoming microbial matter, the dead astronauts are haunting precisely because they are *not* out of the ordinary here. Accordingly, fear and disgust are not the only emotions the courtyard garden elicits. However unnerving, the "planted astronauts"—as Harren titles her visual rendering of the scene—comfort Rachel as she recognizes the corpses as both familiars (almost next of kin) and signs of "people *up there*" (plate 10). As Rachel lingers in the garden, however, she realizes that the astronauts were not aliens from another world but rather casualties of this ransacked one: "They'd died here, like everything died here. Then I realized they were not astronauts but only like astronauts because the sun had bleached the contamination suits white, and I felt perversely less sad" (VanderMeer 2017, 73). How to explain this sudden lessening of melancholy? Harren's illustration offers insight. In the variety of grasses, flowers, and spores it layers over the cracked suit and decaying corpse, the artwork makes legible the duality of the planted astronauts as human corpses killed by toxic labor and humus for botanical life.

Borne grows fixated on the astronauts after he and Rachel pass through the courtyard together during a foraging excursion. He eventually brings the three suits into his rooms at the Balcony Cliffs and hangs them from hooks (the bodies, he assures Rachel, are no longer inside, suggesting that he consumed them). While Rachel experiences this act as one of desecration, the suits give Borne a decidedly uncanny sense of home. A diary Rachel eventually discovers documents his evolving sense of kinship with the astronauts: "I came here from the moon, like the dead / astronauts. / I was made by the Company. / I was made by someone. / I am not actually alive. / I am a robot. / I am a person. / I am a weapon. / I am not / intelligent. / I have nine senses and Rachel only has five." These fragmented thoughts underscore that Borne lacks a stable origin story and taxonomic identity: he is a defunct bioweapon and a person in progress, lab born and self-fashioning, sentient and inert, earthly and alien. He is also, in Rachel's own words, "complex and beautiful, with many levels." The astronauts are a touchstone for this multiplicity. After Wick discards the three suits, Rachel comes across them in the City yet again, this time having been buried to the waist by the Magician and sporting placards that read "Wick, Rachel, Borne." In response to the clear threat, Rachel notes her weariness with "how the dead astronauts kept switching their allegiance, of the way these bodies kept being disrespected, had no fixed address or location" (VanderMeer 2017, 189–90, 200, 201). The astronauts have "no fixed address" precisely because they are vessels for the uncanny narratives and uncanny ecologies that are at once devolving, sustaining, and changing the forms of life in this world, in part by stirring the imagination of a better world to come. It is the work of *Dead Astronauts* to breathe yet new narrative life into "these bodies," which turn out to be a onetime astronaut named Grayson, a former Company man who may also have been a salamander, and a "sentient moss" who is also a woman named Moss (Martine 2019).

Given these revelations in the third book in the series, what the dead astronauts arguably seed in *Borne* is a radical decentering of anthropocentric imaginings of the future. By the novel's end, it is unclear whether there are any humans in this speculative storyworld. But there are many kinds of people living as kin and shoring up a society. The closing pages of *Borne* detail how Rachel and Wick are once again living in the Balcony Cliffs but this time with some of the City's "feral children" who had been biomodified by the Magician to do her bidding—including a child named Teems to whom VanderMeer attributes the authorship of the bestiary in the appendix. As the novel comes to a close, the City is no longer a ghost town of dead bodies and biotech monsters but a place of multispecies family and sociality. "I can stroll down an avenue lined with young trees now," Rachel writes as her narration concludes, "visit a market where people under shelter of makeshift tents barter for goods. . . . Wick tells me we live in an alternate reality, but I tell him the Company is the alternate reality, was always the alternate reality" (VanderMeer 2017, 318–19). Uncanny to the end, the City may be not the real world but just another invention: an alternate reality made by the Company and remade by Borne. But the ambiguity is deliberate rather than a glitch. The tension between Rachel's and Wick's apprehensions of the self-regenerating City underscores the larger ethical stakes of VanderMeer's fiction, which imaginatively expands who counts among the living and what ecological and social forms might evolve down the road if all species of life—born and made—are included.

Making Kin on a "Tough New Planet"

A fictional proxy for the novel's human reader, Rachel models how to make kin with uncanny others on what in his 2011 book *Eaarth* Bill McKibben calls a *tough new planet.* At least according to the history that she remembers and we learn from her as *Borne*'s narrator, Rachel was born in an island archipelago where her father was a council leader and her mother was a doctor. While unnamed, this place of origin "that fell not to war or disease but to rising seas" seems kindred to Fiji, where VanderMeer spent part of his childhood before returning to the United States and making a home on the Gulf Coast of Florida (VanderMeer 2017, 38–39). Having left that home at age six with her parents as climate refugees during "the unraveling of the world," Rachel has scant and unreliable memories of her past. But what she does purport to remember is telling (VanderMeer 2017, 39). While holed up in the Company's ruins during the battle between Borne and Mord, she relays to Wick remembered family stories "of shark deities and island men and women who became trees or birds to outwit monsters" (VanderMeer 2017, 275), tales that allude to the Fijian mythical shark god Dakuwaqa, who appears by name in a previous short story by VanderMeer (2010, 121–32). Like the capital of Fiji, Suva, Rachel's birthplace is a "harbor capital" with a botanical garden featuring a "decorative pond with a dead fountain in the center." A foil to the planted astronauts and to Wick's swimming pool, the garden in Rachel's memory recasts the Suva Botanical Gardens built in Fiji during British colonial occupation as a futuristic habitat for biotech, the products of which were already in Rachel's youth "out in the world more than people knew . . . trying to blend in, to escape notice" (VanderMeer 2017, 238–39). This palimpsest of colonial history, sea level rise, and biotechnology that her memories render thus tethers the novel to our world (see fig. 5.3). At the same time, as we've seen, her origin story might be apocryphal, a figment of her mind after its alteration by the memory beetles Wick administered to numb her pain. But the reliability of her story is beside the point. In the lacunae of a lost home and a lost history, Rachel learns and models for the novel's human reader how to "make kin" with all the other survivors of the Company (Haraway 2015).

With a sly nod to the biblical story of Rachel made fertile by divine intervention, *Borne*'s protagonist is an unconventional figure of the archetypal survivor, a "last woman" who makes her own family by surrendering humanness to biological fluidity. In this sense, she is kindred to the four unnamed women who enter the sentient, ever-evolving environment known as Area X in the first volume of the *Southern Reach Trilogy* and become absorbed into its alien, fungal ecology (VanderMeer 2014). In stark

Figure 5.3. Botanical Gardens, Suva, Fiji (no. 53). Postcard created by Harry Gardiner (Armadale, Victoria, 1920). The Miriam and Ira D. Wallach Division of Art, Prints and Photographs: Picture Collection (PC POC FIJ). Photograph: The New York Public Library Digital Collections.

contrast to the film adaptation, which casts *Annihilation*'s biologist narrator as a White woman, VanderMeer aimed for the novel to stymie expectations about who will inhabit and shape the future and its ecologies: "[O]nce I determined they could not be named in the first novel and that all four were women, I also had to decide if I would describe them or not. And I most definitely decided not to include descriptions to help subvert expectations" (Byrne 2014). This subversion of expectations about characters whose very identities as human (rather than, say, extraterrestrial or fungal) are unstable complements another defining feature of VanderMeer's work: speculative fiction in which unfamiliar organisms are among a collapsing world's most resilient survivors. Resilience in these narratives assumes a meaning that differs from its now clichéd status in arenas such as green engineering and climate change adaptation. In *Area X*, as in *Borne*, *resilience* comes to mean not the rebounding of social and natural systems as they've been under capitalism but, rather, the pliability and durability of *liveliness* itself. In VanderMeer's speculative worlds, the future may be as much or more the provenance of biotechnologies—and yet stranger things—than that of human beings.

VanderMeer has acknowledged that a central concern of his work has been "the question [of] whether we'll have a place" in the future, as he put it in a 2017 interview about a work in progress that became the 2021 novel *Hummingbird Salamander* (Liptak 2017). We have seen that this question permeates *Borne* and its "fantastical post-apocalyptic city" (Liptak 2017). But, in the final analysis, this chapter has argued, *Borne* rejects what Ursula K. Heise terms the *reduced ecologies* of dystopian science fiction, where "only one or two kinds of landscape and a few species" constitute an entire future world. Those landscapes, Heise writes, explore scenarios "in which humans, facing living beings with whom they have not co-evolved, are forced to ask anew the question of what principles should guide their interactions with nonhuman others" (Heise 2012, 99, 100). VanderMeer takes another tack in staging those same interactions between human characters and strange others, one more comparable with the approaches of novelists such as Yamashita and Sinha than with those of eco-dystopian writers. Jolting readers out of habituated notions of ecological wastelands and diminished futures, *Borne* imagines the *vibrant ecologies* that might emerge in the ruins of capitalism and who might make them their home. Put differently, the narrative of *Borne* and the environmental ethics that emerge from it articulate in science-fictional terms how the cultural geographer Jamie Lorimer imagines wildness in a "post-Natural world":

> Wildlife lives among us. It includes the intimate microbial constituents that make up our gut flora and the feral plants and animals that inhabit urban ecologies. Risky, endearing, charismatic, and unknown, wildlife persists in our post-Natural world. Unlike Nature, wildlife also suggests processes. It describes ecologies of becomings, not fixed beings with movements of differing intensity, duration, and rhythm. Wildlife is discordant, with multiple stable states.

In opposition to the commodification and weaponization of bodies on which the Company profited, the storyworld of *Borne* is one in which nature is "discordant" in Lorimer's sense, radically "public, the property of a more-than-human citizenry unable or undisposed to participate in relations of commodified consumption" (Lorimer 2015, 7, 192).

The sequel to *Borne*, a slim novella titled *The Strange Bird*, takes the speculative narrative of such a "post-Natural" ecology and its ethical significance still further. The novella's third-person narrator is known only as Strange Bird. When her story opens, she has fled another corporate compound in another wasted city. The story develops through her aerial and subaltern point of view as a highly sentient and all but immortal creature of flight who is, we quickly learn, a biotechnology. Her narration is lyrical and impressionistic. And the aesthetic and affective experience of following her airborne path while being immersed in her thoughts is uncanny for the human reader. Interspersed with Strange Bird's fast-moving journey over terrestrial landscapes are a series of dreams that interlace the barbaric acts of her engineers back at the lab where she was made with the counsel and compassion of one of those engineers, who seems to have aided her liberation. Her flight proves short-lived as she is taken captive twice during the story, the first time in the subterranean dwelling of a figure known only as the "Old Man," who is the only person living in what was once a prison. After she manages to escape from that hold, she takes flight over a city that readers of *Borne* recognize, within which "moved the outlines of monstrous figures the Strange Bird could not interpret from afar, some that lived below the surface and some that strode across the broken places and still others that flew above" (VanderMeer 2018, 22).

Strange Bird comes in this flight over the City into direct contact with the death of the blue fox and then is ensnared herself by one of the Magician's minions. Weeks and months pass, during which the Magician studies, tortures, dismembers, experiments on, and finally reassembles Strange Bird in order to harness her sophisticated sensing and camouflage properties as a weapon in the Magician's war against Mord. The weapon takes the form of a feathered invisibility cloak that the Magician wears. But, as with both the blue fox and Borne, there is an animism to this bioengineered tool of violence that allows her mind and body to outlast the Magician. The plots of *Borne* and *The Strange Bird* converge at this point in the novella when, on the Magician's death, Rachel and Wick discover the cloak. As Strange Bird lacks language in the ordinary sense, the couple can only speculate as to her provenance and purpose. "'What was it made to do before the Magician?'" Rachel asks, to which Wick replies: "'There could be more than one reason. But before the Magician got hold of her, this bird was a kind of . . . dispersal system for genetic material. It would have been reseeding the world as it flew. Microscopic organisms'" (VanderMeer 2018, 95). Until this point, the reader might have classed Strange Bird as a biotechnology created for surveillance. There is a scene early on, for instance, in which she encounters two drones orbiting Earth in the upper atmosphere, machines that she perceives as fellow airborne creatures. Wick's description recalibrates this militaristic categorization of Strange Bird, confounding the lines between bodies, ecosystems, and machines. Far from a drone, it turns out, the bird-turned-cloak is a kind of seed bank that contains the genetic and microscopic material to propagate new life-forms.

VanderMeer's novella closes with Strange Bird having been remade once again, this time by the relatively benevolent hand of Wick. Recalling his own double status as biotechnology and biotech engineer, Wick transforms the Magician's feathered cloak into three separate but interconnected birds, creating another uncanny and more-than-human family. A dispersed and dispersing body, the birds leave the City in the final pages of the novella. The "compass" that Strange Bird's original engineers genetically hard wired into her makes possible a networked consciousness that calls the three, interconnected creatures to another lab on a remote seaside island:

> It had been a human need, the compass pulsing at her heart, and she was, in the end, much diminished for having followed it. Yet what did it matter. For what are bodies? Where do they end and where do they begin? And why must they be constant? Why must they be strong? So much was leaving her, but of the winnowing, the Strange Bird sang for joy. She sang for joy. Not because she had not suffered or been reduced. But because she was finally free and the world could not be saved, but nor would it be destroyed. (VanderMeer 2018, 108)

If the Company signifies a demonic agent of bioengineering, the animals and plants it made—from the fox with hands to Borne to Strange Bird—become, in the wake of its disappearance, propagators of both ecological novelty and novel society. Although they were made to be weapons of one kind or another, the beings who populate this imagined world that "could not be saved . . . nor . . . destroyed" now live in a world where all kinds of strange birds are vital to sustaining ecological and social life in futures to come.

[CHAPTER 6]

Life after Earth

> History is going to bifurcate along two directions. One path is we stay on Earth forever, and then there will be some eventual extinction event. I do not have an immediate doomsday prophecy, but eventually, history suggests, there will be some doomsday event. The alternative is to become a space-bearing civilization and a multi-planetary species.
>
> —ELON MUSK, "Making Humans a Multi-planetary Species"

It was on a trip between the headlands of Mendocino County and the strand of Morro Bay, the latter known for its twin landmarks of an offshore volcanic rock and a decommissioned power plant, that I began to think about fantasies of space colonization as the subject for the final chapter of *Novel Ecologies*. The world looks wild along much of this four-hundred-mile California route. The midnight blue of the deep ocean collides with the surface disturbance of whitecaps, kelp beds, and rock outcroppings. Birds of prey dot the sky, traveling over redwood groves and chaparral hillsides in parallel to the Pacific Coast Highway (PCH, a.k.a. Highway 1). My experience of these landscapes is hardly novel. Especially since the completion of the highway in the 1960s, this stretch of the Pacific coastline has become a storied place, thick with ideas of the Blue Planet as a wondrous and potentially singular world in its support of all kinds of life. That environmental imagination also informs, if to different ends, the speculative vision of technologically altered bodies and landscapes that the prior chapter traced through *Borne* and *The Strange Bird*.

For decades, however, both storytellers and engineers have written over the picture-postcard view of California as a microcosm of Earth's biodiversity and ecological sublimity by crafting a narrative of the state—and the American West more broadly—as the living lab for pioneering technology, big infrastructure, and terraforming. The last of these borrows directly from the pages of California sci-fi that, since the 1950s, has puzzled out how to remake planets, asteroids, and moons so that at least some humans could live on them (Grabianowski 2010). This corpus now influences the ambitions of both established government institutions like NASA and deep-pocketed corporate ventures to realize what SpaceX CEO Elon Musk proclaimed, at a 2016 meeting of the International Aeronautical Congress, will be a "multi-planetary" future (Musk 2016, 2017a, 2017b; see also Rubenstein 2022, 4–5). Musk's forecast is at once eco-apocalyptic and techno-utopian: it anticipates an abstract "doomsday event"—whether wrought by climate change, nuclear war, or the singularity (discussed in chap. 2)—that would make Earth all but unlivable while taking as a foregone conclusion the "space-bearing" aims of his company (Musk 2016). What's missing from these and other like-minded speculations is any recognition of the entwined history of colonialism and space exploration, which, extrapolated into a future led by a small number of tech companies, likely leads to a doubling down on resource extraction, conscripted labor, and racial inequality. A technology reporter writing for *Wired* gets at the long-standing links between colonial world-building projects on Earth and fantasies of extraterrestrial colonization in a piece about the "deterraforming" of biodiversity hot spots that has had disastrous consequences for local peoples and ecosystems: the Three Gorges Dam in central China, the Alberta Tar Sands in Canada's Athabasca River basin, the Carajás Mine in Brazil's Carajás Mountains, and the Los Angeles River in Southern California, among them (Grabianowski 2010). Such sites support Patrick Murphy's contention, in a comparison of space colony sci-fi and current geoengineering proposals, that "Earth itself is undergoing a largely unplanned global engineering project" and, I would add, has been so for some time now (2009, 56).

Such analyses remind us that the *(de)terraforming* of terrestrial places has provided a test bed for space colonization on the part of the powerful. The environmental historian Peder Anker shows that actual terraforming projects on Earth and aspirational ones in the stars share a political and intellectual history that begins in the 1960s with military-funded research to investigate the possibility of human travel to and settlement on Mars. In the decades since, space colony plans on the part of NASA, the US military, and their private-sector collaborators have come "to represent rational, orderly, and wise management, in contrast to the irrational, disorderly, and ill-managed Earth" (Anker 2005, 240). The assumption is that other worlds could provide controlled environments for determining how human life "should be organized" in the future, which in turn justifies terraforming experiments and space colony simulations in ecosystems classified as close substitutes for Martian environments, from volcanic craters to high deserts (Anker 2005, 240). For space colony true believers and profiteers alike, it is ever-larger-scale engineering that furnishes the models for the future Musk conjures.

That future has required a good story to advance what are astronomical investments in long-shot gambits ripe for failure and primed for dystopian scenarios. In the United States, one such story has built on the national imaginary of frontiers and their settler-pioneers, which turned to space in the second half of the twentieth century. In response to Franklin Delano Roosevelt's postwar call on the Office of Scientific Research and Development (OSRD) to propose strategies for turning wartime technologies into commercial and domestic industries, then OSRD head Vannevar Bush authored "Science, the Endless Frontier." Bush had been offered the presidency of Stanford University in 1941, and, although he declined the post, his ideas of government-backed applied science and technological innovation became a blueprint for the university's postwar evolution and, by extension, Stanford's influence on the development of Silicon Valley as we know it today (Harris 2023, 222–23). That blueprint was implemented by the radio engineer Fred Terman, the dean of engineering at Stanford from 1944 to 1958, who believed in advancing capitalism by way of applied research in the interconnected fields of aerospace, communications, and electronics. As Malcolm Harris explains: "[T]he model worked, and Palo Alto changed. . . . In the 1950s, Palo Alto went straight from rural to something like postindustrial." This in turn was the groundwork that allowed Silicon Valley to become a global tech center as the "space-age settlers who came west to explore the vertical frontier" made Stanford, the region around it, and then California the nexus of technological capitalism (Harris 2023, 223, 225).

Shortly after Terman's tenure as Stanford's engineering dean ended, John F. Kennedy expanded the ideology of American manifest destiny to encompass the moon and the planetary bodies beyond, anticipating what would be dubbed "Project Apollo." In his now famous acceptance speech at the 1960 Democratic national convention, he explicitly aligned his presidential candidacy with the "New Frontier . . . of science and space" (Kennedy 1960). The US space program in the next decade leaned heavily on this narrative of innovation to marshal nationalist support for Apollo, interlacing tropes drawn from American westerns with the genre of space opera. Tuned for the US pursuit of geopolitical power, space opera spins episodic stories of "space travel, [intergalactic] conflict, huge vistas, and Big Dumb Objects" like the *Star Wars* Death Star (Sawyer 2009, 505). During the Cold War, Kennedy and Soviet premier Nikita Khrushchev became self-styled heroes of a real-world space opera whose plot revolved around their nations' contest to control the world order, for which the space race became a proxy. That contest fueled California's aerospace industry and, in particular, the growth of the Pasadena-based Jet Propulsion Laboratory (JPL) from a Caltech research group into a NASA juggernaut (Benford 2013; Conway 2015; Koppes 1982). As a result, Southern California became a major aerospace hub during the same period that Silicon Valley became the nerve center of computing. But, decades before the space race, William Mulholland planted the seed for the notion that exploration, innovation, and world-building were California's own manifest destiny. At the 1913 opening of the Los Angeles Aqueduct, Mulholland uttered about the water that had been newly diverted from the Owens River the now notorious line: "There it is—take it!" (Ulin 2013). The brash claim exalted the reconfiguration of a vital watershed into a 280-mile gravity flow system that today delivers some 430 million gallons of water daily to Los Angeles (see fig. 6.1). The history of such gigantic infrastructure in California provides a kind of template for *designs on space* that hinge on the abilities of engineers to construct life-support systems out of whole cloth. With the LA Aqueduct and the state's other manufactured water systems, engineers effectively did just that by rewiring California's topography and waterways.[1] The results were as Mulholland, city leaders, and land developers intended: the population of the Los Angeles basin increased exponentially over the next century. A cautionary tale for terraforming, this water system has had numerous ecological and social repercussions. Among others, Los Angeles has become dependent on increasingly precarious water sources imported from across the western United States, while communities outside the Los Angeles basin have been dispossessed of local waterways, from the Paiute Shoshone and agricultural settlers in the Owens Valley to Mexican towns in the Sonoran Desert where Río Colorado now runs dry (Lakhani 2019; Los Angeles County Public Works, n.d.; Owen 2017; Reisner 1986; Sahagun 2013).

It is the premise of this chapter that, from waterworks to space colonies, California's history of and stake in world-making seeks to actualize the concept *Spaceship Earth*. The term comes from the eccentric theory that the architect and inventor Buckminster Fuller hashed out during the first space race, a theory that conceived of the planet as a complex machine requiring engineers to ensure its operation and update its systems on a regular basis (Díaz 2011, 86; Fuller 1969; Pak 2016, 100). California has served as a microcosm of Spaceship Earth for those who believe planets are machines to disassemble and reassemble. Notably, Fuller relocated to California in 1980 and lived out his brief remaining life in the Pacific Palisades, a coastal development located between Santa Monica

Figure 6.1. "Crowd Gathered around the Newhall Spillway as the Aqueduct First Fills Up with Water" (San Fernando Valley, 1913). From the *Los Angeles Times* (November 1913). Photograph: Picture Collection (Collection 99), Charles E. Young Research Library, UCLA Library Special Collections (LSC_99_Aq_004).

and Malibu that overlooks the PCH. He died there in 1983 just two weeks after JPL's *Pioneer 10* became the first spacecraft to travel past Jupiter and reach the outer solar system (NASA, n.d.). In the twenty-first century, the desire of California engineers to make worlds has turned increasingly to the stars. Known for sci-fi novels about terraforming Mars, Mercury, and the asteroid belt, Kim Stanley Robinson observes that California has been a major source of inspiration for such fictions. In an interview, the novelist muses that the state is itself a "science fictional place": "The desert has been terraformed. The whole water system is unnatural and artificial. . . . It's big. It's various. It's an entire country. *It's an entire planet*" (Robinson 2013, 4–6; emphasis added). The photographer Barron Bixler concurs: "When I began photographing [the state's] sprawling network of mines, pits, quarries and materials-processing plants in the early days of the new millennium, I was drawn to the landscapes by their terraformed brutalism, which seemed at odds with the California imaginary" (Bixler, n.d.-a).

Figure 6.2. Barron Bixler, "Ball Mill, Lehigh Cement, Tehachapi, California." From "Industrial Materials: Mining California," analog photograph captured on black-and-white film (2003). By permission of the artist. Photograph: Barron Bixler.

Foregrounding landscapes that are jarringly "at odds" with a breezily picturesque California, Bixler elaborates (see figs. 6.2–6.3):

> When Curiosity began beaming back images of the surface of Mars to NASA's Jet Propulsion Laboratory in August 2012 . . . I thought to myself just how much like Mars my pictures of denuded mining landscapes looked, and how Curiosity, in its many Martian selfies, resembled the hulking machines that have been used to dismantle and scrape bare the California landscape. A part of me was comforted to see novel photographic evidence of a sister planet with a recognizable, Earthlike geology. But another part—the part that has an affinity for dystopian sci-fi stories—was unsettled. Given that our drive to create world-altering technologies is outpacing our ability to mitigate their consequences, I thought, how long will it be before California comes more closely to resemble the surface of Mars? (Bixler 2015, 65)

This reflection by my spouse and longtime collaborator, whose influence on *Novel Ecologies* I shared in the prologue, sparked this chapter's "unsettled" interest in space colony fantasy and its possible realization in my lifetime by

Figure 6.3. Barron Bixler, "Conveyors, Gravel Piles, and Smokestack, San Francisco, California." From "Industrial Materials: Mining California," analog photograph captured on black-and-white film (2003). By permission of the artist. Photograph: Barron Bixler.

California world-builders like Musk. That California itself has been deconstructed and remade many times over such that certain landscapes can pass for "denuded" Martian landscapes haunts that fantasy and reminds us that world-building and world-destroying often go hand in hand. Through this lens, the new space race is extending to Mars-and-beyond terrestrial narratives of the American frontier, its settlers, and its engineers. What follows puts the Silicon Valley architects of twenty-first-century rockets and Martian settlements into conversation with artists, scientists, and writers who illuminate the perils of space races, old and new, and imagine the universe as too big, alive, and manifold to be an inert terrain for world-making. The writers who are central to this critique of a multiplanetary future for a human elite—namely, the novelists T. C. Boyle and Octavia Butler and the poet Tracy K. Smith—perceive the engineer's quest to settle other worlds as variously hubristic, absurd, and violent. Their work shows a paradox at the heart of contemporary space colony ventures: the belief that Earth is already a lost cause, hurdling toward doomsday, entwined with the promise that these ventures are rescue missions that will secure *life after Earth* for at least a chosen few.[2]

"Your Oasis in Space"

The race to space in this century has powerful proponents. What the religious studies scholar Mary-Jane Rubenstein (2022) terms *NewSpace* has been popularized as the latest expression of American exceptionalism, evident in such best-selling books as *Rocket Billionaires* (Fernholz 2018), *The Space Barons* (Davenport 2018), and *When the Heavens Went on Sale* (Vance 2023). While occasionally critical, these upbeat narratives make the ambitions of Elon Musk and others "one of the most exciting tales of our time" (Vance 2023, dust jacket) about "a budding rivalry" between billionaires to decide who controls and profits from the next generation of space travel (Davenport 2018, 4). While page-turners, these accounts isolate NewSpace from its geopolitical, social, and ecological conditions and consequences as a small group of White men who have made their fortunes in the digital economy turn to other worlds as their next frontier. In the endeavor to expand his holdings beyond Earth, Musk is in the company of Amazon CEO Jeff Bezos, who launched Blue Origin as the culmination of a lifelong obsession, Google cofounder Larry Page, who was an initial investor in Planetary Resources, and dozens of less famous tech billionaires whose sights are set on the off-world mining of minerals needed to power both the digital and the renewable energy economies (Bhaimiya 2023; Foer 2019; Levy 2018; Rubenstein 2022; Thompson 2020).[3] As this list intimates, such ventures are rapidly moving the center of gravity for aerospace from nations like the United States and government institutions like NASA to private individuals and their corporations. (Think, recalling the prior chapter, of the Company, which trashed the world of Borne only to decamp for another one.) As Rubenstein writes about the "fine print" of the SpaceX Starlink contract for prospective passengers to the Red Planet, Musk has declared Mars "free from death, free from Earth, free from gravity—at least most of it—and even free from international regulation" (2022, 5).

As I noted above, NewSpace takes some of its cues from a sci-fi canon in which corporations—acting as governments—build cities, mining operations, and colonies across the solar system. Put differently, "the rocket billionaires" are rebooting an established and arguably clichéd story, one from which institutions like NASA have long borrowed (Messeri 2016; Vertesi 2020). Unlike the self-promotion of SpaceX & Co., however, the literary canon has often speculated about the military conflicts, ecological and social exploitation, and resource wars that would define both space colonization and alien contact. Such fictional stories pit authoritarian governments and technological elites against oppressed and oppositional groups, such as the antiterraforming "Reds" in Kim Stanley Robinson's Mars trilogy (1993,

1994, 1996),[4] the "belter" opposition to asteroid mining in *The Expanse* 2015–22 television series (Fergus and Ostby 2015), and the nomadic underground in Charlie Jane Anders's novel about a partly terraformed planet called January, *The City in the Middle of the Night* (2019).[5] Sci-fi has also grappled with the environmental risks of human exploration and inhabitation of other worlds. In the Mars trilogy, this concern finds expression in the commitments of the Reds to protect the planet's native atmosphere and surface conditions from geoengineering. In their fight for Martian ecologies, the Reds echo the actual scientific field of planetary protection: an area of research and a set of protocols that took shape in the late 1950s around "the practice of protecting solar system bodies from contamination by Earth life" as well as the other way around (NASA/OSMA 2023; see also Wolfe 2002). In the same decade that scientists and policymakers worked out the first international frameworks on planetary protection, Ray Bradbury's novel *The Martian Chronicles* (1950/1997) depicted an advanced Martian society whose native people and their built environment are all but decimated by the planet's first American settlers, themselves in exile from nuclear war on Earth. In a related vein, Anders's 2019 novel invents a species endemic to January known as *crocodiles* by the planet's human colonists, who see them only as deadly predators to be hunted and eliminated. When a bond forms between one of these creatures and the novel's protagonist, the reader realizes that the crocodiles are not monstrous beasts but sentient citizens of a complex society.

SpaceX & Co. alternately overlook and misread this tradition of speculative narrative in support of their ambitions. But, as Colin Milburn writes about terraforming discourse, their extraterrestrial drives are "born from science fiction and still laden with the semiotic residue of science fiction" (2012, 81 n. 49). Robinson's Mars trilogy, for instance, offers at once a schema for and a social satire of the outer-space pursuits of Musk, Bezos, and others. In the trilogy, the human settlers of Mars who identify as Blues achieve their goal of terraforming the planet over the course of just two centuries despite the determined resistance of the Reds. Motivated by a dogma they call *viriditas*, the Blues engineer a biosphere hospitable to human beings on the Red Planet that eventually comes to "grow and spread until it covered everything, with an ocean in the north, and lakes in the south, and streams, forests, prairies, cities and roads" (Robinson 1996, 46). In contrast to the techno-utopianism that SpaceX and Blue Origin promote to win government contracts and public support, however, Robinson dwells at length on the biological, ecological, and cultural practicalities of space colonization. To quote Milburn again, the Mars trilogy thinks in detailed ways about "elementary particles on the one hand and trans-planetary ecosystems on the other" to imagine how "a long-term greening of the solar system" might occur and, I would add, to think through the ways such a future could go wrong (2012, 75).

By comparison, the rhetoric of tech companies like SpaceX and Blue Origin is light on details and inattentive to how their plans might affect the people on whose labor they will increasingly depend, the people their rockets will leave behind, and the people they will shuttle away as well as the worlds their technologies will reach and settle. Blue Origin—which notably changed its public tagline from "Earth . . . is just our starting place" (Blue Origin 2018) to "For the benefit of Earth" (Blue Origin, n.d.)—casts itself as the hero of a hazily defined "future where millions of people are living and working in space" (Blue Origin 2022). Although the company's plans hinge on mining colonies and the people who would work in them, its marketing taps into what David Nye (1994) calls the *American technological sublime*. The term refers to the physical scale and sweeping discourse of major engineering projects in the United States since the nineteenth century, from the transcontinental railroad to the moon landing. The future championed by contemporary space corporations leverages the technological sublime to cast the futures for which they pine as a universal humanitarian one.

But alongside the soaring rhetoric is an inattention to justice that space colony simulation has already exhibited and a cavalier attitude about the violence of actual space colonization on the part of the rocket billionaires. The same month that NASA put a crew on Hawaiʻi's Big Island at the Mars simulation habitat known as HI-SEAS, Musk quipped on Twitter: "Terraforming a new home (Mars) is a far better use for nuclear weapons than genocide" (Musk 2015). The tweet referred to an outrageous remark Musk had made the same day on *The Late Show*. Responding to questions from Stephen Colbert about whether the CEO's drive to monopolize electric cars and their raw materials on Earth and human colonies on Mars made him a hero or a supervillain, Musk gave credence to the latter interpretation when he hazarded that there would be people on Mars within the decade (Colbert 2015). How would the Red Planet—whose surface temperature can plummet to −225 degrees Fahrenheit and whose atmosphere is 95 percent carbon dioxide—be made Earthlike so quickly? In reply to his provocation, Musk suggested that a conglomerate of companies and state actors led by SpaceX would make Mars habitable "the fast way," by "dropping nuclear weapons at the poles" (Colbert 2015). This brazen proposal for the use of nuclear warheads to advance space colonization disavows the historical violence and enduring consequences of nuclear weapons across this planet—from the Pacific Islands to the California coastline, where SpaceX launches its rockets from Vandenberg Air Force Base, an intercontinental-ballistic-missile testing site since the 1950s (DeLoughrey 2019, 63–97; Hayden 2017; National Park Service 2020). Cutting through such cartoonish bravado, the *New Republic* reporter David Beers has detailed the punishing labor conditions of SpaceX during the COVID-19 pandemic to show that Musk's rhetoric papers over a business model that disregards the welfare of the company's own employees, especially in manufacturing facilities. Comparing Musk to the Nazi engineer and US rocket maker Wernher von Braun, Beers argues that the "wildly expensive and deadline-driven business" of space exploration has long deployed utopianism to maintain a "loyal workforce" and to keep government contracts and capital investments flowing (2020). This self-serving recourse to utopianism is evident in presentations that Musk has given about the SpaceX rocket known as Starship (or, more crassly, BFR, for Big Fucking Rocket) and the Martian settlements to which it would ferry people. Space opera meets slick slide deck in these vignettes, which portray a lone woman leaving the Blue Planet for her Martian estate: a trip that Musk once claimed could happen as early as 2022 at a cost of $200,000 per traveler, a projection he pushed out when that deadline came and went to a still spectacularly optimistic date of 2030 (Bhaimiya 2023; Rathi 2016; Skipper and Roulette 2023; Torchinsky 2022).

Unabashedly White, the SpaceX brand of private travel to a Martian escape from this world echoes portrayals of space colonization on the part of popular science boosters. Consider *National Geographic*'s *Mars*, a limited-run series. The series alternates between an episodic and fictionalized story of astronauts sent to Mars for the first phase of a terraforming project and documentary-style interviews with NASA scientists, SpaceX engineers, sci-fi authors, and Mars colony devotees like Robert Zubrin (a former Lockheed Martin engineer who founded the Mars Society to advance "the settlement of the planet Mars") (Mars Society, n.d.; see also Mason and Wilkes 2016–18). In a kindred vein, JPL released to a broad public audience a series of posters that domesticates what the theoretical physicist Michio Kaku (2018) describes as "our destiny beyond Earth" and was titled *Visions of the Future*. Through portraits of individuals and small groups of people going about day-to-day life on other worlds, *Visions of the Future* adapts the *See America* posters that were commissioned in the 1930s by the US Works Progress Administration (WPA) to promote national park tourism in each state (plate 12). Drawing explicitly on the midcentury typography and design of the WPA posters, *Visions of the Future* combines wilderness sublime with nostalgic Americana: a Hollywood-style studio gate marks an arrival entrance on the asteroid Ceres, a pack of trading cards advertises the giant gas planet 51 Pegasi b, and a white picket fence protects onlookers from a red rock desert on Kepler-186f (a dwarf planet that is over 550 light-years away from Earth) (plates 13–14). Connecting distant worlds to nationalist iconography, *Visions of the Future* restages the US frontier mythology of manifest destiny and its protagonist, the White explorer and settler. While some posters foreground the technological advances requisite for space tourism and settlement, others invoke the familiar landscapes of Yosemite, Yellowstone, Moab, the Grand Canyon, and Big Sur. Much like the marketing for SpaceX, the JPL posters whitewash space colonies of their geopolitical and social conditions and conflicts while depicting Earth as "your oasis in space"—an oasis populated, if at all in this imagined future, by people coded White who enjoy a respite from space travel for the Blue Planet's breathable air and big vistas (NASA/JPL 2020).

In step with *Visions of the Future*, the tech companies that are fueling NewSpace are propagating images of multiplanetary life as a new form of exploration and conquest. For one noteworthy illustration, consider Amazon's Spheres. Erected at the company's downtown Seattle headquarters between 2015 and 2018, the Spheres takes the form of three interlocking "biodomes" (pentagonal hexecontahedrons, to be precise). The combined size totals seventy thousand square feet, while the facade comprises an estimated twenty-six hundred panes of glass whose function is to provide sufficient light to the estimated forty thousand plants inside (plate 15). A curated archive of four hundred species collected from "the cloud forest regions of over thirty countries" among other biomes, the Spheres living garden rekindles the imperial science of botanical prospecting and collecting (Amazon, n.d.). To quote architecture critic Timothy Schuler, this structural engineering marvel, whose undisclosed cost likely exceeded $1 billion, is now a "bona fide conservatory" that has joined the ranks of established institutions of colonial science and ecological conservation: from the Kew Gardens outside London to the Huntington Library and Botanical Gardens located just a few miles from JPL.

But the Spheres are best understood as a template for space colony architecture, and they have become iconic precisely in this way. Landmarks of the futuristic city and extraterrestrial futurism, they update Seattle's Space Needle. They also literalize Amazon's name, which Bezos landed on shortly after founding the company in 1995 when consultants warned that his first pick, "Cadabra," sounded too much like *cadaver* (Foer 2019). The runner-up, Amazon, served pragmatic and symbolic functions at once, placing the online bookstore at the top of Google search results at a time when those results were still delivered alphabetically, while signaling that the rapidly growing company was, in a boorish reference to its riparian namesake, "the center of the e-commerce universe" (Brooker 1999). The Spheres deliver on these perhaps apocryphal origins of Amazon's brand by bringing to its mothership an entire world of rare, medicinal, and otherwise highly valued plants (Roush 2005).[6] The architectural team modeled the design on the equatorial cloud forest because it translates well into an enclosed ecosystem that supports the comfort and productivity of Amazon employees as well as the biological needs of "a broad range of unique and interesting plants" indigenous to the Americas, Asia, and Africa (Schuler 2019, 3). Putting a fine point on the aims of this hothouse approach to both biodiversity stewardship and tech labor, the northern and southern domes carry the titles the "New World Garden" and the "Old World Garden," respectively, while the large middle dome functions as a corporate space station organized around modular compartments where Amazon employees can work, meet, eat, rest, and, above all, be inspired to create the "tiny seeds" of new ideas that fuel the profits Bezos has long wanted to parlay into a space venture (Foer 2019; Schuler 2019).

This last detail indicates that the Spheres are less a botanical garden than a space colony simulation. However horticultural they appear at first glance, the interlocking domes are actually an AI-powered machine, engineered to monitor every moment of every day of every person inside via the microchip embedded in each Amazon employee's badge (Bloomberg 2018). As this spectral presence in the Spheres reflects, a macabre view of capitalist productivity underlies Bezos's preoccupation with putting humans in space: "[W]hat worries Bezos is that in the coming generations the planet's growing energy demands will outstrip its limited supply. The danger, he says, 'is not necessarily extinction,' but stasis 'we will have to stop growing'" (Foer 2019). This anxiety correlates the end of capitalist growth with the end of the human story, an apocalyptic dread abated, for Bezos, by keeping people working perpetually here on Earth while expanding capitalism off world (think Mechanical Turk on a mining colony in the asteroid belt). A high-tech Eden, the Spheres create a hermetically sealed world for Amazon professional and programming workers. In this, they are in good company with other tech headquarters. To take another example, Apple's 175-acre headquarters in Cupertino, California, has been dubbed the Spaceship Campus: a circular, doughnut-shaped structure totaling nearly three million square feet. The building, which has been identified with "neofuturist" architecture but could also double as a Hollywood sci-fi set, seems poised to lift off for interstellar travel (Schuler 2019). The inverse of the Spheres, Apple's spaceship surrounds an open-air park planted with eight thousand trees intended to "restore the natural landscape that once blanketed Silicon Valley" (Schuler 2019). If Amazon has curated the world's exoticized flora under the domes of its Spheres, Apple is cultivating a native California arboretum at its headquarters while requiring, as do its competitors, rare earth minerals from around the globe to make the chips that operate its ever-expanding product portfolio. Thickening the irony of the fledgling forest that sits within the doughnut hole of Spaceship Campus, Silicon Valley takes its name from the mineral integral to semiconductor chip manufacturing, which has been a major source of groundwater pollution in tech centers like the Bay Area and no doubt has taken a toll on the trees (Heppler 2017; Pellow and Sun-Hee Park 2002; Solnit 2010). The historian Margaret O'Mara interprets these space-age tech campuses as Walden Pond under glass: "a retreat, a cathedral away from the hubbub of the city" (quoted in Wingfield 2016; see also O'Mara 2019a). More accurately, however, these enclosed worlds tap into old American myths of both self-sufficiency and world-making, offering themselves as proofs of concept for an otherworldly future to come.

HI-SEAS

The maximalist architecture of today's tech headquarters obscures the stripped-down form that space colonies would assume for the foreseeable future. Most prototypes for the robots and semiautonomous machines that will go ahead of people to fabricate critical infrastructure, for the rockets that will ferry astronauts and tourists beyond the moon, and for the habitats that will support first-generation space colonists are spartan and small by necessity. Similarly, the first Martian homesteaders "would need to live in underground bunkers, grow food in inflatable greenhouses, figure out how to manufacture things in 37 percent gravity, and send rovers to find water and metal deposits"—as Rubenstein (2022, 132) puts it in showing that one genealogy for NewSpace is the US Homestead Act and its colonial function of enlisting predominantly White citizens to settle Indigenous land by performing the manual labor of farming it. The terrestrial simulations that prepare for future space colonies are, accordingly, bare-bones and purpose-built: inflatable "habs" that could fit inside a suburban home, pressurized greenhouses whose fresh vegetable yield is measured in milligrams, and water recyclers that would nourish just a few people at a time. While novelists like Robinson and billionaires like Musk and Bezos forecast entire planets made blue and green, the work of terraforming a world like Mars is easier to dream up than to pull off, and indoors is where multiplanetary people probably would live for many generations, if not indefinitely. In other words, the science fiction and speculative science around spacefaring outrun the realities of making other worlds livable and, in the process, deflect crucial debates about the motivations, risks, and consequences of extending settler colonialism beyond Earth.

The very tight quarters and regimented routines on the International Space Station illustrate the gap between space colony epic and actual human life in space (NASA 2020b, 2023). So too does HI-SEAS, a NASA-funded project located on Mauna Loa and coordinated by the University of Hawaiʻi at Mānoa. A two-story geodesic dome, HI-SEAS (which stands for Hawaiʻi Space Exploration Analog and Simulation) is a fairly rudimentary habitat that boasts recycled air and water systems but virtually no biological life beyond a small human crew and its dehydrated food supply. Measuring just thirteen thousand cubic feet, HI-SEAS features five common areas—kitchen, laboratory, bathroom, simulated airlock, and engineering bay area—along with six compact bedrooms (HI-SEAS 2022a). From its launch in 2013 through 2023, it has housed eighteen missions. Each crew has lived there for between a few weeks and a full year, conducting what mission control describes as "long duration Mars analog simulation" (HI-SEAS 2022b; NASA 2024a). The HI-SEAS media kit that advertised mission 4, which ran from 2015 to 2016, offers a window into what life under the dome is like. That year, six people from three countries entered HI-SEAS for a yearlong Mars colony simulation. The crew was made up of a geophysicist, a soil scientist, an astrobiologist, an architect, a science writer, and an aeronautics specialist. Their immediate surroundings—described in press releases as "an abandoned quarry on the northern slope of Mauna Loa . . . next to an escarpment formed from a string of cinder cones dotting a collapsed lava tube"—were selected for having "little vegetation, no rare, threatened or endangered species, and no archaeological sites or cultural practices" (see fig. 6.4). Sealed off physically and culturally from the world around them, the crew was charged with "seeing how isolation and the lack of privacy in a small group affects social aspects of would-be explorers" while putting in long days of work to test "the budding technologies future Mars explorers could employ during real expeditions to the Red Planet" (Siceloff 2015). NASA's assumptions about the attributes of prospective space colonists pervade this portrayal of the HI-SEAS site. Contra the botanical wonderland of the Spheres, which aims to produce productive Amazon workers who never want to leave, NASA suggests that the ideal space colonists must be able to survive sensory deprivation. On this view, the function of an extraterrestrial living simulation is to offer as "few signs of [one's] home planet" as possible (Siceloff 2015).

This framework informs a mischaracterization of Mauna Loa as an optimal proxy for Mars, a notion that decouples the volcano from Hawaiian histories of and ongoing struggles against US colonization and military occupation. NASA accounts of the HI-SEAS location as a Martian proxy ignore, in particular, the Native Hawaiian (Kānaka Maoli) sovereignty

Figure 6.4. HI-SEAS dome, exterior photograph showing two crew members, Mauna Loa, Hawai'i (n.d.). Reprinted with permission of HI-SEAS Director. Photograph: NASA/JPL.

movement, the religious and ecological significance of the islands' five volcanic mountains (of which Mauna Loa is one), and the contested status of international aerospace institutions on nearby Mauna Kea, which Noelani Goodyear-Ka'ōpua (Kānaka Maoli) and others have detailed (Goodyear-Ka'ōpua, Hussey, and Kahunawaika'ala Wright 2014; Lander and Puhipau 2006).[7] Taken together, these Indigenous claims and countermobilizations challenge the idea that a simulated Martian space station could ever be devoid of "archaeological sites" and "cultural practices," as NASA claims about HI-SEAS (see Sammler and Lynch 2021). The apprehension of Mauna Kea as barren ground goes hand in hand with the notion that other planets are blank slates for human settlement. However small and self-contained as a simulation, HI-SEAS thus reproduces in miniature the long history of American colonialism and its fixation on new frontiers for settlement and development.

Environmental artists have taken up such simulations of space colonization. Two examples, which draw on, respectively, the conceptual resources of parody and participatory engagement, are especially germane to this chapter's critical analysis of SpaceX & Co.: the New York artist Natalie Jeremijenko's 2007 project "Urban Space Station" ("USS") and the "starship sculptures" and ecological installations of the "transdisciplinary and cross-cultural collective" Space Ecologies Art and Design (SEADS) (see SEADS, n.d.-a, n.d.-b). As for the first, Jeremijenko classifies "USS" as an enactment of "parasitic mutualism," a mock-up of an airlocked structure that would "generate its own energy" while producing a surplus for the "building it rests upon" (Jeremijenko and Cubero 2016). The drawings and models for the project riff on infrastructures of renewable energy and green urban design. But the project also plays with the architecture of simulations like HI-SEAS and the geopolitics and discourses behind them. In an artist's statement, Jeremijenko describes "USS" in a tongue-in-cheek vein as a "*frontier* of urban space and energy harvesting" (Jeremijenko and Cubero 2016; emphasis added). A visual rendering develops this parody of terrestrial and extraterrestrial colonialism alike. In the former, seven White children and one Black child frolic in isolated pods on a small plot of scraggly grass outside the sealed structure, which is notably empty of any sign of organic life save one lone White child. Within the categorization of "USS" as a "space station," the trope of childhood innocence intermingles with invocations of social alienation and racial segregation, intimating that terraformed environments in the future—whether in cities or on off-world colonies—would be far from utopian. Moreover, although the drawing depicts "USS" as an organic form evocative of a caterpillar, the model that Jeremijenko and her collaborators built on an urban rooftop in New York was mechanistic and lifeless. In notable contrast to the Spheres, this urban space station is a claustrophobic and inorganic machine built primarily for harvesting energy. By extension, the future it portends is one without regenerative ecosystems or lively cultures.

The "USS" engagement with space colonization turns on a macabre joke: life under glass—a common trope for extraterrestrial habitats and their earthly imitations—will be lonely, monotonous, and machine operated. One of the founding members of SEADS, Angelo Vermeulen, has developed an entire collaborative practice around imagining space futures as other than mechanistic and alienating. Vermeulen has been developing artistic interventions in terraforming and space travel for over two decades, work that landed him a spot in the inaugural 2013 HI-SEAS mission—for which he was described as a "space researcher, filmmaker, visual artist, community organizer, and author" (Kelleher 2013). One imagines that he accepted the offer partly out of a searching skepticism about how scientists and aerospace institutions envision "the future of human habitation and survival" (Vermeulen 2011). The mission was animated by NASA's Artemis mission to "land the first woman and next man on the Moon by 2024" and then take "our next greatest leap—human exploration of Mars" (NASA 2020a). Three of the SEADS projects that speak in particularly complex ways to this mission have evolved over the years before and after Vermeulen's HI-SEAS stint: the Biomodd, Merapi Terraforming, and Seeker Projects interrogate the nationalist and techno-utopian forces that fuel twenty-first-century space exploration (SEADS, n.d.-a, n.d.-c, n.d.-d). Each has involved sustained collaborations with artists, activists, and researchers at the locales where the projects have been developed or installed.[8] One of the stated aims of these site-specific collaborations is to stir public dialogue and introspection about the "technological, ecological, and social systems" that would facilitate and develop from "interstellar exploration" (Vermeulen, n.d.). The Merapi Terraforming Project, for instance, is a participatory experiment to grow plants in highly challenging environmental conditions (SEADS, n.d.-c). At first glance, the experiment appears akin to HI-SEAS in its interest in creating a "vertical laboratory . . . explicitly inspired by terraforming" on an Indonesian volcano chosen because its nitrogen-poor soils are hostile to plant life (Vermeulen 2011). However, unlike the NASA-funded dome on Mauna Loa, the Merapi terraforming experiment is a "biological artwork" created to engender "discussions about the future use of destroyed land" as well as the "imaginary" of terraforming extraterrestrial ground (Vermeulen 2011).[9]

This community-based work is apposite to the gigantism of space colonization and its billionaire-backed investment in terraforming whole worlds. The SEADS projects and their accompanying artist statements employ a kind of contemplative exploration of possible space living arrangements that implicitly critique any multiplanetary future that forecloses on "meaningful relationships between biology, computers, and people" and lauds the "colonization of barren worlds in outer space" (Vermeulen, n.d.). Installations of the Biomodd project throw into relief how architecturally and ecologically barren space pods like HI-SEAS and other such prototypes have also been bereft of cultural complexity (plate 20). In a process that is a prototype for "symbiotic relationships between plants and computers," the Biomodd structure grows algae that cool data processors that in turn create greenhouse conditions with their heat. In the makers' words, the project "creates new relationships between nature and technology across different cultures around the world": "In 'Biomodd,' nature and technology are fused into hybrid interactive art installations. The core idea is the co-creation of experimental systems in which recycled computers and living ecosystems coexist and mutually reinforce one another" (SEADS, n.d.-a). The project here calls attention, I would argue, to the pitfalls of space settlement experiments on Earth, their desiccated ecologies, and their geopolitical and capitalistic designs on other worlds. It does so, in particular, by invoking the illusionist's water tank as well as Dr. Who's TARDIS time machine/spacecraft. Through these visual citations of magic and sci-fi, the interior becomes a kind of curiosity cabinet of plants, tubes, wires, and anachronistic computers and monitors (Vermeulen 2007). In the Philippine versions of the project, a statue representing Marie Makiling, a nature spirit in Filipino culture, was affixed to the installation. Collaborating on the statue with local woodcarvers, the team envisioned the figure as an embodiment of ecological guardianship. Through my lens here, the figure spotlights the masculinist bent of the engineer's drive to create and colonize worlds while also retooling that drive's attachments to alchemy and the supernatural. Juxtaposed with JPL's *Visions of the Future* and the space-age tech headquarter, artist-led experiments like "USS" and Biomodd powerfully challenge the alternately epic, sublime, and ecofascist visions of NewSpace.

The Terranauts

The Santa Barbara–based writer T. C. Boyle offers a literary analogue to these artist space colony engagements with his fictional narrative of engineers, venture capitalists, and their aerospace fantasies: *The Terranauts*. The 2016 novel adds to a body of fiction that has taken California to task for both its environmental and its technological imaginaries. That work includes Boyle's story of the social inequality and wildfire risk of suburban Los Angeles, *Tortilla Curtain* (1995), the partly speculative narrative *A Friend of the Earth* (2005) in which a once-zealous activist who fought deforestation in the 1980s finds himself in a near-future California beset by torrential rain and stifling heat taking care of a pop star's menagerie of endangered animals, and the trenchant satire of a Los Angeles developer's conflict over the Channel Islands with his environmentalist foe, *When the Killing's Done* (2011). With *The Terranauts*, Boyle shifts the target of satire to a space colony experiment and terraforming project in the Arizona desert. More specifically, the novel recounts the notorious history of Biosphere 2 (B2), a "scaled-down replica of Earth replete with a desert, a savanna, a rainforest and a wave-machine-rippled ocean, as well as its own sealed and calibrated atmosphere," an enclosed architecture not unlike the Amazon Spheres that two different crews called home from 1991 to 1994 (Cohn 2007; Koch 2021; Miles 2016). Riddled with mechanical failures and social scandals, this "monument of geodesic domes and pyramids" located outside Tucson was shuttered as a habitat in 1994 and has functioned since then as a research facility operated first by Columbia University and then by nearby Arizona State University (University of Arizona Biosphere 2, n.d.; Zimmer 2019). Today, the biosphere feels like a relic of both technological hubris and its failure to launch, its blaring white facade and ornate architecture looming over the high-desert landscape on which it sits—as photographs taken after a snowstorm during an academic gathering I attended in 2019 at the adjacent conference center capture (plates 16–18).

The plot of *The Terranauts* revolves around the biosphere's leadership in "Mission Control" and the all-White, eight-person crew that lived inside the habitat for two years. That plot, with its satiric orientation to the historical narrative on which Boyle based the novel, embodies a distinctly "US utopian fantasy of the all-encompassing, human-constructed environment" centered in the American West, as the critic John Schwetman argues (Schwetman 2021, 57). Modeled on the four men, four women crews that made up the first two B2 missions, the terranauts are motivated by a mix of messianic ambitions and venal desires. Boyle renames the habitat Ecosphere 2 (E2), thus underscoring its design as a miniature Earth to be replicated on Mars. In the novel, the project's backer is a shadowy billionaire called GF, for "God the Financier," a cheeky nod to Ed Bass, who invested an estimated $150–$200 million in B2 (Koch 2021, 41). But the "visionary" behind E2 is the head of Mission Control, Jeremiah Reed, whom the crew nicknames GC, for "God the Creator." Prone to megalomania, GC is a devotee of Fuller's theory of Spaceship Earth (with its call for active intervention in the planet's ecological and social systems) as well as the trained chemist and onetime NASA consultant James Lovelock's "cosmology of Gaia" (which views Earth as a self-regulating organism that should be left as undisturbed as possible) (Boyle 2016, 41–42). These contradictory influences connect GC with the actual founding director of B2, the engineer and inventor John Allen, who built an ecovillage outside Santa Fe, New Mexico, in the 1970s called Synergia Ranch where he and Bass first met and later hatched the plan for the biosphere (Koch 2021, 41–42; Zimmer 2019).

Drawing on published memoirs about B2, *The Terranauts* zeroes in on the public relations machine that Mission Control orchestrates to advance GC's secular theology about space colonization. Shaped by sci-fi tropes, the Mission Control triumvirate dreams of "forty-eight closures to come after" the first crew and a still more distant future when "the children of E2 . . . will be pioneers to the stars" (Boyle 2016, 388). Although the novel identifies them as members of mission 2 and dates their entry as March 6, 1994 (the same date as the second B2 crew began its mission), Boyle's terranauts mirror in their backgrounds the inaugural B2 crew.[10] The enclosed world of the novel quickly deteriorates, lampooning the purported humanitarian underpinnings of the crew's mission. Throughout the narrative, Boyle juxtaposes repeated systems failures with the ongoing conflicts among E2's eight human inhabitants. Rather than being a self-sustaining ecosystem capable of supporting complex biological life, the biosphere fails to nourish its inhabitants while reproducing the morass of social relationships—and dysfunctions—on Earth. Boyle organizes this satire into four parts: a brief "pre-closure" period during which the eight terranauts are selected by GC and his chief of staff, Judy, from a larger pool of candidates; the first and second years of "closure" inside E2, during which the crew's mission is to maintain the airlock seal no matter what biological, technological, or interpersonal calamities happen inside; and, finally, the much anticipated "reentry" of the crew into the Arizona desert and the outside world. Each part alternates among three first-person narrators: the animal husbandry expert Dawn (a.k.a. "E."), the communications officer Ramsay (a.k.a. "Vodge"), and the biologist Linda, one of the candidates who does not make the E2 cut and is relegated to a Mission Control staff position. Linda is the only person of color in the story, a detail that highlights, whether by design or not, the whiteness of both the original B2 and other space colony simulations. Central to this structure, the three narrators begin most chapters in medias res, creating gaps and digressions that make the novel akin to a mockumentary rife with narrative unreliability. Form thus amplifies content, as gossip, backstabbing, and self-promotion on either side of the glass throw into doubt the viability of E2 as a prototype for the multiplanetary future.

Contra futuristic fictions about space exploration and terraforming, Boyle employs a mix of literary realism and parody to narrativize the banality of living in a space colony simulation that deliberately severs the ties of its inhabitants to the home world that E2 reductively re-creates (Hüpkes and Dürbeck 2022). Dawn captures the isolation, tedium, and manual labor that define daily life under the glass. After over a year of closure, she muses, E2 has become a purgatory: "We'd been inside a long time—forever it seemed. To think about the world beyond the glass was like looking down the wrong end of a telescope, everything shrunk to irrelevance. We were on another planet and nothing that happened back on the home planet really mattered anymore" (Boyle 2016, 271). This confession suggests that E2's expressed mission to pave the way for a privately funded colony on the Red Planet relies on alienating would-be Martians from the world they know. Over the course of the novel, there are twenty-nine references to Mars. Taken together, they depict space colonization as a quasi-religious enterprise for engineers seeking new ground for terraforming: a religious mythology that Rubenstein tracks through NewSpace as what she terms *astrotopia* (2022).

Early on, Ramsay rehearses hypothetical critiques of himself as "a corporation man" who unabashedly promotes E2, in response to which he muses:

> The whole notion of the Ecosphere, of eight people confining themselves willingly in a man-made world for twenty-four months, caught the public's imagination precisely because of that hook, the conceit of voluntary imprisonment—not to mention the Mars connection. If E2 was supposed to be an experiment in world-building, it was also about business, the kind of potentially remunerative enterprise that enticed a man like Darren Iverson to put up his money in the first place. The earth was running out of resources, global warming was beginning to be recognized as science fact and not science fiction, and if man was to evolve to play a part in things instead of being just another doomed organism on a doomed planet, if the technosphere was going to replace pure biological processes, then sooner or later we'd have to seed life elsewhere—on Mars to begin with. (Boyle 2016, 29)

In reading this passage, one wonders whether Boyle had encountered Musk's manifesto on life after Earth before the novel went to press. The tone is typical of Ramsay and other characters who serve as spokespeople for E2: a resignation to Earth's "doomed" fate mingles with a swagger about the drive to "seed life elsewhere." This narrative sees E2 as an ideal "technosphere," a concept that, as we saw in chap. 1, was first developed by the environmental engineer Peter Haff to normatively describe large-scale technological systems that run on their own and rival atmospheric, oceanic, and biospheric ones (Haff 2014). The novel shows up this theory by way of how little in the habitat works according to its design. The basic physical needs of the terranauts and the other flora and fauna with which they live and that are meant to help regulate their atmosphere, provide their sustenance, and offer multispecies companionship prove difficult for the biosphere to meet. A devotee of technological determinism, Ramsay imagines that the recurrent biological and ecological problems in E2 are just temporary setbacks and that the future for which E2 is prepping will be a wholly engineered and managed one where "pure biological processes" of life no longer matter.

One could imagine Musk and Bezos nodding in agreement but so too Stewart Brand (chap. 4). In his *Whole Earth Discipline: An Ecopragmatist Manifesto*, Brand updates the conditional syntax of the founding statement for *The Whole Earth Catalog* (1968–98) to read: "We are as gods and HAVE to get good at it" (Brand 2009). The reformulated manifesto challenges what Brand describes as environmental "pieties" in making the case for nuclear energy, transgenic foods, and geoengineering as essential technologies for addressing the twenty-first century's mounting problems. Brand identifies these technologies as "planet craft," an unwitting synonym, I would note, to Nature Remade. It is the deification of planet craft that *The Terranauts* most satirizes. Ramsay echoes the dogma of Brand, Musk, and other eco-pragmatists with his suggestion that the technosphere is fated to supplant the biosphere and, in turn, will make it possible to seed an anthropogenic and anthropocentric society on Mars. This belief informs a cynical interpretation of the first E2 crew's decision to break closure to access medical care when one of its members severs a finger. Responding to an imagined interlocutor who would say, "[B]ut you're not really on Mars. It isn't life or death," Ramsay retorts: "[A] pledge is a pledge; *nothing in, nothing out.*" There is a messianic mythology at work here: "This was the moon, this was Mars, this was material closure, not some greenhouse you could just stroll in and out of whenever you had the urge." If to outsiders the biosphere is a very large hothouse, to the initiated it is all the world they need, "Gaia in miniature" (Boyle 2016, 32–33, 42).

Rather than a corporation man, Ramsey fashions himself as an explorer. He compares the terranauts to a line of White colonial explorers that includes Ernest Henry Shackleton, who led British surveying expeditions to Antarctica in the early twentieth century, and Edmund Hilary, who, in the 1950s, became the first White person to reach the summit of Mount Everest as well as the North and South Poles (Boyle 2016, 32). Dawn is initially more reticent about the grandiose narratives of E2 that Mission Control and Ramsey promulgate. Over the first half of the novel, her interior monologues portray E2 as a spectacle. She notes, for example, that the team enters E2 with only "the basics" chiefly to dramatize for the press and the broader public that its mission is a dry run for the real thing on Mars. In this same chapter, Dawn reveals that the team could have smuggled into E2 all sorts of modern comforts during the months leading up to closure. The point of showcasing E2's expressed requirements of subsistence agriculture, renewable energy, recycled water, and so on is that, in Dawn's words, "this was theatre": "[I]t was designed to show the world that we were dead serious about absolute closure and living with the basics—Mars, we were going to Mars!" (Boyle 2016, 84–85).

This exposé of E2 as techno-utopian theater dovetails with GC's mandate to produce and perform a live play each year, with two mirror productions composed of the terranauts and the Mission Control staff, respectively. The plays selected over the two years of closure are puzzling at first blush: Thornton Wilder's 1942 comedy *The Skin of Our Teeth* (where planetary disasters, from a new Ice Age to a worldwide flood, structure the three acts) and Eugène Ionesco's 1950 drama *The Bald Soprano* (which revolves around nonsensical banter among two bourgeois couples, a domestic servant, and her lover). Sketching the plot of *The Bald Soprano*, Linda observes: "[W]hat [the plays have] to do with us, with the environment, with closure, I can't imagine" (Boyle 2016, 267). But, taken together, the two plays call attention to both the apocalypticism that motivates space colonization and the petty, domestic conflicts among the terranauts. According to GC, the performances serve as an exercise in method acting: by inhabiting their assigned roles, the terranauts will reflexively experience the mission as essential to the human story. Rather than a stunt, living through the simulation acts as a work of *science theater*. This notion of E2 as science theater appears with the one and only reference in the novel to Fuller's Spaceship Earth, which Ramsay glosses as a theory of "everything connected, everything one" (Boyle 2016, 42). This coincidence disturbs the promotion of E2 as a scientific training ground for Mars and, hence, as a research station for the future technosphere and shows it instead to be a performance to keep the outside world interested.

It is Dawn in the end, rather than Ramsay, for whom this science theater becomes all too real. The turning point in Dawn's character arc speaks to the heterosexual bias and authoritarian reproductive mandate of E2 (as with its real-world inspiration) that teeters on ecofascism. Dawn gets pregnant after a fling with Ramsay. Refusing to "break closure," the team physician intimates that abortion is not a safe option in E2. Choice ostensibly foreclosed, Dawn takes the pregnancy to term and then marries Ramsay as good publicity for the intergenerational potential of a Mars colony. The most significant narrative outcome of this storyline is that Dawn becomes a true believer. Her onetime excitement for reentry morphs into a zealous belief that she, Ramsay, and their daughter (named Eve for the obvious symbolism) remain in E2 for another mission and perhaps indefinitely. Ramsay goes along with this plan over the objections of the other terranauts, only to balk during the first day of reentry when Dawn and Eve remain inside and he elects to join the celebration outside. Overcome by the cornucopia of food and fresh air, Ramsay flees. The novel ends with the perspectives of both Ramsay and Linda, who each describe E2 from the vantage of the Arizona desert. From this view, the space colony simulation appears at once solipsistic and inhuman: "aglow with the morning sun, the struts shining and the glass so invested with it the structure seemed to be generating its own light from within . . . a material presence slapped down there in the middle of the desert," "a mystery ship" (Boyle 2016, 490, 507). In what is an anticlimactic ending that deflates the techno-utopianism of SpaceX & Co., *The Terranauts* closes with the whimper of a nuclear family's dissolution.

The novel thus parodies endeavors like B2 and HI-SEAS and, by extension, the space colony plans of tech billionaires by cutting them down to size as "spaceframes," blank slates devoid of planetary and sociocultural complexity made chiefly to fulfill the fantasies of the few (Boyle 2016, 507).

Alien Ecologies

Since at least H. G. Wells's 1898 novel about a Martian invasion of Earth, *War of the Worlds*, with its adaptation by Orson Welles forty years later as a mock radio news bulletin, imaginative literature has alternately inspired and challenged the ambitions of astrotopia (to cite a core concept from Rubenstein [2022] again). Running through these myriad storyworlds of life on other worlds and human life beyond Earth is a leitmotif that the poet Tracy K. Smith captures in her metaphor of a universe "choc-full of traffic," congested with stars, planets, moons, suns, and (possible) lifeforms we may barely comprehend (T. K. Smith 2011, 10). From blockbuster franchises like *Star Trek* (1966–), *Star Wars* (1977–), and *Guardians of the Galaxy* (2014–23) to cinematic adaptations of cult sci-fi novels like *Dune* (the original film appeared in 1984, remakes from 1992 to 2024) and *The Hitchhiker's Guide to the Galaxy* (film: 2005), movie studios, for their part, have brought to the screen an intergalactic array of alien species and their home worlds so varied that one would be hard-pressed to catalog them all.[11] However fantastic those fictional worlds are, real environments on Earth have been the fodder for their alien ecologies. As one illustration, *National Geographic* has cataloged the terrestrial locations that have made the *Star Wars* universe, observing that the franchise's "planetary Pantone has ranged from the burnt orange of an arid planet, to the bright white of a frozen one, . . . via swampy, woody, watery worlds of every kind. And absolutely none of them are real places—meaning that before the advent of CGI technology, producers had to find a suitable substitute here on Earth" (Ingram 2019). The worlds of *Star Wars*, in other words, build on four of Earth's major biomes (temperate forest, arid desert, tropical jungle, and Arctic tundra) as well as the urban environments of cities like Los Angeles and Shanghai. Especially before computer-generated imagery afforded wondrously biodiverse planets like *Avatar*'s Pandora, sci-fi movies often have been filmed on location in landscapes that viewers perceive as unearthly: glaciers and fjords in the Arctic, dolomite peaks in the Italian Alps, karst mountains in Thailand and China, and, with particular frequency given the proximity to Hollywood, the deserts of California.

Modeled on alien terrestrial environments (for many audiences), the invented extraterrestrial landscapes of sci-fi have also enlivened the scientific fields of astrophysics and astrobiology. The academic communities who search, respectively, for exoplanets outside our solar system and for extraterrestrial intelligence (known as the SETI [search for extraterrestrial intelligence] community) often refer to science fiction to illustrate both theoretical possibilities and observational indicators of alien life. Today, researchers in these fields are identifying more and more planets that exhibit Earthlike conditions, that is, *Goldilocks planets*, named for atmospheric and biochemical signatures suggesting that they are "just right" for life (whether microbial, botanical, animal, or otherwise). This research thinks of Earth as a yardstick by which other worlds are measured for the ingredients that support complex biological life, however unlike life on Earth it may be. At the same time, as Stefan Helmreich explains, the scientists who spend their careers looking to the stars consider Earth to be "not only one planet among others, but also a planet that points to and even contains its others" (Helmreich 2012, 1133; see also Helmreich 2011). This "ricochet effect" conceives of alien organisms and ecosystems in relationships to anomalous species and outlier ecosystems on Earth, thus decentering humans from the story of both this planet and the multiplanetary future (Helmreich 2012, 1133). We can observe the ricochet effect in findings that microbes from California's Mono Lake might live on arsenic rather than phosphorus (the latter traditionally understood as an essential building block for all biological life) and in the hypothesis that hydrothermal vents in the deep ocean house archaebacteria whose origins are Martian rather than earthly (Helmreich 2012, 1130, 1133). One consequence of such discoveries is, in Helmreich's words, "extraterrestrial relativism," a view of organic matter and the planetary or lunar conditions that sustain it as highly variable both on Earth and throughout the universe (Helmreich 2012, 1130; see also Messeri 2017, 331; Salazar 2017; and Vertesi 2015). This paradigm presents an *alienating* theory of life for which the human is just one "air-lover" among amphibians, anaerobes, and other known and unknown biological beings that may inhabit the universe (Helmreich 2012, 1129).

The interrelated scientific paradigms of an alive cosmos and an alien Earth radically unsettle the human ambitions of a few to develop, settle, and dwell in space, ambitions that confront a universe understood to be *many worlded* (to hark back to chap. 1 and its discussion of *A Tale for the Time Being*) yet quite unwelcoming to human beings. If advocates for space colonization hold tight to an anthropocentrism that privileges oxygen and water and in turn hinges on remaking other worlds in Earth's image, the alien ecologies that astroscientists conjure and conceptualize rupture such designs on the universe. Consider, in stark and provocative contrast to SpaceX & Co., the future hoped for by Natalie Batalha, an astrophysicist at UC Santa Cruz and a former lead scientist for JPL's Kepler mission to survey the Milky Way galaxy (NASA 2024d). While Batalha does envisage a future in which humans are spacefaring, she is quick to observe that those prospective travelers will be not architects of space colonies but fish out of water, aliens to other species who have plans of their own. Her speculations resonate with those of the late Pasadena-based novelist Octavia Butler, who wrote much of her body of science fiction not far from JPL's headquarters. Butler's *Xenogenesis* trilogy (*Dawn* [1987], *Adulthood Rites* [1988], and *Imago* [1989]) tells the story of the spacefaring Oankali people and their first contact with human beings. This fictional species arrives in our solar system—after a total war among Earth's nations—as "gene traders" whose highly malleable biology allows them to hybridize with human survivors, as they have done in their many encounters with other sentient species in the universe. Much has been written about the trilogy, generally focused on how Butler's narrative of Oankali reproductive conscription and cultural assimilation of humans—and the new bodies and societies that result—projects eugenics and slavery, on the one hand, and queer sexualities, on the other, into a future in which a supersentient, superevolved alien race embodies a liminal space between colonizer and kin (Greenwald Smith 2009; Johns 2010; Sendur 2020; Wallace 2009).

In the context of *Novel Ecologies* and Nature Remade, the Oankali are also striking as an alien society whose home world is a living, breathing spaceship, a biosphere wherein they have mutualistic rather than extractive relationships to the flora and fauna and to the ship itself. The trilogy opens with humans on the brink of extinction. The Oankali enter this postapocalyptic world and proceed to rebuild the "salvaged Earth" by biologically pairing with human survivors and then endeavoring to integrate them into their ways of life. In Earth's recent past, human societies had their sights set on space exploration, ambitions that accelerated the collapse: "people who believed space was our destiny" were disabused by "the missiles" of planetary warfare, in the words of the trilogy's protagonist Lilith. By comparison, the Oankali have been successful both as space travelers and as world-makers while also sustaining their own *spaceship planet*. In the trilogy, they become alien terraformers of a decimated Earth: building anew its atmosphere, soils, and biodiversity "from prints, from collected specimens from [their] own creations, and from altered remnants" (Butler 2012, 290). The world they so regenerate is a fundamentally and forever different one from the Blue Planet.

In terms akin to Butler's astrobiological speculations in *Xenogenesis*, Batalha wonders whether space could one day generate interplanetary relationships that transform entrenched ideas of the human and the world. She asks: "I wonder what will happen to us as a species as we transition from land to space. What potential will be released? . . . How will we evolve?" (Batalha 2013). In response to this query, she connects the time when Earth was in its biological infancy (the Cambrian period, during which invertebrate marine life emerged) to an imagined future when contact with aliens forever alters the ecological and sociocultural ways of life on Earth. Contra space colony proponents, moreover, she situates this future in which some humans visit or reside on other worlds in highly intimate and interpersonal terms: a story of a galactic romance centered on initially novel but eventually domesticated *transplanetary* experiences of love, sex, kinship, and sociality that restructure the boundaries of Earth and outer space as well as human and alien. Socially utopian, this long view of the universe foresees ever-widening forms of connection and community. The ideas of scientists like Batalha thus resonate with ecofeminist theories of posthuman affinities or what Stacy Alaimo calls the *transcorporeal* relationships and bonds that can knit people to all kinds of other beings (microbial, synthetic, plant, animal, and so on) (Alaimo 2010, 2016). If from a different intellectual vantage, Batalha can be understood as extending transcorporeality to other worlds: "[W]e are stardust and here I am, this bag of stardust, and it took how many billions of years for the atoms that make up my body to come together and make this being that's able to take a conscious look at the universe" (Batalha 2013). This line of thought views space exploration as an aesthetic, visceral, and cultural endeavor, one whose ethical considerations it is more essential to wrestle with than are the engineering challenges of rocket design and terraforming.

Smith's 2011 volume of poetry *Life on Mars* pursues a related line of thought, giving lyrical expression to the belief that humans are neither alone in nor masters of the universe. The volume toggles between familial, sociopolitical, and intergalactic scales of existence, melding, in terms of its literary form, elegy and protest poetry with Afrofuturism. The four-part book opens "eons from even our own moon," calling on images from NASA's Hubble Telescope and popular sci-fi references that include David Bowie's avatar Ziggy Stardust and Stanley Kubrick's film *2001: A Space Odyssey* (T. K. Smith 2011, 7, 13). Later poems bring the reader back to Earth. Part 2 is organized around an elegy for Smith's father, a mechanical engineer who worked on the optical instruments for Hubble and died in 2008 as Smith was beginning to write *Life on Mars* (T. K. Smith 2011, 40, 48–53). The second half of the book moves between searing poems that explore racial and sexual violence, White supremacy, and warfare and experimental lyrics about love, desire, childbirth, and poetry itself. The multiplicity of subjects and speakers lends *Life on Mars* the structure of a constellation, an intricate work of poetry that links matters of life and death, the intimate and the interstellar, the sociopolitical and the technological. Connecting the volume to the work of Butler and other writers associated with Afrofuturism, James Edward Ford asks how the early "science-fictional poems" of *Life on Mars* converse with the later poems about American militarism and police violence in Black communities as well as those structured around daily rhythms of love, family, and work. What links them, he persuasively concludes, is an expansive investigation of "what new forms of ethical connectedness must be thought and expressed, based on the phenomena we witness in the universe" (Ford 2014, 162). A lens on poetic form and planetary upheaval that speaks to these same dimensions of *Life on Mars* is Min Hyoung Song's category of "revived lyric" in *Climate Lyricism*: poetic expression "which is not concerned with the spotlighting of an individual 'I' or the exploration of a profound psychic interior, with which the lyric is often associated, but focuses instead on the space between a first-person speaker and a second-person addressee" (2022, 5).

The title poem of *Life on Mars*, to this point, pays homage to Bowie's iconic song released on the album *Hunky Dory* in 1971, the year before Smith was born. As dramatized in the song's music video, "Hunky Dory" opens with the scene of an adolescent girl leaving her arguing parents at home for a movie theater, where a montage of clichéd violence first bombards and then bores the young viewer and leaves her dreaming about "life on Mars." The lyrics stage a two-part commentary on White suburbia and US consumerism as entwined affronts to artistic expression and political radicalism. In this allusion, Smith knits into *Life on Mars* Bowie's surreal approach to social critique, which the titular poem adapts to a dialogue on "dark matter" and filial love interwoven with scenes of sexual trauma and militaristic violence (T. K. Smith 2011, 37–42). By comparison, other poems in part 1 draw on the comedic tenor of Bowie's 1972 concept album *The Rise and Fall of Ziggy Stardust and the Spiders from Mars*. The album tells the story of an alien "space invader" turned rock and roll star who promises to save Earth from a looming apocalypse but ends up crashing and burning on the fickle whims of celebrity culture (Bowie 1972). A "starman" in two senses, then, Bowie's well-known avatar melds the gender-fluid camp of glam rock with pulp sci-fi about alien invasions of Earth.

Smith's lyric recitations of Ziggy Stardust highlight the partly parodic lens on both astrophysics and science fiction in *Life on Mars*. Against positivist efforts to survey galaxies and anthropocentric dreams of alien contact, Smith makes the universe a

party
Your neighbors forgot to invite you to: bass throbbing

Through walls, and everyone thudding around drunk
On the roof. . . .

(T. K. SMITH 2011, 13)

Left out of the cosmic fun, would-be space colonizers come across in these poems as narrow-minded and navel-gazing, if also profiteering. "We like to think of it as parallel to what we know," one speaker muses about dominant ways of seeing and exploring the universe before going on to catalog a string of sci-fi plots that revolve around White, male, American heroes:

One man against the authorities
Or one man against a city of zombies. . . .
. . . .
Man on the run.
Man with a ship to catch, a payload to drop,
This message going out to all of space. . . .

(T. K. SMITH 2011, 8)

In conversation with Bowie's albums, *Life on Mars* employs camp to juxtapose machismo and militarism with procedures of the imagination that are at once politically subversive and artistically experimental. Traveling from California's "Regan years" to a distant and future world where human spacefarers no longer remember the sun of our solar system, Smith figures the universe in alternative ways than NASA and Hollywood do (not to mention SpaceX & Co.) (T. K. Smith 2011, 7). Her poems figure the universe, more pointedly, in terms that flout techno-utopian stories of spacefaring driven by aspirational land and power grabs. The universe in *Life on Mars* is many things, but what it is not is ready-made for NewSpace. It is, instead, "silent, / Buoyant, bizarrely benign," and at the same time "bursting at the seams with energy we neither feel / Nor see" (T. K. Smith 2011, 8, 10).

In the pair of poems that constitute the volume's second section, memories of a father's death collide with the, by last count in early 2024, 1.6 million pictures that Hubble has captured since 1990, when NASA launched it into low Earth orbit (NASA 2024c). Those photographs depict "objects near and far—from small colliding asteroids in our solar system, to distant star-forming galaxies that date back to when the universe was only three percent of its current age" (NASA 2024b). In Smith's poems, these distant corners of space that Hubble arrests on film function, to quote one reviewer, "as a metaphor for the unknowable zone into which her father has vanished and as a way of expressing the hope that his existence hasn't ceased, merely changed" (Brouwer 2011). Dedicated "*in memoriam,* Floyd William Smith 1935–2008," the poem opens with the scene of a hospital room "made quiet by waiting" for the speaker's father to die:

> A room where we'd listen for the rise
> Of breath, the burble in his throat.
>
> I didn't want the orchids or the trays
> Of food meant to fortify that silence,
>
> Or to pray for him to stay or to go then
> Finally toward that ecstatic light.
>
> (T. K. SMITH 2011, 27)

This scene of waiting is relayed through the perspective of an adult daughter (Smith the reader assumes) gathered with family members and expecting the loss of her father. A moment of anticipatory grief, it refrains from eschatological understandings of death while unsettling hierarchical taxa of family, race, and species. Written in seven parts, the poem mixes expressions of mourning for a parent who built telescope optics for JPL but also collected seeds for a home garden, with descriptions of cross-cultural grieving rituals, the violence of slavery, and the human-accelerated extinction of other species. Throughout, the poem moves between spiritual faith in an "ecstatic light" as the afterlife of individual death and the scientific principle that nothing in the universe ever disappears but only changes physical form, a juxtaposition of belief systems that the unrhymed, irregular couplets echo structurally (T. K. Smith 2011, 29).

A surreal sequence brings these threads together. It begins with allusions to the modern extinctions of the Javan, Bali, and Caspian tigers and concludes with a metaphor of Smith's deceased father as "the only heat of your kind for miles" (T. K. Smith 2011, 32). Akin to the tigers, the ghost of her father stalks prey, wades through streams, and makes his bed in a "heaven of leaves":

> Of all the original tribes, the Javan has walked into the dappled green light.
> Also the Bali, flicking his tail as the last clouds in the world dissolved at his back.
> And the Caspian, with his famous winter mane, has lain down finally for good.

Or so we believe. And so I imagine you must be even more alone
now,

The only heat of your kind for miles. A solitary country. At dawn you
listen
Past the birds rutting the trees, past even the fish at their mischief. . . .
. . . .
You raise your head and the great mouth yawns. You swallow the
light.

(T. K. SMITH 2011, 32)

These lines posit that Earth's lost beings eventually join the stars, undergoing a state change from planet-bound body to interstellar matter. The first and last lines end with the word *light,* whereby the green luminescence of an extinct species filters into Smith's deceased father. To quote Jia Tolentino's review of *Life on Mars,* the long elegy thus "travels through stages [of grief] that feel as discrete and expansive as galaxies" (2017). The speaker wonders whether "one day it will be enough to live a few seasons and return to ash. / No children to carry our names. No grief. Life will be a brief, hollow walk" (T. K. Smith 2011, 29). The conjecture calls forth a future in which bonds of kin, race, species, and world submit to ways of being and of perpetuating life that cross earthly boundaries as well as interplanetary ones (T. K. Smith 2011, 29). That possibility lightens the weight of intergenerational trauma and grief in the poem. Or, rather, "The Speed of Belief" puts side by side the feelings of the poet remembering the death of her father and the perspective of Hubble reflecting back to Earth the vast universe. To peer through Hubble's eye is to see that only matter has staying power in the universe while individual bodies and the lives they lead and the attachments they forge are at once painfully momentary and wondrously mutable.

The volume thus mingles familiar elegiac tropes—the passage of time and the ephemerality of life—with concepts drawn from the physical sciences. This mixture comes into focus when "The Speed of Belief" cites its own title, at the point when the speaker imagines that her father has

spun out of himself
And landed squarely in *that there,* his new
Body capable, lean, vibrating at *the speed*
Of belief. . . .

(T. K. SMITH 2011, 30; EMPHASIS ADDED)

There is no antecedent in the stanza for the phrase *that there*, whose downbeat spondaic meter intimates that the *there* refers to something elemental, molecular, and subatomic—but also cosmic. If the poem's earlier metaphor of a dead parent as an extinct species turns on the poetic trope of metamorphosis, the centrifugal figure of speech here ("spun out of himself") articulates the strangeness of quantum physics, calling my own reader back to the conceptual terrain of Ozeki's novel *A Tale for the Time Being* (chap. 1). The poem ends with a return to the conventions of elegy via the trope of immortality granted to a lost loved one through the act of writing:

> And if you are bound
> By habit or will to be one of us
> Again, I pray you are what waits
> To break back into the world
>
> Through me.
>
> (T. K. SMITH 2011, 33)

The enjambment in this quatrain suspends readers between faith in an afterlife ("I pray you are what waits") and a meditation on theoretical physics ("To break back into the world"). The latter implies that, like the speed of light itself, both the poet and the person she mourns transcend ordinary scales of human embodiment and temporality. With its last breath, "The Speed of Belief" illuminates a central idea of *Life on Mars*: aerospace technologies like Hubble and literary forms like lyric share a capacity to perceive otherwise imperceptible forms of life "out there" and thus to dwell in *alien ecologies*.

If "The Speed of Belief" develops this disposition to the life both on and beyond Earth through elegy, the first section of *Life on Mars* does so through dramatic monologue, with speakers who intermix the actual discoveries of Hubble with references to works of contemporary literature, film, and music that have variously pictured and pined for alien worlds. The cover of *Life on Mars*, which reproduces a photograph of the Cone Nebula that Hubble first captured in 1995, frames the book as a rumination on where different lives on Earth fit in the cosmos (plate 19). Seven light-years in length, the photographed portion of the nebula equates to a staggering "23 million roundtrips to the Moon," a scale that dwarfs not only Earth but also any prospective travel in our solar system to visit and settle Mars (NASA 2008). As we've seen, *Life on Mars* as a poetic project interleaves cosmic bodies like the Cone Nebula with the intimate meditations of elegy and the social witnessing of protest poetry. This structure of the book is especially evident in a poem that reenacts the moment when the first images came back from Hubble on May 20, 1990. Smith describes that moment from the vantage of her childhood home in Northern California, where the poem depicts her father and his fellow engineers watching the historic event on a television screen (T. K. Smith 2011, 16). (The telescope was built by Lockheed Martin in Sunnyvale, California, in the heart of Silicon Valley.) Recalling Hubble's transmission of otherworldly images, the poem slips its coordinates of late twentieth-century California for those of a wormhole:

> The second time,
> The optics jibed. We saw to the edge of all there is—
>
> So brutal and alive it seemed to comprehend us back.
>
> (T. K. SMITH 2011, 16)

As the perspective shifts from optical engineers to the optics of a telescope, a machine that orbits Earth opens onto a sensing, sentient universe that "comprehends" us. In turn, the poem recasts engineering as "brutally" insignificant while correlating an aerospace industry that not only observes but also explores and orders the universe with the apparatus of police and military surveillance. The final poem of *Life on Mars* ("Us & Co.") crystallizes these engagements with space exploration and its logics of power. The poem's choral speaker reflects: "[W]e are here for what amounts to a few hours, / a day at most" (T. K. Smith 2011, 70). The miniature span of one life on Earth has its formal analogue in the eight-line brevity of the poem, which counters the epic sweep of space colony discourse and development. Smith ends *Life on Mars* by making space and time, rather than nations and technologies, that which "contains multitudes":

> Moments sweep past. The grass bends
>
> then learns again to stand.
>
> (T. K. SMITH 2011, 70)

Traveling from *Ziggy Stardust* to the Cone Nebula to a single spot of presumably California grass, the volume constructs a capacious poetic account of a "universe choc-full of traffic" that offers a salient alternative to the view of space as inorganic, inert, and, hence, at the ready for world-makers here on Earth.

If SpaceX & Co. places a few humans and their inventions at the nucleus of multiplanetary futures, writers such as Butler and Smith and scientists such as Batalha rethink space as replete with life-forms that likely have their own social worlds and ways of knowing the universe. They thus join the artistic, scientific, and activist voices articulating what Rubenstein poetically calls *other space-times*. With reference to the Afrofuturist composer Sun Ra as well as novelists like Butler and N. K. Jemisin and the Navajo astronaut Tazbah Redhouse, Rubenstein concludes her account of "the lofty religious" vision being deployed to sell NewSpace by foregrounding models of "a different kind of interworldly transport: one not to conquer the spaceways but to find 'another kind of living'" (2022, 4, 170). Through these optics, space is seen as an infinitely complex place for communication, connection, and creativity rather than as a terrain for discovery, extraction, and occupation. In the final analysis, the literary and scientific projects that this closing chapter of *Novel Ecologies* has centered as imaginative checks on space colonization and its terrestrial simulations powerfully question the race to make new worlds and its fervent engineers. Contra such anthropocentric designs on life after Earth, these imaginaries invite us to stay with the here and now of this world and its urgent need for better ways of living on it and with one another while also dwelling in the unknowable expanse of alien ecologies.

Epilogue

It's early December 2023 on the New Jersey Cape. I'm here to finish this book, and I've been staring at a blank page earmarked for its epilogue. It's here that I begin to bring the book to a close, a book started three thousand miles away in the place that has most made and remade its contents—California.

The tides of the Delaware Bay rise and fall dramatically on the western side of the peninsula where I'm staying in a small cottage a hundred feet from the water. At low tide, you can walk far from the shore's high-water line across the mudflats for what looks like a mile. At high tide, it's a different coastline altogether. On this visit to the Cape, high tide coincides with dusk, when the temperature dips and the wind whips across the dunes. I stand at the water's edge, watching gulls, sandpipers, and sanderlings, wondering how many more years it will be before this spit of sand between the beach houses and the bay disappears. Each evening of the last week, the sun has disappeared slowly through a sliver of open sky below the winter clouds as muted shades of pink, blue, and gray along the horizon slowly fade into night. But the sunset I see tonight is of another order, difficult to capture by camera or convey in words. Its culmination could have been mistaken for a bomb or perhaps some cosmic event, the landing of an impossibly luminous alien spacecraft. For an hour, I sit mesmerized as the sky shape-shifts into a technicolor ball of fire that reflects and refracts back on itself, making it nearly impossible to say where the water ends and the sky begins, and opening a portal into some other, imaginative world.

But, as I peer across this chasm from the deserted winter beach, the reverie breaks, and I'm thrust back into the painful, urgent, and also beautiful real world, a world in which all of us are living through a sea change of ecological loss and climatic disorder but in no way equally. And I think to myself, This place we call the Blue Planet is both more brutalized than I once thought and more complexly alive than the utopias dreamed up by those who aim to remake nature and rebuild Earth.

The poet Franny Choi helps me clarify what I mean to say here as a conclusion to *Novel Ecologies*. In "How to Let Go of the World" (alluding to a climate change documentary by that name), Choi writes of wildfire "brimstone eating California," of water pipes in Flint that deliver "war wrapped in putrid cellophane," and of "photos of bleached reefs" (Choi 2019). Layering these and other markers of global warming and the particularized harms of environmental racism, Choi interknits unnatural disaster with mundane routine and visceral loss. I learned of the poem from Min Hyong Song. Song turns to the poem in his conclusion to *Climate Lyricism*, where he recalls a walk taken with his spouse in the first spring of the COVID-19 pandemic during which they passed by a group holding a vigil for and standing in protest of George Floyd's murder by Minneapolis police. Digressing from that recollection, Song describes Choi's poem as "conjur[ing] explicitly the ways in which the specter of the police, . . . especially among Black and other minority peoples, can conjure a visceral feeling of alarm, maybe even terror, before it reveals that what lies beyond this feeling is a much larger, and perhaps not unrelated, threat," what Choi calls "the sky, shocked with dying" (Song 2022, 209–10). Song goes on to highlight the poem's formal moves between the speaker's memories of a lover who she suggests committed suicide and the proliferation of climatic and other large-scale alterations of the planet. As Song does, I'll reproduce the final stanza of the poem in full:

> In lieu of proximity to firefighters; in lieu of the ability to speak the airlesss [*sic*] language of ghosts; or to reverse the logic of molecules; or to force Exxon to call the hurricane by its rightful name; or to convince my friends not to launch themselves from the rooftops of every false promise made by every rotten idol; in lieu of all I can't do or undo; I hold. The faces of the trees in my hands. I miss them. And miss and miss them. Until I fly out of grief's arms, and the sky. Catches me in its thousand orange hands. It catches me, and I stay there. Suspended against the unrelenting orange. I stay there splayed, and dying. And shocking the siren sky. (Choi 2019)

Written as prose, the lines come to the reader as a single breath and, hence, in the terms of lyric poetry, as a single unravelable thought: invocations of wildfires and hurricanes, ghosts of coral reefs and lost lovers, the naming of Exxon as a synecdoche for fossil fuel energy and extractive capitalism, the sentience of forest and sky, and, then, the unmitigated shock at the world people have *unmade* (some much more than others). Condensed into just 126 words, the sweep of its epic catalog of what the novelist N. K. Jemisin calls *the broken Earth* is gutting (Jemisin 2015). But then, in that same breath, there is a call to "hold"—to take a long pause (to recall the end of Jennifer Egan's *A Visit from the Goon Squad* from chap. 2) and stay with the violence and vulnerability of *the world as it is* and, simultaneously, the world as it might be if it were different enough to be more livable, more just.

The poem stays with "these difficult emotions," in Song's words, that insist: "[W]e are still here and . . . we, too, refuse to give up. We hold. We are caught. We stay" (Song 2022, 210). This reading of the poem opens onto both a provisional environmental politics and a tacit suggestion that the work of environmental imagination—including its more scholarly forms—is by necessity collective and unfinished. He writes: "In many ways we are in the middle of the story. We just can't imagine how bad things can get (maybe our worst-case scenarios aren't bad enough?), and we can't convince ourselves that we can make better worlds—and not just better worlds, but stupendously, wildly, deliriously better worlds" (Song 2022, 210–11). He concludes: "These thoughts beg the question of what terrifies us more: the worst-case scenarios or the idea of making the world better?" (Song 2022, 210–11). I read *Climate Lyricism* and "How to Let Go of the World" as I was endeavoring to finish *Novel Ecologies*, a book I've written in a thousand spots of times over seven years of life lived with my husband and then too our son—a project that has been interrupted by intimate losses and exhilarating sojourns and rethought several times over in the hopes that its final form would offer something that might endure. Song's reflections throw into relief what might be most meaningful to say in closing about this book and the places and people who have most inspired it. Above all, *Novel Ecologies* has confronted the stories and schemes of Nature Remade with literary expressions that refuse to surrender *the world as it is* to worldbuilders—insisting that the future is not theirs to design and determine, holding space for yet bleaker futures if the status quo prevails, and, in the same breath, hazarding what *wildly better worlds* might look like.

This may be the last book I write in which writers and their environmental imaginings are central and in which close reading as a method propels an argument. Whether or not that intuition holds, I'm inclined in this final paragraph to make a strong case for the *ecological speculations* that *Novel Ecologies* has put forward to counter the speculative gambits of Nature Remade: capacious novels that immerse readers in microcosms of the globe, like *A Tale for the Time Being*; sci-fi narratives of other worlds, like *A Psalm for the Wild-Built* and *Borne*; and lyric poems that exceed poetic conventions to channel voices (in some cases extraterrestrial ones) other than those of their human speakers. These works of narrative and poetry—all of them hybrid in their literary forms—have offered portals into worlds as they are and worlds as they could be, illuminating the planetary ambitions of tech in this century as far from utopian. These literary imaginings are extraordinarily powerful tools for real-world transformation. And, even when that inherent potential falters or comes to naught, they carry into the future stories, voices, and, yes, whole worlds that might otherwise have been lost. By comparison, the world-building designs of Nature Remade—which at times have held me in their alluring sway—now seem claustrophobic. Foregone conclusions. Hothouses of technological determinism and endless capitalist growth. As I've dwelled with the wildly otherwise imaginings to the illusions of tech that run through this book, I have come to know that other futures for this world are conceivable, if we hold fast to them.

Acknowledgments

The path I followed from curiosities and questions to the final form of *Novel Ecologies* was far from linear. Over the seven years I spent researching, drafting, rethinking, and finally writing the book, I was fortunate to be in conversation with and to learn from scholars, storytellers, artists, and scientists who have expanded the boundaries of environmental knowledge and reimagined past and future relationships between nature and technology.

The initial ideas for the book took shape at UCLA, where colleagues in the English department, the Institute of the Environment and Sustainability, and across campus changed how I both think about and practice research. I thank especially Ali Behdad, Chris Chism, Dana Cuff, Elizabeth DeLoughrey, Louise Hornby, Rachel Lee, Marissa López, Kathleen McHugh, Anahid Nersessian, Cully Nordby, Todd Presner, David Schaberg, Brad Shaffer, Aradhna Tripati, and Maite Zubiaurre. The compatriots who helped launch the Laboratory for Environmental Narrative Strategies (LENS) at UCLA collaborated on a range of public-facing projects, and our work together transformed the shape and scope of this book. On this score, I thank Jessica Cattelino, Kristy Guevara-Flanagan, Cailey Hall, Spencer Robins, Shouhei Tanaka, and the other faculty and students in the LENS community as well as our partners at KCET/SoCal PBS. Above all, I am grateful to my LENS cofounders and longtime colleagues and friends Jon Christensen and Ursula K. Heise. Ursula: You have been a mentor for two decades. I can only begin to convey the myriad ways in which your brilliant scholarship and generous mentorship have contributed to my own work within and beyond these pages.

In 2021, I moved from California to New Jersey to join the faculty at Princeton University. It was there that *Novel Ecologies* cohered. For generous research support, I thank the Offices of the Dean of Research and the Dean of the Faculty and the Humanities Council as well as my home departments, the Effron Center for the Study of America and the High Meadows Environmental Institute (HMEI). Both have afforded ideal interdisciplinary spaces and provided subvention funding to support the inclusion of color plates. To the stellar professional staff at Effron and HMEI, thank you for making it possible for me to complete this book while teaching and learning the ropes at a new institution. I am especially grateful, at Effron, to Jordan Dixon, Yelz Góchez, Karyn Greco, Genesis Manyari, and Bianca Toliver and, at HMEI, to Emily Ahmetaj, Kathy Hackett, and Amber Lee.

To my new colleagues, thank you for the warm welcomes to Princeton and for inspiring me to hone the stakes of *Novel Ecologies*. Thanks especially to Aisha Beliso-De Jésus, Anne Cheng, Luc Deike, Rachel DeLue, Matt Desmond, Tessa Desmond, Patricia Fernández-Kelly, Lorgia García Peña, Filiz Garip, Hanna Garth, Bill Gleason, Judith Hamera, John Higgins, Shamus Khan, Reed Maxwell, Laure Resplandy, Sarah Rivett, Kate Stanton, Tim Szetla, and Corina Tarnita. To Anne Cheng and Judith Hamera, I extend my gratitude for reading an early draft of the book's introduction and offering feedback at a pivotal moment that put much-needed wind in my sails. (Nature Remade is the capitalized keystone concept of the book because of those conversations with each of you.)

During my first three years at Princeton, alongside the writing of *Novel Ecologies*, I launched Blue Lab, a multidisciplinary group of researchers, storytellers, and artists that has become an extraordinary community of people with whom to think and create. To Barron Bixler, Braeden Carroll, Jayme Collins, Patrick Jaojoco, Kavya Kamath, Diana Little, Kyra Morris, Jessica Ng, Alex Norbrook, Nate Otjen, Asela Perez-Ortiz, Maggie Poost, Juan Rubio, Mario Soriano, Grace Wang, and Max Widman as well as to our partners at Kouvenda Media, thank you for pouring your imagination, expertise, and time into making the lab all that it is. Our collaborations have enlivened the solitary work of writing this book, and you have all inspired me to try to make *Novel Ecologies* resonate across our various disciplinary, generational, and cultural backgrounds.

Over the years of bringing this book to fruition, I have had a sustaining network of mentors, collaborators, and friends in and beyond the fields of environmental studies, the environmental humanities, science and technology studies, and American literature and culture. In addition to those already mentioned, I am grateful for Alenda Chang, Harris Feinsod, Heather Houser, Cat Keyser, Ju Yon Kim, Stephanie LeMenager, Claire Seiler, Amy Tigner, Kyla Wazana Tompkins, Janet Walker, Bethany Wiggin, and Marina Zurkow.

For opportunities to present nascent sections of and ideas from *Novel Ecologies*, I thank Princeton's Anschutz Distinguished Lecture series, the Humanities Center at the University of Tennessee at Knoxville, the Penn Program in Environmental Humanities, and the Environmental Humanities

Working Group at the University of Texas at Austin for invitations to be in dialogue with their communities. The project was also supported and improved by exceptional research assistance from Cailey Hall, Shouhei Tanaka, and Diana Little and was reanimated at a crucial inflection point by the feedback of Gareth Cook at Verto Literary. The project in its initial conception and the manuscript in its complete form benefited from four different anonymous reviewers who believed in its potential and catalyzed some of its most significant revisions. At the University of Chicago Press, Alan Thomas offered invaluable intellectual and editorial expertise and encouraged me to write a book that would reach across disciplinary silos in a voice of my own. I also thank Randolph Petilos, Christine Schwab, freelance copyeditor Joseph Brown, and other members of the copyediting, design, production, and marketing teams at the press for their professional acumen and for the time and skill it takes to create a book out of a manuscript.

Over the years it took to finish *Novel Ecologies*, it was the good humor and good company of friends from different chapters of my life that kept me going, including during the many months when we saw one another only over Zoom. To Claire, Harris, Heather, Ju Yon, Laura, Michael, Heather and Brian, Stephanie and Manu, Johan and Bene, Kate and John, Sheila and Kurt, Matt and Tessa, Hanna and Crystel, Filiz and Mert, and the "happiest of hours" crew (Betsy, Filiz, Fred, Hanna, Shamus, and Tessa), I am fortunate to count you as friends old and new. The raucous book launch party I most want to throw would include all of you.

Finally, I acknowledge my wonderfully blended family, beginning with my parents, Pat Carruth and Dennis and Penney Carruth, and my sister, Ashley Carruth. For your collective belief in me and support of the academic career I've been working at for some twenty-five years, I am grateful. I also thank my in-laws, Pat and Harold Hilker, for loving me as your own and for making me feel so at home in what has become one of my favorite nooks of coastal California. Morro Bay has been both a crucial writing retreat and a much-needed retreat from writing. Because I became a parent during the final three years of working on *Novel Ecologies*, it feels especially fitting to offer another word of thanks to my mother, Pat Carruth. Mom: I will be forever thankful that my memories of finishing this book are intertwined with all the days I got to spend with you in Colorado as part of your "Kicking the Shit Out of Cancer" team. Witnessing your strength, grace, and fierce love of all of us has put this book into the best kind of perspective.

It is to my husband, Barron Bixler, and our son, Julian Bixler, that I dedicate *Novel Ecologies*. Julian: While it will be a long time before you might read this book that got its start years before you came along, I want you to know that its final form has been indelibly changed by you and is filled with you. Embarking on this new and sometimes wild adventure of parenthood has meant that the book took longer to finish than it might otherwise have. But what a beautiful detour it's been. In the end, *Novel Ecologies* is a better book for the extra time and space you unwittingly gave to it, to say nothing of the urgency your life, and my profound love for you, has lent my hopes and fears about our possible environmental futures and who will decide them. Barron: I love you. This book simply wouldn't exist without you. Only we know what it took for these pages to come together as they have and all we went through along the way. Your searching eye as a photographer and your way with words as a writer and as the best reader of my work have shaped how I think about the places, stories, and gambits that form the backbone of this book. If California as a place of world-builders and storyworlds lies at the heart of *Novel Ecologies*, it is because of how I've come to see that place of dreams through our unfurling story, which began in a San Francisco café one unforgettable sunny afternoon two decades ago and, with a potent undertow, keeps drawing us back to the place where we feel most deeply at home.

Notes

Introduction

1. For this analysis, I am drawing on extended studies of the environmental impacts of Silicon Valley's manufacturing history (see, e.g., Pellow and Sun-Hee Park 2002; Schlossberg 2019; Solnit 2010).

2. I drafted *Novel Ecologies* following the convention of capitalizing *Black*, *Indigenous*, and other terms indicating racial and ethnic identities and lowercasing *white*. In the final form of the book, I follow the practice of the University of Chicago Press as well as new conventions in publishing more broadly and also capitalize *White* when referring to its racial meaning.

3. I'm indebted to and in dialogue with a wide range of ecocritical and environmental humanities scholars whose work I cite throughout *Novel Ecologies*. Along with DeLoughrey and Wenzel, I would give special mention here to Ursula K. Heise's *Imagining Extinction* (2016a), Heather Houser's *Infowhelm* (2020), Cajetan Iheka's *African Ecomedia* (2021), Stephanie LeMenager's *Living Oil* (2014), Nicole Seymour's *Bad Environmentalism* (2018), and Min Hyoung Song's *Climate Lyricism* (2022).

4. There are by custom and practice multiple spellings of *Chamoru*, as with other words in the Chamoru language, with *Chamorro* being the most common alternative spelling. Throughout, I follow Craig Santos Perez's predominant use of *Chamoru*.

5. I'm grateful to one of my anonymous readers for throwing into relief these stakes of the book.

6. Over the past decade, the discussion of climate fiction (shorthanded as cli-fi) has become a subfield of ecocriticism as well as a topic of environmental arts and culture reporting (Abraham 2017; Evancie 2013; Ghosh 2016a; Harper 2023; LeMenager 2017; Marshall 2015; Rothman 2022; Sullivan 2020; Taylor 2018; Tuhus-Dubrow 2013; Vitale 2023). The term *postnatural fiction* comes from Jonathan Levin (2011), while *novels of the Anthropocene* is attributed to Kate Marshall (2015).

7. The geoscientist Robert Socolow explains the particular importance for climate science of data taken from Mauna Loa: "In 1958, Charles David Keeling began measuring the concentration of carbon dioxide (CO_2) in the atmosphere, at a site 11,000 feet above sea level near the top of Mauna Loa. . . . The time series of monthly averages, the 'Keeling Curve,' is the iconic figure of climate change" (2012, 1455; see also Callison 2014, 81–87).

Chapter 1

1. Marco Caracciolo convincingly argues that Ozeki's novel "resists narrative's tendency to sink into digital oblivion" by foregrounding "the incredible wealth of human experiences forgotten in the 'garbage patch of history and time'" (2019, 285).

2. In *Global Appetites* (Carruth 2013, 117–53) and elsewhere (see Carruth 2016), I have written about Ozeki's first two novels, *My Year of Meats* (1998) and *All over Creation* (2003).

3. Since a team of scientists at the Woods Hole Oceanographic Institution first coined the term, there have been a number of studies that have corroborated the ecological and climatic significance of the plastisphere (Amaral-Zettler, Zettler, and Mincer 2020; Kirstein et al. 2019; Thomas 2021; Wallbank et al. 2022; Wright, Langille, and Walker 2021; Zettler, Mincer, and Amaral-Zettler 2013).

4. In Oliver Kellhammer's various online writing about the project, there are variants of the spelling *NeoEocene* as *Neo Eocene* and *Neo-Eocene*. As *A Tale for the Time Being* consistently spells it as *NeoEocene*, I follow suit.

Chapter 2

1. As for the first of these, the Life Products Line "distills transformative energies from luminescent rocks, effectively 'hybridizing' its users and expanding their mind" (Johnson 2015).

2. Of Facebook's first three data centers, e.g., two were located in regions where over 60 percent of electricity comes from coal.

3. Second Life is known as "a MUVE (multi-user virtual environment), aka OVSW (online virtual social world), that enables its users to enact alternative identities and social practices without any preconceived rules or narratives, with the exception of the actual building blocks, landscapes, and customization options offered in-world" (Ensslin 2017, 403).

Chapter 3

1. OpenAI repeatedly attests in publicly available white papers and blog posts that both the initial training and the ongoing human-supervision and AI-assisted monitoring and retooling are working to "align" AIs with human values and needs—alignment being a key concept in the field of AI research and development. Setting aside the question of who determines with which values and needs to align any one AI, however, the technology is already being used for self-dealing, hate speech, and nefarious activities. Moreover, it remains unclear—likely to the coders themselves—whether human-AI values alignment is even an attainable goal.

2. Other examples of this narrative association in American sci-fi run the gamut: from films and television series such as *Soylent Green* (1973), *The Matrix* (1999), the *Battlestar Galactica* remake (2004–9), and the Netflix adaptation of *Altered Carbon* (2018–20) to novels such as William Gibson's *Neuromancer* (1984) and Jeff VanderMeer's *Borne* series (2017–19), which chap. 5 takes up at length (Fleischer 1973; Gibson 1984; Kalogridis 2018–20; Moore 2004–9; VanderMeer 2017, 2018, 2019; Wachowski and Wachowski 1999).

3. I have written about this comedic strain of the trilogy in "Wily Ecologies" (Carruth 2018).

4. Writing for *Vox*, Aja Romano (2018) describes hopepunk as "weaponized optimism," indicative of a tendency in popular culture to collapse what Rebecca Solnit (2004) has termed *hope in the dark* into more reductive or naive habits of looking on the bright side.

5. Not unlike Chambers, "Ishiguro is optimistic about the technological revolution coming down the line, and says he finds AI 'alarming and exciting at the same time.'" This ambivalent curiosity stems, for Ishiguro, partly from the potential of AIs to compete with human writers as storytellers: "'It's not just that AI might produce a novel that you can't distinguish from an Ian McEwan novel. It's that I think it might produce a new kind of literature . . . because AI does see things in a different way'" (quoted in Stewart 2021).

Chapter 4

1. The guest list included the sci-fi novelists Ursula LeGuin and J. G. Ballard, the farmer and writer Wendell Berry, the geneticist James Watson, technology scholars like Marshall McLuhan, and environmentalists like Brower.

2. Minteer describes new conservation and especially Brand's version of ecopragmatism as an "environmental appropriation" of the philosophical tradition of American pragmatism, which, in contrast to new conservation, advances "contingency and restraint" and recognizes the limits of human agency in the natural world (2019, 10–11).

3. Guha (2000, 26) traces global conservation science and the codification of wilderness to the rise of academic forestry research first in the United States and England and then throughout the British Empire and the Americas—a history he dates to the 1864 publication of the Vermont-based George Perkins Marsh's *Man and Nature*. His study offers a transnational history of conservation that covers not just American scientists like Marsh and Gifford Pinchot (who founded the Yale School of Forestry) but also Alexander von Humboldt, a Prussian naturalist who studied Venezuelan forests on a 1799–1800 Spanish colonial expedition, and Miguel Angel de Quevado, a Mexican architect and engineer who, in 1922, started the Mexican Forestry Society.

4. Cronon refers here to Frederick Jackson Turner's *The Frontier in American History*, first composed as a short essay in 1893 and then published in an extended form in 1920. Turner's analysis correlates US nation building with access to "free" space, understood as wilderness rather than Indigenous land.

5. In 2018 alone, federally controlled lands and waters "produced 39 percent of total US coal (282 million tons), 21 percent of total US oil (826 million barrels) and 14 percent of total US gas (4.3 trillion cubic feet)" (Ruas 2020).

6. Ecologists coined the term *charismatic megafauna* to characterize modern species, from polar bears to bottlenose dolphins, that captivate human curiosity and compassion and, thus, help garner "funding and support" for conservation research (Lorimer 2015, 139).

7. Lorena Becerra-Valdivia and Thomas Higham (2020, 93) contend that pre-Clovis cultures were in the hemisphere before, during, and after the Last Glacial Maximum (which began about twenty-six thousand years ago in what is now North America). On the basis of the evidence for this longer timescale of human occupation, they suggest

that it is plausible that human activities and their environmental impacts were connected to megafauna extinctions.

8. Between 1992 and 2004, there were approximately two dozen peer-reviewed papers published about rewilding that used *rewilding* anywhere in the text, as keyword and full-text searches I ran in the Princeton University Library Articles+ database showed.

9. Between 2009 and 2010, the US Fish and Wildlife Service and the Guam Department of Agriculture agreed to create a refuge for the rails free of invasive predators on Cocos and Rota Islands (US Fish and Wildlife Service 2023).

10. As an illustration, when a team of Japanese scientists announced in 1996 that they were "planning to fertilize elephant eggs" with the preserved sperm of a woolly mammoth, the media coverage was scant. In English-language news sources, only three articles appeared about the announcement: in *The Guardian, Nature,* and the *Washington Post. The Guardian* ran only a brief story about the announcement, focused on the skepticism of other scientists (Radford 1996, 11).

11. In addition to Church's Woolly Mammoth Project, the most visible de-extinction teams include two small groups in Shapiro's lab (one working on the giant beaver and the other on the passenger pigeon), a mammoth group led by Hendrik Poinar in Ontario, and a team in Leipzig led by Svant Paabo focused on Neanderthals.

12. The Revive and Restore visualizations can be viewed on the organization's website: https://reviverestore.org/about-the-passenger-pigeon.

13. Perez and his publisher, Omnidawn, list the poetry volumes in this series in lowercase with the volume title in brackets after the series title, as in, *from unincorporated territory [hacha].* I have followed that convention.

Chapter 5

1. Other examples include fireflies that are "the work of amateur bioengineers" and a type of flounder that is a "dual-purpose fish and living map" (VanderMeer and Nyquist 2017). There are also outright fantastic creatures: the leviathan of biblical fame along with the "digging leviathan" (a reference to an obscure 1984 sci-fi novel) and the "fire slug," which Harry Potter fans know as "a magical creature found in the Amazon rainforest of Brazil" (Blaylock 1984; "Fire Slug," n.d.). This nod to the Harry Potter series and to J. K. Rowling's own metafictional bestiary *Fantastic Beasts and Where to Find Them by Newt Scamander* (Rowling 2001), whose first edition attributed its authorship to Scamander in the title, accentuates the prominence of genre remixing and sampling in VanderMeer's speculative narratives.

2. Identifying the field's purpose as "preserving biological diversity," Soulé argues that ecosystems tend toward equilibrium if minimally disturbed but that, while under human influence, they become "disequilibrial [*sic*]" (1985, 727–29). This principle has led to two maxims for conservation biology and wilderness-centered environmentalism: "ecological complexity is good" and "biotic diversity has intrinsic value" (Soulé 1985, 730–31).

3. While WorldCat lists approximately 801 publications of all formats between 1980 and 1988 that use *biodiversity* in the title, from 1988 through 2022 that number swelled to nearly 85,000 (OCLC 2018, 2023).

4. The *Weird Tales* magazine launched in the 1920s, continues at the time of this writing in 2024, and has published writers ranging from H. P. Lovecraft to twenty-first-century authors.

Chapter 6

1. Those two systems are the Colorado Aqueduct and the California State Water Project.

2. As Stacy Alaimo poignantly writes: "Like conservation, sustainability has become a plastic but potent signifier, meaning, roughly, the ability to somehow keep things going despite the economic and environmental crisis that, we fear, may render this impossible" (Alaimo 2012, 559).

3. As an addition to this list, by last count, £20 billion mothership, Virgin founding CEO Richard Branson launched Virgin Galactic in 2004.

4. Ursula K. Heise glosses the environmentalist resistance in the trilogy as follows: "Robinson starts out his trilogy with a cast of one hundred scientists, the 'First Hundred' who are sent from Earth to settle Mars. Tens of thousands, hundreds of thousands, and finally millions of settlers follow them over the next few decades as Earth suffers crisis after crisis from population growth, climate change, and the ever-increasing power of transnational corporations. As Fredric Jameson has pointed out, what would be called a 'green' perspective on Earth becomes the perspective of the 'Reds' on Robinson's Mars, a group of migrants and, as time passes, of Martian natives who want to preserve the planet as much as possible in its original condition. . . . The 'Greens,' by contrast, are those who want to terraform Mars by gradually heating up its atmosphere, introducing plants and animals many of which were genetically engineered to fit into their extraterrestrial habitats, and making the planet more and more suitable for human habitation" (2011, 452).

5. For extended discussions of this sci-fi canon, see Alaimo (2007), Buhle (1998), Heise (2011, 2016b), Markley (1997), and Pak (2016).

6. Among many other endangered plants, the Spheres contain "a genetic clone of one of seven surviving genetically distinct golden fascia" from Chiapas, Mexico, a species that is extinct in the wild.

7. Mauna Kea's peak is the location of over a dozen international telescopes managed by major American universities and the governments of Argentina, Brazil, Britain, Canada, Chile, France, Japan, the Netherlands, Taiwan, and the United States (Maunakea Observatories 2020).

8. To date, these installations have taken place in Belgium, Brazil, Germany, Indonesia, Kosovo, New Zealand, the Philippines, Taiwan, and the United States, among other places.

9. The project was developed in collaboration with an Indonesian artist collective called House of Natural Fiber (HONF) and Gadjah Mada University.

10. This detail is confirmed by their two-year mission (the second crew to enter B2 lived inside for only six months) and by source material Boyle consulted (two nonfiction works by "the original Biospherians"). Those titles are, respectively, *Life under the Glass: The Inside Story of Biosphere 2* (Alling and Nelson 1993) and *The Human Experiment: Two Years and Twenty Minutes inside Biosphere 2* (Poynter 2006).

11. Fan sites for *Star Wars* have tallied across the franchise's twelve films over 300 populated planets and 250 sentient species, among which Ewoks, Hutts, and Wookiees are some of the best known (see also Greshko 2019).

Works Cited

Abbey, Edward. 1968. *Desert Solitaire: A Season in the Wilderness*. New York: Ballantine.

Abbey, Edward, Dave Foreman, and Bill Haywood, eds. 1987. *Ecodefense: A Field Guide to Monkeywrenching*. Tucson, AZ: Ned Ludd.

Abraham, John. 2017. "CliFi—a New Way to Talk about Climate Change." *The Guardian*, October 18. https://www.theguardian.com/environment/climate-consensus-97-per-cent/2017/oct/18/clifi-a-new-way-to-talk-about-climate-change.

Ackerman, Diane. 2014. *The Human Age: The World Shaped by Us*. New York: Norton.

Advanced Conservation Strategies. n.d.-a. "About ACS." https://advancedconservation.org/about-acs. Accessed July 15, 2024.

———. n.d.-b. Home page. https://advancedconservation.org. Accessed July 15, 2024.

———. n.d.-c. "Sustainability Science." https://advancedconservation.org/sustainability-science. Accessed July 15, 2024.

Alaimo, Stacy. 2007. "Dying Planet: Mars in Science and the Imagination, and: Red Planet: Scientific and Cultural Encounters with Mars (Review)." *Configurations* 15 (3): 355–57.

———. 2010. *Bodily Natures: Science, Environment, and the Material Self*. Bloomington: Indiana University Press.

———. 2012. "Sustainable This, Sustainable That: New Materialisms, Posthumanism, and Unknown Futures." *PMLA* 127 (3): 558–64.

———. 2016. *Exposed: Environmental Politics and Pleasures in Posthuman Times*. Minneapolis: University of Minnesota Press.

Alling, Abigail, and Mark Nelson. 1993. *Life under the Glass: The Inside Story of Biosphere 2*. Oracle: Biosphere.

Amaral-Zettler, Linda A., Erik R. Zettler, and Tracy J. Mincer. 2020. "Ecology of the Plastisphere." *Nature Reviews Microbiology* 18 (3): 139–51. https://doi.org/10.1038/s41579-019-0308-0.

Amazon. n.d. "The Spheres: Learn about the Plants." https://www.seattlespheres.com/the-plants. Accessed July 15, 2024.

Amazon Web Services. n.d. "What Is a Neural Network? Artificial Neural Network Explained." https://aws.amazon.com/what-is/neural-network. Accessed July 15, 2024.

Amin-Hong, Heidi. 2023. "Craig Santos Perez's Poetics of Multispecies Kinship: Challenging Militarism and Extinction in the Pacific." *Atlantic Studies* 20 (2): 292–307. https://doi.org/10.1080/14788810.2021.2013678.

Anders, Charlie Jane. 2019. *The City in the Middle of the Night*. New York: Macmillan.

Anker, Peder. 2005. "The Ecological Colonization of Space." *Environmental History* 10 (2): 239–68.

Aquarium of the Pacific. n.d. "Pacific Sea Nettle." https://www.aquariumofpacific.org/onlinelearningcenter/species/pacific_sea_nettle. Accessed July 16, 2024.

Asafu-Adjaye, John, Linus Blomqvist, Stewart Brand, Barry Brook, and Ruth Defries. 2015. "An Ecomodernist Manifesto." Available at https://www.ecomodernism.org.

Atwood, Margaret. 2003. *Oryx and Crake*. New York: Anchor.

———. 2009. *The Year of the Flood*. New York: Anchor.

———. 2013. *MaddAddam*. New York: Anchor.

Aune, K., D. Jørgensen, and C. Gates. 2017. "American Bison (*Bison bison*) (errata version published in 2018)." IUCN Red List of Threatened Species. https://www.iucnredlist.org/species/2815/123789863.

Bacigalupi, Paolo. 2009. *The Windup Girl*. San Francisco: Night Shade.

Bahner, Beth, Aliza Baltz, and Ed Diebold. 1998. "Micronesian Kingfisher Species Survival Plan: Husbandry Manual." Philadelphia: Zoological Society of Philadelphia.

Bakhtin, Mikhail. 1981. *The Dialogic Imagination: Four Essays*. Edited by Michael Holquist. Austin: University of Texas Press.

Ball, Matthew. 2022. *The Metaverse: And How It Will Revolutionize Everything*. New York: Liveright.

Bansal, Sheel, J. Bradley St. Clair, Constance A. Harrington, and Peter J. Gould. 2015. "Impact of Climate Change on Cold Hardiness of Douglas-Fir (Pseudotsuga Menziesii): Environmental and Genetic Considerations." *Global Change Biology* 21 (10): 3814–26. https://doi.org/10.1111/gcb.12958.

Bardini, Thierry. 2011. *Junkware*. Posthumanities. Minneapolis: University of Minnesota Press.

Batalha, Natalie. 2013. "Exoplanets and Love: Science That Connects Us to One Another." Interview by Krista Tippett. *On Being* (podcast), February 14, updated August 29. https://onbeing.org/programs/natalie-batalha-exoplanets-and-love-science-that-connects-us-to-one-another.

Bawdy, T. 2016. "Global Warming: Data Centres to Consume Three Times as Much Energy in Next Decade, Experts Warn." *The Independent UK*, January 23. https://www.independent.co.uk/climate-change/news/global-warming-data-centres-to-consume-three-times-as-much-energy-in-next-decade-experts-warn-a6830086.html.

Beauregard, Guy. 2015. "On Not Knowing: *A Tale for the Time Being* and the Politics of Imagining Lives beyond the Nation." *Canadian Literature* 227:96–112.

Becerra-Valdivia, Lorena, and Thomas Higham. 2020. "The Timing and Effect of the Earliest Human Arrivals in North America." *Nature* 584 (7819): 93–97. https://doi.org/10.1038/s41586-020-2491-6.

Beckwith, Naomi. 2009. "Saya Woolfalk's Utopia: Sensation as a Space of Critique." *Nka: Journal of Contemporary African Art* 25 (1): 150–57.

Beers, David. 2020. "Selling the American Space Dream: The Cosmic Delusions of Elon Musk and Wernher von Braun." *New Republic*, December 7. https://newrepublic.com/article/160268/selling-american-space-dream.

Begley, Sharon. 2018. "Scientists Have Reconstructed the Genome of a Bird Extinct for 700 Years." *Scientific American*, February 27. https://www.scientificamerican.com/article/scientists-have-reconstructed-the-genome-of-a-bird-extinct-for-700-years.

Benford, Gregory. 2013. "Sunshine Technopolis: Southern California's Utopian Futures." *Los Angeles Review of Books*, August 15. https://v2.lareviewofbooks.org/article/sunshine-technopolis.

Bennett, Jane. 2009. *Vibrant Matter: A Political Ecology of Things*. Durham, NC: Duke University Press.

Benton, Michael J. 2016. "Origins of Biodiversity." *PLOS Biology* 14 (11): 1–7. https://doi.org/10.1371/journal.pbio.2000724.

Berke, Deborah. 2018. "Apple Park [by Foster + Partners]." *Arquitectura Viva*, January 5. https://arquitecturaviva.com/works/apple-park-1.

Berlant, Lauren, and Sianne Ngai. 2017. "Comedy Has Issues." *Critical Inquiry* 43 (2): 233–49. https://doi.org/10.1086/689666.

Bhaimiya, Sawdah. 2023. "Elon Musk Says It's 'Highly Likely' Man Will Go to Mars within 10 Years Because He's 'Congenitally Optimistic.'" *Business Insider*, February 10. https://www.businessinsider.com/elon-musk-says-man-will-go-mars-within-10-years-2023-2.

Bhopal Medical Appeal. n.d. "What Happened." https://www.bhopal.org/continuing-disaster/the-bhopal-gas-disaster/union-carbides-disaster. Accessed April 2, 2024.

Biello, David. 2016. *The Unnatural World*. New York: Scribner.

Biggerstaff, Sarah. 2019. "Saya Woolfalk: Expedition to the Chimacloud, March 1–Sept. 1, 2019." *KC Studio*, March 8. https://kcstudio.org/saya-woolfalk-expedition-to-the-chimacloud-march-1-sept-1-2019.

BirdLife International. 2019. "Guam Rail (*Hypotaenidia owstoni*)." IUCN Red List of Threatened Species. https://www.iucnredlist.org/species/22692441/156506469.

Bixler, Barron. 2015. "Industrial Materials." *Boom: A Journal of California* 5 (2): 64–77.

———. n.d.-a. "Industrial Materials: Mining California." Barron Bixler Photographs. https://barronbixler.com/projects/industrial-materials-california-mining-landscapes.

———. n.d.-b. "Watershed: A Speculative Atlas of California." Barron Bixler Photographs. https://barronbixler.com/projects/watershed-california-water-system-images.

Blaylock, James P. 1984. *The Digging Leviathan*. New York: Ace.

Bloomberg, Spencer Soper. 2018. "Amazon Brings Tropical Relaxation to Seattle Headquarters." *Toronto Star*, January 29.

Blue Origin. 2018. Home page. Archived July 1 at the Wayback Machine. https://web.archive.org/web/20180701222305/https://www.blueorigin.com.

———. 2022. "About Blue Origin." Archived June 1 at the Wayback Machine. https://web.archive.org/web/20220601043224/https://www.blueorigin.com/about-blue/.

———. n.d. Home page. https://www.blueorigin.com. Accessed July 15, 2024.

Blumenfeld, Jacob. 2017. "Modern Humans Are Probably Easier to Unwrap: Jeff VanderMeer with Jacob Blumenfeld." *Brooklyn Rail*, August. https://brooklynrail.org/2017/07/books/Modern-Humans-Are-Probably-Easier-to-Unwrap-Jeff-Vandermeer-with-Jacob-Blumenfeld.

Botkin, Daniel B. 1990. *Discordant Harmonies: A New Ecology for the Twenty-First Century*. Oxford: Oxford University Press.

———. 2012. *The Moon in the Nautilus Shell: Discordant Harmonies Reconsidered*. Oxford: Oxford University Press.

Bouson, J. Brooks. 2016. "A 'Joke-Filled Romp' through End Times: Radical Environmentalism, Deep Ecology, and Human Extinction in Margaret Atwood's

Eco-apocalyptic *MaddAddam* Trilogy." *Journal of Commonwealth Literature* 51 (3): 341–57. https://doi.org/10.1177/0021989415573558.

Bowie, David. 1971. *Hunky Dory*. Vinyl. New York: RCA Records.

———. 1972. *The Rise and Fall of Ziggy Stardust and the Spiders from Mars*. Vinyl. New York: RCA Records.

Boyce, James K. 2015. "Rethinking Extinction: Toward a Less Gloomy Environmentalism." *Harper's Magazine*, November. https://harpers.org/archive/2015/11/rethinking-extinction.

Boyle, T. Coraghessan. 1995. *Tortilla Curtain*. New York: Viking.

———. 2001. *A Friend of the Earth*. New York: Penguin.

———. 2011. *When the Killing's Done*. New York: Penguin.

———. 2016. *The Terranauts*. New York: HarperCollins.

Bradbury, Ray. 1950/1997. *The Martian Chronicles*. New York: William Morrow.

Brady, Amy. 2018. "Rewilding Your Lawn in the Anthropocene: An Interview with Author Jeff VanderMeer." *Orion Magazine*, July 28. https://orionmagazine.org/2018/07/rewilding-your-lawn-in-the-anthropocene-an-interview-with-author-jeff-vandermeer.

Brand, Stewart. 1978. Letter from Stewart Brand to David Brower. MSS 7/9 (carton 5, folder 41), David Ross Brower Papers, 1924–2000, Bancroft Library, University of California, Berkeley.

———. 2009. *Whole Earth Discipline: An Ecopragmatist Manifesto*. New York: Viking.

———. 2013. "The Dawn of De-extinction. Are You Ready?" TEDx, February, 18 min., 7 sec. https://www.ted.com/talks/stewart_brand_the_dawn_of_de_extinction_are_you_ready.

Brean, Joseph. 2017. "Dream of Jurassic Park Moves Closer to Reality; But Experts Fear 'De-extinction' Could Fuel New Moral Quandaries and Unknown Ecological Risks." *National Post*, October 28.

Brocade. 2012a. "About Brocade." Archived September 8 at the Wayback Machine. https://web.archive.org/web/20120908084553/http://www.brocade.com/company/about-brocade/index.page.

———. 2012b. "Where on Earth Is Your Data Center Now?" Online ad.

Brooker, Katrina. 1999. "Amazon vs. Everybody." *Fortune*, November 8.

Broughton, Jack M., and Elic M. Weitzel. 2018. "Population Reconstructions for Humans and Megafauna Suggest Mixed Causes for North American Pleistocene Extinctions." *Nature Communications* 9 (1): 5441. https://doi.org/10.1038/s41467-018-07897-1.

Brouwer, Joel. 2011. "Poems of Childhood, Grief and Deep Space." *New York Times*, August 26. https://www.nytimes.com/2011/08/28/books/review/life-on-mars-by-tracy-k-smith-book-review.Html.

Brower, David Ross. Papers. BANC MSS 79/9 c, Bancroft Library, University of California, Berkeley. See https://oac.cdlib.org/findaid/ark:/13030/hb8g5011x4/entire_text.

———. 1974. "How to Get to the Twenty-First Century from Here (Life in Post-industrial America)." MSS 7/9 (carton 5, folder 41), David Ross Brower Papers, 1924–2000, Bancroft Library, University of California, Berkeley.

———. 1975. "Third Planet Operating Instructions." *New York Times Magazine*, March 16.

———. 1976. "Comments on O'Neill's Space Colonies." *CoEvolution Quarterly*, 1976:17. https://wholeearth.info/p/coevolution-quarterly-spring-1976?format=spreads&index=17.

Brower, David Ross, and Sierra Club. 1961. *Wilderness: America's Living Heritage*. New York: Gillick.

Buhle, Paul. 1998. "Fear of a Green Planet: Kim Stanley Robinson's Ecotopian Science Fiction." *Village Voice*, July 14.

Burgess, Jean. 2023. "Everyday Data Cultures: Beyond Big Critique and the Technological Sublime." *AI and Society* 38 (3): 1243–44. https://doi.org/10.1007/s00146-022-01503-1.

Butler, Octavia. 1987. *Dawn*. New York: Warner.

———. 2012. *Lilith's Brood: The Complete Xenogenesis Trilogy*. New York: Open Road Integrated Media.

Byrne, Monica. 2014. "The Rumpus Interview with Jeff VanderMeer." *The Rumpus*, December. http://therumpus.net/2014/12/the-rumpus-interview-with-jeff-vandermeer.

Callison, Candis. 2014. *How Climate Change Comes to Matter*. Durham, NC: Duke University Press.

Calma, Justine. 2021. "The Climate Controversy Swirling around NFTs." *The Verge*, March 15. https://www.theverge.com/2021/3/15/22328203/nft-cryptoart-ethereum-blockchain-climate-change.

Cameron, James, dir. 2009. *Avatar*. Twentieth Century Fox.

Campos, Luis A., Michael R. Dietrich, Tiago Saraiva, and Christian C. Young, eds. 2021. *Nature Remade: Engineering Life, Envisioning Worlds*. Convening Science. Chicago: University of Chicago Press.

Caracciolo, Marco. 2019. "Form, Science, and Narrative in the Anthropocene." *Narrative* 27 (3): 270–89. https://doi.org/10.1353/nar.2019.0016.

Caracciolo, Marco, and Gry Ulstein. 2022. "The Weird and the Meta in Jeff VanderMeer's *Dead Astronauts*." *Configurations* 30 (1): 1–23.

Carey, John. 2016. "Rewilding." *Proceedings of the National Academy of Sciences* 113 (4): 806–8.

Carney, Judith A., and Richard Nicholas Rosomoff. 2009. *In the Shadow of Slavery: Africa's Botanical Legacy in the Atlantic World*. Berkeley: University of California Press.

Caro, Tim. 2007. "The Pleistocene Re-Wilding Gambit." *Trends in Ecology and Evolution* 22 (6): 281–83. https://doi.org/10.1016/j.tree.2007.03.001.

Carr, Nicholas G. 2010. *The Shallows: What the Internet Is Doing to Our Brains*. New York: Norton.

Carruth, Allison. 2013. *Global Appetites: American Power and the Literature of Food*. New York: Cambridge University Press.

———. 2014. "The Digital Cloud and the Micropolitics of Energy." *Public Culture* 26 (2): 339–64.

———. 2016. "Open Source Foodways: Agricultural Commons and Participatory Art." *ASAP/Journal* 1 (1): 95–122.

———. 2018. "Wily Ecologies: Comic Futures for American Environmentalism." *American Literary History* 30 (1): 108–33.

Carson, Rachel. 1962. *Silent Spring*. Boston: Houghton Mifflin.

Carver, Steve, Ian Convery, Sally Hawkins, Rene Beyers, Adam Eagle, Zoltan Kun, Erwin Van Maanen, et al. 2021. "Guiding Principles for Rewilding." *Conservation Biology* 35 (6): 1882–93. https://doi.org/10.1111/cobi.13730.

Chakrabarty, Dipesh. 2009. "The Climate of History: Four Theses." *Critical Inquiry* 35 (2): 197–222.

Chambers, Becky. 2019. *To Be Taught, If Fortunate*. New York: HarperCollins.

———. 2021. *A Psalm for the Wild-Built. Monk and Robot*, bk. 1. New York: Tordotcom, a Tom Doherty Associates Book.

———. 2022. *A Prayer for the Crown-Shy. Monk and Robot*, bk. 2. New York: Tordotcom, a Tom Doherty Associates Book.

Chapin, F. Stuart, and Anthony M. Starfield. 1997. "Time Lags and Novel Ecosystems in Response to Transient Climatic Change in Arctic Alaska." *Climatic Change* 35 (4): 449–61.

Charo, R. Alta, and Henry T. Greely. 2015. "CRISPR Critters and CRISPR Cracks." *American Journal of Bioethics* 15 (12): 11–17.

Choi, Franny. 2019. "How to Let Go of the World." *PEN America* (blog), October 3. https://pen.org/how-to-let-go-of-the-world.

Church, George M. 2023. "George M. Church's Tech Transfer, Advisory Roles, and Funding Sources." Updated October 27. https://arep.med.harvard.edu/gmc/tech.html.

Church, George M., and Edward Regis. 2012. *Regenesis: How Synthetic Biology Will Reinvent Nature and Ourselves*. New York: Basic.

Churchwell, Sarah. 2011. Review of *A Visit from the Goon Squad* by Jennifer Egan. *The Guardian*, March 12. https://www.theguardian.com/books/2011/mar/13/jennifer-egan-visit-goon-squad.

Cohn, Jeffrey P. 2007. "Biosphere 2, Version 3.0." *BioScience* 57 (9): 808. https://doi.org/10.1641/B570921.

Colbert, Stephen. 2015. "Elon Musk Might Be a Super Villain." *The Late Show with Stephen Colbert*, September 10. CBS. Available at https://www.youtube.com/watch?v=gV6hP9wpMW8.

Colossal. n.d.-a. "Company: The Science of Genetics, the Business of Discovery." https://colossal.com/company. Accessed July 15, 2024.

———. n.d.-b. Home page. https://colossal.com. Accessed July 15, 2024.

———. n.d.-c. "Species: De-extinction for the Survival of Our Planet." https://colossal.com/species. Accessed July 15, 2024.

Comfort, Alex, ed. 1972. *The Joy of Sex: A Cordon Bleu Guide to Lovemaking*. New York: Crown.

Condon, Robert H., Carlos M. Duarte, Kylie A. Pitt, Kelly L. Robinson, Cathy H. Lucas, Kelly R. Sutherland, Hermes W. Mianzan, et al. 2013. "Recurrent Jellyfish Blooms Are a Consequence of Global Oscillations." *Proceedings of the National Academy of Sciences* 110 (3): 1000–1005. https://doi.org/10.1073/pnas.1210920110.

Congressional Research Service. 2005. "Wilderness: Overview, Management, and Statistics." Updated 2022. RL31447. https://crsreports.congress.gov/product/pdf/RL/RL31447.

Connolly, John. 2019. "The Future of Sci-Fi Never Looked So Bright." *Irish Times*, August 26. https://www.irishtimes.com/culture/books/the-future-of-sci-fi-never-looked-so-bright-1.3994109.

Conway, Erik M. 2015. *Exploration and Engineering: The Jet Propulsion Laboratory and the Quest for Mars*. Baltimore, MD: John Hopkins University Press.

Cook, Gary, Tom Dowdall, David Pomerantz, and Yifei Wang. 2014. "Clicking Clean: How Companies Are Creating the Green Internet." Washington, DC: Greenpeace International.

Cook, Gary, Jude Lee, Tsai Tamina, Ada Kong, John Deans, Brian Johnson, and Elizabeth Jardim. 2017. "Clicking Clean: Who Is Winning the Race to Build a Green Internet?" Washington, DC: Greenpeace International.

Cook, Gary, and David Pomerantz. 2015. "Clicking Clean: A Guide to Building the Green Internet." Washington, DC: Greenpeace International.

Cooper, A., C. Turney, K. A. Hughen, B. W. Brook, H. G. McDonald, and C. J. A. Bradshaw. 2015. "Abrupt Warming Events Drove Late Pleistocene Holarctic Megafaunal Turnover." *Science* 349 (6248): 602–6. https://doi.org/10.1126/science.aac4315.

Cooper, Melinda. 2001. "Transgenic Life: Controlling Mutation." *Theory and Event* 5 (3). https://muse.jhu.edu/article/32630.

———. 2007. "Life, Autopoiesis, Debt: Inventing the Bioeconomy." *Distinktion: Scandinavian Journal of Social Theory* 8 (1): 25–43. https://doi.org/10.1080/1600910X.2007.9672937.

Coupland, Ken. 1996. "The Metaverse Is Coming." *Graphis* 52 (303): 16.

Crawford, Kate. 2021. *Atlas of AI: Power, Politics, and the Planetary Costs of Artificial Intelligence*. New Haven, CT: Yale University Press.

Crease, Robert P. 2019. "The Bizarre Logic of the Many-Worlds Theory." *Nature* 573 (7772): 30–33. https://doi.org/10.1038/d41586-019-02602-8.

Crichton, Michael. 1990/1991. *Jurassic Park*. New York: Ballantine.

Cronon, William. 1991. *Nature's Metropolis: Chicago and the Great West*. New York: Norton.

———. 1996. "The Trouble with Wilderness; or, Getting Back to the Wrong Nature." *Environmental History* 1 (1): 7–28. https://doi.org/10.2307/3985059.

Crosby, Alfred W. 2004. *Ecological Imperialism: The Biological Expansion of Europe, 900–1900*. 2nd ed. Cambridge: Cambridge University Press.

Cross, Emily S., Ruud Hortensius, and Agnieszka Wykowska. 2019. "From Social Brains to Social Robots: Applying Neurocognitive Insights to Human-Robot Interaction." *Philosophical Transactions of the Royal Society* 374 (1771): 1–8. https://doi.org/10.1098/rstb.2018.0024.

Crutzen, Paul, and Eugene Stoermer. 2000. "The Anthropocene." *IGBP Newsletter* 41:17–18.

Darrow, Barb. 2017. "Apple, Facebook, and Google Top Greenpeace Energy Report Card." *Fortune*, January 10. https://fortune.com/2017/01/10/greenpeace-energy-report-apple-facebook-google.

Davenport, Christian. 2018. *The Space Barons: Jeff Bezos, Elon Musk, and the Quest to Colonize the Cosmos*. New York: PublicAffairs.

Davidson, Cathy N., and David Theo Goldberg. 2009. *The Future of Learning Institutions in a Digital Age*. Cambridge, MA: MIT Press.

Davidson, John. 2023. "Is ChatGPT a Form of Magic or the Apocalypse?" *Australian Financial Review*, January 23. https://www.afr.com/technology/is-chatgpt-a-form-of-magic-or-the-apocalypse-20230117-p5cd4p.

Davis, Rocío G. 2015. "Fictional Transits and Ruth Ozeki's *A Tale for the Time Being*." *Biography* 38 (1): 87–103.

Dawson, Ashley. 2016. *Extinction: A Radical History*. New York: OR Books.

Defenders of Wildlife. n.d. "Bison." https://defenders.org/wildlife/bison. Accessed July 15, 2024.

DeLoughrey, Elizabeth. 2014. "Satellite Planetarity and the Ends of the Earth." *Public Culture* 26 (2): 257–80. https://doi.org/10.1215/08992363-2392057.

———. 2019. *Allegories of the Anthropocene*. Durham, NC: Duke University Press.

Deutscher, Maria. 2020. "Google: Our Data Centers Are Now Twice as Energy-Efficient as a Typical Enterprise Facility." *SiliconANGLE* (blog), February 27. https://siliconangle.com/2020/02/27/google-data-centers-now-x2-energy-efficient-typical-enterprise-facility.

de Vries, Alex, Ulrich Gallersdörfer, Lena Klaaßen, and Christian Stoll. 2022. "Revisiting Bitcoin's Carbon Footprint." *Joule* 6 (3): 498–502. https://doi.org/10.1016/j.joule.2022.02.005.

Díaz, Eva. 2011. "Dome Culture in the Twenty-First Century." *Grey Room* 42:80–105.

Dick, Philip K. 1968. *Do Androids Dream of Electric Sheep?* New York: Random House.

Dimock, Wai Chee. 2017. "There's No Escape from Contamination above the Toxic Sea." *New York Times*, May 5. https://www.nytimes.com/2017/05/05/books/review/borne-jeff-vandermeer.html.

———. 2020. "AI and the Humanities." *PMLA* 135 (3): 449–54. https://doi.org/10.1632/pmla.2020.135.3.449.

Doerr, Anthony. 2009. "Am I Still Here: Looking for Validation in a Wired World." *Orion*, February.

Donlan, Josh. 2014. "De-extinction in a Crisis Discipline." *Frontiers of Biogeography* 6 (1): 25–28. https://doi.org/10.21425/F5FBG19504.

Donlan, Josh, Joel Berger, Carl E. Bock, Jane H. Bock, David A. Burney, James A. Estes, Dave Foreman, et al. 2006. "Pleistocene Rewilding: An Optimistic Agenda for Twenty-First Century Conservation." *American Naturalist* 168 (5): 660–81. https://doi.org/10.1086/508027.

Donlan, Josh, Harry W. Greene, Joel Berger, Carl E. Bock, Jane H. Bock, David A. Burney, James A. Estes, et al. 2005. "Re-Wilding North America." *Nature* 436 (7053): 913–14. https://doi.org/10.1038/436913a.

Doudna, Jennifer. 2020a. "The Promise and Challenge of Therapeutic Genome Editing." *Nature* 578 (7794): 229–36. https://doi.org/10.1038/s41586-020-1978-5.

———. 2020b. "'A Viable Path toward Responsible Use': A Discussion with Jennifer Doudna on the Risks and Rewards of CRISPR/Cas9 Gene Editing." *Issues in Science and Technology* 36 (3): 37–39.

Doudna, Jennifer, and Samuel H. Sternberg. 2017. *A Crack in Creation: Gene Editing and the Unthinkable Power to Control Evolution*. Boston: Houghton Mifflin Harcourt.

Duarte, Carlos M., Kylie A. Pitt, Cathy H. Lucas, Jennifer E. Purcell, Shin-ichi Uye, Kelly Robinson, Lucas Brotz, et al. 2013. "Is Global Ocean Sprawl a Cause of Jellyfish Blooms?" *Frontiers in Ecology and the Environment* 11 (2): 91–97. https://doi.org/10.1890/110246.

Duhigg, Charles. 2023. "The Inside Story of Microsoft's Partnership with OpenAI." *New Yorker*, December 1. https://www.newyorker.com/magazine/2023/12/11/the-inside-story-of-microsofts-partnership-with-openai.

Ecological Society of America. n.d. "What Is Ecology?" https://www.esa.org/about/what-does-ecology-have-to-do-with-me. Accessed July 15, 2024.

Edwards, Paul N. 1996. *The Closed World: Computers and the Politics of Discourse in Cold War America.* Inside Technology. Cambridge, MA: MIT Press.

Eftaxiopoulos, Georgios. 2020. "The Largest Room in the World." *AA Files* 77:89–101.

Egan, Jennifer. 2010. *A Visit from the Goon Squad.* New York: Knopf.

———. 2012. "Black Box." *New Yorker*, May 28. https://www.newyorker.com/magazine/2012/06/04/black-box.

Ellis, Erle. 2015. "Too Big for Nature." In *After Preservation: Saving American Nature in the Age of Humans*, ed. Ben A. Minteer and Stephen J. Pyne, 24–31. Chicago: University of Chicago Press.

El-Mohtar, Amal. 2021. "A Monk and a Robot Meet in a Forest . . . and Talk Philosophy in This New Novel." NPR, July 18. https://www.npr.org/2021/07/18/1017119290/a-monk-and-a-robot-meet-in-a-forest-and-talk-philosophy-in-this-new-novel.

Ensmenger, Nathan. 2018. "The Environmental History of Computing." *Technology and Culture* 59 (4): S7–S33. https://doi.org/10.1353/tech.2018.0148.

Ensslin, Astrid. 2017. "Linden Lab's Second Life." In *The Routledge Companion to Imaginary Worlds*, ed. Mark J. P. Wolf, 402–9. New York: Routledge.

Evancie, Angela. 2013. "So Hot Right Now: Has Climate Change Created A New Literary Genre?" *Weekend Edition Saturday*, NPR, April 20. https://www.npr.org/2013/04/20/176713022/so-hot-right-now-has-climate-change-created-a-new-literary-genre.

Everard, Mark. 2013. *Hydropolitics of Dams: Engineering or Ecosystems?* London: Bloomsbury.

Farrell, Justin. 2020. *Billionaire Wilderness: The Ultra-wealthy and the Remaking of the American West.* Princeton, NJ: Princeton University Press.

Fergus, Mark, and Hawk Ostby, developers. 2015–22. *The Expanse.* Television series. Based on the novels by James S. A. Corey (pen name of Daniel Abraham and Ty Franck). Alcon Entertainment.

Fernholz, Tim. 2018. *Rocket Billionaires: Elon Musk, Jeff Bezos, and the New Space Race.* Boston: Houghton Mifflin Harcourt.

Finney, Carolyn. 2014. *Black Faces, White Spaces: Reimagining the Relationship of African Americans to the Great Outdoors.* Chapel Hill: University of North Carolina Press.

———. 2020. "The Perils of Being Black in Public: We Are All Christian Cooper and George Floyd." *The Guardian*, June 3. https://www.theguardian.com/commentisfree/2020/jun/03/being-black-public-spaces-outdoors-perils-christian-cooper.

"Fire Slug." n.d. Harry Potter Wikia. http://harrypotter.wikia.com/wiki/Fire_slug. Accessed July 15, 2024.

Fisher, Max. 2022. *The Chaos Machine: The Inside Story of How Social Media Rewired Our Minds and Our World.* New York: Little, Brown.

Flavelle, Christopher, and Ian C. Bates. 2024. "Warming Is Getting Worse: So They Just Tested a Way to Deflect the Sun." *New York Times*, April 2. https://www.nytimes.com/2024/04/02/climate/global-warming-clouds-solar-geoengineering.html.

Fleetwood, Nicole R. 2014. "Performing Empathies: The Art of Saya Woolfalk." *Callaloo* 37 (4): 973–89. https://doi.org/10.1353/cal.2014.0145.

Fleischer, Richard, dir. 1973. *Soylent Green.* MGM.

Foer, Franklin. 2019. "Jeff Bezos's Master Plan." *The Atlantic*, November. https://www.theatlantic.com/magazine/archive/2019/11/what-jeff-bezos-wants/598363.

Ford, James Edward, III. 2014. "'Space Is the Place': Afrofuturist Elegy in Tracy K. Smith's *Life on Mars*." *Black Scholar* 44 (1): 161–66.

Foreman, Dave, John Davis, David Johns, Reed Noss, and Michael E Soulé. 1993. "The Wildlands Project." *Earth Island Journal* 8 (2): 25.

"Foster City: A Story of Filling the Bay." 2009. *SFGate*, June 14. https://www.sfgate.com/bayarea/article/foster-city-a-story-of-filling-the-bay-3295665.php.

Francis, Abby. 2022. "Tla'amin First Nation Harvests for the Future and Cultural Values." *Cortes Currents* (blog), March 2. https://cortescurrents.ca/first-nation-harvests-for-the-future-and-cultural-values.

François, Anne-Lise. 2003. "'O Happy Living Things': Frankenfoods and the Bounds of Wordsworthian Natural Piety." *Diacritics* 33 (2): 42–70.

Freud, Sigmund. 1919/2003. "The Uncanny." In *The Uncanny*, trans. David Mclintock, 123–62. London: Penguin.

"From Gene Editing to A.I., How Will Technology Transform Humanity?" 2018. *New York Times Magazine*, November 18. https://www.nytimes.com/interactive/2018/11/16/magazine/tech-design-medicine-phenome.html.

Fuller, R. Buckminster. 1969. *Operating Manual for Spaceship Earth*. Carbondale: Southern Illinois University Press.

Gabrys, Jennifer. 2013. *Digital Rubbish: A Natural History of Electronics*. Ann Arbor: University of Michigan Press.

———. 2015. "Powering the Digital: From Energy Ecologies to Electronic Environmentalism." In *Media and the Ecological Crisis*, ed. Richard Maxwell, Jon Raundalen, and Nina Lager Vestberg, 3–18. New York: Routledge.

Galchen, Rivka. 2011. "Dream Machine." *New Yorker*, May 2. https://www.newyorker.com/magazine/2011/05/02/dream-machine.

Geiger, Susi. 2020. "Silicon Valley, Disruption, and the End of Uncertainty." *Journal of Cultural Economy* 13 (2): 169–84.

Ghosh, Amitav. 2016a. "Amitav Ghosh: Where Is the Fiction about Climate Change?" *The Guardian*, October 28. https://www.theguardian.com/books/2016/oct/28/amitav-ghosh-where-is-the-fiction-about-climate-change-.

———. 2016b. *The Great Derangement: Climate Change and the Unthinkable*. Chicago: University of Chicago Press.

Gibson, Abraham. 2021. "Harvesting Hogzillas: Feral Pigs and the Engineering Ideal." In *Nature Remade: Engineering Life, Envisioning Worlds*, ed. Luis A. Campos, Michael R. Dietrich, Tiago Saraiva, and Christian C. Young, 60–69. Chicago: University of Chicago Press.

Gibson, William. 1984. *Neuromancer*. New York: Ace.

———. 2001. "My Own Private Tokyo." *Wired*, September 1. https://www.wired.com/2001/09/gibson.

Gilles, Nathan. 2022. "Pac NW's 'Trees of Life' Are Dying: Now We Know Why." *Columbia Insight* (blog), August 18. https://columbiainsight.org/pac-nws-trees-of-life-are-dying-now-we-know-why.

Glanz, James. 2011. "Google Details, and Defends, Its Use of Electricity." *New York Times*, September 8. https://www.nytimes.com/2011/09/09/technology/google-details-and-defends-its-use-of-electricity.html.

———. 2012. "Power, Pollution and the Internet." *New York Times*, September 22. https://www.nytimes.com/2012/09/23/technology/data-centers-waste-vast-amounts-of-energy-belying-industry-image.html.

Glassie, Alison. 2020. "Ruth Ozeki's Floating World: *A Tale for the Time Being*'s Spiritual Oceanography." *Novel: A Forum on Fiction* 53 (3): 452–71. https://doi.org/10.1215/00295132-8624642.

Goodyear-Ka'ōpua, Noelani, Ikaika Hussey, and Erin Kahunawaika'ala Wright, eds. 2014. *A Nation Rising: Hawaiian Movements for Life, Land, and Sovereignty.* Durham, NC: Duke University Press.

Google Real Estate. 2022. "Bay View and Gradient Canopy." Short film, 4 min., 58 sec. https://realestate.withgoogle.com/bayview.

Google Sustainability. n.d. "Operating on 24/7 Carbon-Free Energy by 2030." https://sustainability.google/progress/energy. Accessed July 15, 2024.

Gorvett, Zaria. 2023. "The AI Emotions Dreamed Up by ChatGPT." BBC, March 22. https://www.bbc.com/future/article/20230224-the-ai-emotions-dreamed-up-by-chatgpt.

GPT4 (OpenAI). 2023. Personal communication with Allison Carruth. Correspondence in author's possession.

Grabianowski, Ed. 2010. "Terraforming Earth: How to Wreck a Planet in 3,000 Years (Part 1)." *Wired*, September 24. https://www.wired.com/2010/09/terraforming-part-1.

Greenbaum, Dov. 2022. "The Virtual Worlds of the Metaverse." *Science* 377 (6604): 377. https://doi.org/10.1126/science.add5905.

Greenpeace Reports. 2010. "Make IT Green: Cloud Computing and Its Contribution to Climate Change." Greenpeace International. March 30. https://www.greenpeace.org/international/publication/7099/make-it-green-cloud-computing-and-its-contribution-to-climate-change.

———. 2011. "How Dirty Is Your Data? A Look at the Energy Choices That Power Cloud Computing." Greenpeace International. April. https://www.greenpeace.org/static/planet4-international-stateless/2011/04/4cceba18-dirty-data-report-greenpeace.pdf.

———. 2012. "How Clean Is Your Cloud?" Greenpeace International. April 17. https://www.greenpeace.org/international/publication/6986/how-clean-is-your-cloud.

———. 2020. "Oil in the Cloud." Greenpeace USA, May 19. https://www.greenpeace.org/usa/reports/oil-in-the-cloud.

Greenwald Smith, Rachel. 2009. "Ecology beyond Ecology: Life After the Accident in Octavia Butler's *Xenogenesis* Trilogy." *Modern Fiction Studies* 55 (3): 545–65. https://doi.org/10.1353/mfs.0.1627.

Greshko, Michael. 2019. "The Real Science Inspired by 'Star Wars.'" *National Geographic*, December 1. https://www.nationalgeographic.com/science/article/151209-star-wars-science-movie-film.

Grossman, Elizabeth. 2006. *High Tech Trash: Digital Devices, Hidden Toxics, and Human Health.* Washington, DC: Island.

Grossman, Lev. 2007. "The Hyperconnected." *Time*, April 5. https://content.time.com/time/subscriber/article/0,33009,1607260,00.html.

"The Guardian View on De-extinction: Jurassic Park May Be Becoming Reality." 2022. *The Guardian*, August 19. https://www.theguardian.com/commentisfree/2022/aug/19/the-guardian-view-on-de-extinction-jurassic-park-may-be-becoming-reality.

Guha, Ramachandra. 1989. "Radical American Environmentalism and Wilderness Preservation: A Third World Critique." *Environmental Ethics* 11 (1): 71–83.

———. 2000. *Environmentalism: A Global History*. New York: Longman.
Haff, Peter K. 2014. "Technology as a Geological Phenomenon: Implications for Human Well-Being." In *A Stratigraphical Basis for the Anthropocene*, Geological Society Special Publication 395, ed. C. N. Waters, J. A. Zalasiewicz, M. Williams, M. Ellis, and A. M. Snelling, 301–9. London: Geological Society.
Hance, Jeremy. 2018. "How Native American Tribes Are Bringing Back the Bison from Brink of Extinction." *The Guardian*, December 12. https://www.theguardian.com/environment/2018/dec/12/how-native-american-tribes-are-bringing-back-the-bison-from-brink-of-extinction.
Hand, Elizabeth. 2017. "Jeff VanderMeer's New Dystopian Novel 'Borne' Is Lyrical and Harrowing; Elizabeth Hand Reviews." *Los Angeles Times*, April 27. http://www.latimes.com/books/jacketcopy/la-ca-jc-borne-vandermeer-20170413-story.html.
Hao, Karen, and Charlie Warzel. 2023. "Inside the Chaos at OpenAI." *The Atlantic*, November 20. https://www.theatlantic.com/technology/archive/2023/11/sam-altman-open-ai-chatgpt-chaos/676050.
Haraway, Donna J. 1991. *Simians, Cyborgs and Women: The Reinvention of Nature*. London: Free Association.
———. 2015. "Anthropocene, Capitalocene, Plantationocene, Chthulucene: Making Kin." *Environmental Humanities* 6 (1): 159–65.
———. 2016. *Staying with the Trouble: Making Kin in the Chthulucene*. Durham, NC: Duke University Press.
Harper, Tyler. 2023. "What *The Last of Us*, *Snowpiercer* and 'Climate Fiction' Get Wrong." BBC, April 19. https://www.bbc.com/culture/article/20230418-what-snowpiercer-and-climate-fiction-get-wrong.
Harris, Malcolm. 2023. *Palo Alto: A History of California, Capitalism, and the World*. New York: Little, Brown.
Hayden, Tyler. 2017. "Nukes of Hazard: Vandenberg, Star Wars, and North Korea." *Santa Barbara Independent*, June 1. https://www.independent.com/2017/06/01/nukes-hazard-vandenberg-star-wars-and-north-korea.
Hayles, N. Katherine. 1999. *How We Became Posthuman: Virtual Bodies in Cybernetics, Literature, and Informatics*. Chicago: University of Chicago Press.
Heise, Ursula K. 2006. "The Hitchhiker's Guide to Ecocriticism." *PMLA* 121 (2): 503–16.
———. 2009. "The Android and the Animal." *PMLA* 124 (2): 503–10.
———. 2011. "Martian Ecologies and the Future of Nature." *Twentieth-Century Literature* 57 (3/4): 447–71.
———. 2012. "Reduced Ecologies: Science Fiction and the Meanings of Biological Scarcity." *European Journal of English Studies* 16 (2): 99–112. https://doi.org/10.1080/13825577.2012.703814.
———. 2016a. *Imagining Extinction: The Cultural Meanings of Endangered Species*. Chicago: University of Chicago Press.
———. 2016b. "Terraforming for Urbanists." *Novel: A Forum on Fiction* 49 (1): 10–25.
Helmreich, Stefan. 2011. "What Was Life? Answers from Three Limit Biologies." *Critical Inquiry* 37 (4): 671–96.
———. 2012. "Extraterrestrial Relativism." *Anthropological Quarterly* 85 (4): 1125–39.
Heppler, Jason A. 2017. "Green Dreams, Toxic Legacies: Toward a Digital Political Ecology of Silicon Valley." *International Journal of Humanities and Arts Computing* 11 (1): 68–85.

HI-SEAS. 2022a. "About HI-SEAS." Hawai'i Space Exploration Analog and Simulation. https://www.hi-seas.org/about-hi-seas.
———. 2022b. Home page. Hawai'i Space Exploration Analog and Simulation. https://www.hi-seas.org/.
Hobbs, Richard J., Salvatore Arico, James Aronson, Jill S. Baron, Peter Bridgewater, Viki A. Cramer, Paul R. Epstein, et al. 2006. "Novel Ecosystems: Theoretical and Management Aspects of the New Ecological World Order." *Global Ecology and Biogeography* 15:1–7.
Hoefler, Dan. 1971. "Silicon Valley U.S.A." *Electronic News*, January 11.
Hohn, Donovan. 2007. "Moby-Duck; or, the Synthetic Wilderness of Childhood." *Harper's Magazine*, January. https://harpers.org/archive/2007/01/moby-duck.
———. 2008. "Sea of Trash." *New York Times Magazine*, June 22. https://www.nytimes.com/2008/06/22/magazine/22Plastics-t.html.
Holden, Emily. 2020. "Trump 'Turns Back the Clock' by Luring Drilling Companies to Pristine Lands." *The Guardian*, February 12. https://www.theguardian.com/environment/2020/feb/12/trumps-legacy-drilled-public-lands-and-the-resulting-carbon-emissions.
"HollyFrontier and Holly Energy Partners Announce Completion of Transactions with the Sinclair Companies and Establishment of New Parent Company, HF Sinclair Corporation." 2022. *Business Wire*, March 14. https://www.businesswire.com/news/home/20220313005024/en/HollyFro . . . s-and-Establishment-of-New-Parent-Company-HF-Sinclair-Corporation.
Houser, Heather. 2014. "The Aesthetics of Environmental Visualizations: More Than Information Ecstasy?" *Public Culture* 26 (2): 319–37. https://doi.org/10.1215/08992363-2392084.
———. 2020. *Infowhelm: Environmental Art and Literature in an Age of Data*. New York: Columbia University Press.
Hsu, H. L. 2012. "Guåhan (Guam), Literary Emergence, and the American Pacific in *Homebase* and *from unincorporated territory*." *American Literary History* 24 (2): 281–307. https://doi.org/10.1093/alh/ajs021.
Huang, Jiawei, Melissa S. Lucash, Robert M. Scheller, and Alexander Klippel. 2021. "Walking through the Forests of the Future: Using Data-Driven Virtual Reality to Visualize Forests under Climate Change." *International Journal of Geographical Information Science* 35 (6): 1155–78. https://doi.org/10.1080/13658816.2020.1830997.
Huang, Michelle N. 2017. "Ecologies of Entanglement in the Great Pacific Garbage Patch." *Journal of Asian American Studies* 20 (1): 95–117. https://doi.org/10.1353/jaas.2017.0006.
Hulme, Mike. 2017. *Weathered: Cultures of Climate*. London: Sage.
Hüpkes, Philip, and Gabriele Dürbeck. 2022. "The Technical Non-reproducibility of the Earth System: Scale, Biosphere 2, and T. C. Boyle's *Terranauts*." *Anthropocene Review* 9 (2): 161–74. https://doi.org/10.1177/20530196211048935.
Hurdle, John. 2009. "Philadelphia Zoo on a Mission to Save Birds." Reuters, May 28. https://www.reuters.com/article/idUSN28333690.
Hurly, Adam. 2019. "How Private Land Reserves Are Saving Endangered Species." *Men's Journal*, August 12. https://www.mensjournal.com/adventure/how-private-land-reserves-are-saving-endangered-species.
Huxley, Aldous. 1932. *Brave New World*. London: Chatto & Windus.

Iheka, Cajetan Nwabueze. 2021. *African Ecomedia: Network Forms, Planetary Politics.* Durham, NC: Duke University Press.

Ingram, Simon. 2019. "Not So Far, Far Away: Star Wars Location Shrines around the World." *National Geographic*, December 18. https://www.nationalgeographic.co.uk/travel/2019/12/not-so-far-far-away-star-wars-location-shrines-around-world.

Irfan, Umair. 2017. "Energy Hog Google Just Bought Enough Renewables to Power Its Operations for the Year." *Vox*, December 6. https://www.vox.com/energy-and-environment/2017/12/6/16734228/google-renewable-energy-wind-solar-2017.

Ishiguro, Kazuo. 2021. *Klara and the Sun.* New York: Knopf.

IUCN. n.d. "Raw Data to Red List." IUCN Red List of Threatened Species. https://www.iucnredlist.org/assessment/process. Accessed July 15, 2024.

James, Erin. 2015. *The Storyworld Accord: Econarratology and Postcolonial Narratives.* Lincoln: University of Nebraska Press.

James, Erin, and Eric Morel. 2018. "Ecocriticism and Narrative Theory: An Introduction." *English Studies* 99 (4): 355–65. https://doi.org/10.1080/0013838X.2018.1465255.

Jasanoff, Sheila. 2016. *The Ethics of Invention: Technology and the Human Future.* New York: Norton.

Jemisin, N. K. 2015. *The Fifth Season. Broken Earth*, bk. 1. New York: Orbit.

Jennings, Hope. 2010. "The Comic Apocalypse of *The Year of the Flood.*" *Margaret Atwood Studies* 3 (2): 11–18.

Jeremijenko, Natalie, and Angel Borrego Cubero. 2016. "Urban Space Station." Office for Strategic Spaces. https://www.o-s-s.org/work/urban-space-station.

Johns, J. Adam. 2010. "Becoming Medusa: Octavia Butler's *Lilith's Brood* and Sociobiology." *Science Fiction Studies* 37 (3): 382–400.

Johnson, Greg. 2022. "Dozens of Refinery Workers Face Layoffs in Sinclair." *Wyoming Tribune Eagle*, July 14. https://www.wyomingnews.com/news/local_news/dozens-of-refinery-workers-face-layoffs-in-sinclair/article_a4b54973-6a81-53e4-bfcc-0130265a398f.html.

Johnson, Ken. 2015. "Saya Woolfalk: 'ChimaTEK: Hybridity Visualization System.'" *New York Times*, February 19. https://www.nytimes.com/2015/02/20/arts/design/saya-woolfalk-chimatek-hybridity-visualization-system.html.

Johnson, Kira. 2019. "Private Lands Protecting Species." *Voices for Biodiversity* (blog), January 2. https://voicesforbiodiversity.org/articles/private-lands-protecting-species.

Johnson, Steven. 2022. "A.I. Is Mastering Language. Should We Trust What It Says?" *New York Times Magazine*, April 15. https://www.nytimes.com/2022/04/15/magazine/ai-language.html.

Johnston, Katherine D. 2017. "Metadata, Metafiction, and the Stakes of Surveillance in Jennifer Egan's *A Visit from the Goon Squad.*" *American Literature* 89 (1): 155–84. https://doi.org/10.1215/00029831-3788753.

Jones, Benjamin A., Andrew L. Goodkind, and Robert P. Berrens. 2022. "Economic Estimation of Bitcoin Mining's Climate Damages Demonstrates Closer Resemblance to Digital Crude Than Digital Gold." *Nature: Scientific Reports* 12 (14512). https://doi.org/10.1038/s41598-022-18686-8.

Jordal, J. 2019. "Splendid Waxcap (*Hygrocybe splendidissima*)." IUCN Red List of Threatened Species. https://www.iucnredlist.org/species/147321990/147999041.

Jørgensen, Dolly. 2015. "Rethinking Rewilding." *Geoforum* 65 (October): 482–88. https://doi.org/10.1016/j.geoforum.2014.11.016.

———. 2019. *Recovering Lost Species in the Modern Age: Histories of Longing and Belonging*. Cambridge, MA: MIT Press.

Kaku, Michio. 2018. *The Future of Humanity: Terraforming Mars, Interstellar Travel, Immortality, and Our Destiny beyond Earth*. New York: Doubleday.

Kalogridis, Laeta, developer. 2018–20. *Altered Carbon*. Television series. Based on the novel by Richard Morgan. Mythology Entertainment and Skydance Television.

Kareiva, Peter, and Michelle Marvier. 2012. "What Is Conservation Science?" *BioScience* 62 (11): 962–69. https://doi.org/10.1525/bio.2012.62.11.5.

———. 2013. "Shared Conservation Goals but Differing Views on How to Most Effectively Achieve Results: A Response from Kareiva and Marvier." *BioScience* 63 (4): 242–43.

Karuka, Manu. 2019. *Empire's Tracks: Indigenous Nations, Chinese Workers, and the Transcontinental Railroad*. Oakland: University of California Press.

Kehe, Jason. 2021. "Is Becky Chambers the Ultimate Hope for Science Fiction?" *Wired*, September 16. https://www.wired.com/story/is-becky-chambers-ultimate-hope-science-fiction.

Keith, David. 2021. "What's the Least Bad Way to Cool the Planet?" *New York Times*, October 1. https://www.nytimes.com/2021/10/01/opinion/climate-change-geoengineering.html.

Kelleher, Jennifer Sinco. 2013. "Mars Food Study Researchers Emerge from Dome." *Seattle Times*, August 13. https://www.seattletimes.com/nation-world/mars-food-study-researchers-emerge-from-dome.

Keller, Evelyn Fox. 1995. *Refiguring Life: Metaphors of Twentieth-Century Biology*. New York: Columbia University Press.

———. 2005. "Ecosystems, Organisms, and Machines." *BioScience* 55 (12): 1069–74.

Kellhammer, Oliver. 1988. "Forest-Model of the Universe." Oliverk:Projects. http://oliverk.org/art-projects/installations/forest-model-of-the-universe.

———. 1992. "The State of the Forest: The Canadian Landscape as Propaganda." *FUSE* 22:22–30.

———. 1997. "Memory Trees." Oliverk:Projects. http://oliverk.org/art-projects/land-art/memory-trees.

———. n.d.-a. "Biography." http://oliverk.org/node/85. Accessed July 16, 2024.

———. n.d.-b. "Neo Eocene Project." Oliverk:Projects. http://oliverk.org/art-projects/land-art/neo-eocene-project. Accessed July 15, 2024.

Kelman, Lori M., and Zvi Kelman. 1999. "The Use of Ancient DNA in Paleontological Studies." *Journal of Vertebrate Paleontology* 19 (1): 8–20.

Kennedy, John F. 1960. "The New Frontier." Acceptance speech presented at the Democratic National Convention, Los Angeles, July 15. https://www.jfklibrary.org/Asset-Viewer/AS08q5oYz0SFUZg9uOi4iw.aspx.

Kennedy, Max J. 1991. "The Evolution of the Word 'Biotechnology.'" *Trends in Biotechnology* 9: 218–20.

Kent, Charlotte. 2022. "Can You Be an NFT Artist and an Environmentalist?" *Wired*, February 17. https://www.wired.com/story/nfts-art-environment-cryptocurrency-climate-change.

Kerridge, Jake. 2021. "The Inventor of the Metaverse: 'What Matters Is Who Is Paying for It.'" *Irish Independent*, November 20. https://www.independent.ie/

entertainment/books/the-inventor-of-the-metaverse-what-matters-is-who-is-paying-for-it/41069430.html.

Kettle, Jeff. 2021. "The Internet Consumes Extraordinary Amounts of Energy: Here's How We Can Make It More Sustainable." *The Conversation*, June 9. https://theconversation.com/the-internet-consumes-extraordinary-amounts-of-energy-heres-how-we-can-make-it-more-sustainable-160639.

Kiester, A. R., R. Palomo-Ramos, J. Ríos-Arana, and E. V. Goode. 2018. "Bolson Tortoise (*Gopherus flavomarginatus*)." IUCN Red List of Threatened Species. https://www.iucnredlist.org/species/9402/112660985.

Kim, E. Tammy, and Damon Winter. 2021. "Can This Tribe of 'Salmon People' Pull Off One More Big Win?" *New York Times*, October 22.

Kincaid, Ellie. 2016. "Coming Back from Captivity." *Scienceline*, May 2. https://scienceline.org/2016/05/coming-back-from-captivity.

Kirk, Andrew G. 2007. *Counterculture Green: The Whole Earth Catalog and American Environmentalism*. Lawrence: University Press of Kansas.

Kirschenbaum, Matthew. 2023. "Prepare for the Textpocalypse." *The Atlantic*, March 8. https://www.theatlantic.com/technology/archive/2023/03/ai-chatgpt-writing-language-models/673318.

Kirstein, Inga Vanessa, Antje Wichels, Elisabeth Gullans, Georg Krohne, and Gunnar Gerdts. 2019. "The Plastisphere—Uncovering Tightly Attached Plastic 'Specific' Microorganisms." *PLOS One* 14 (4): e0215859. https://doi.org/10.1371/journal.pone.0215859.

"Kistler in New Company." 1926. *New York Times*, September 18.

Klein, Naomi. 2014. *This Changes Everything: Capitalism vs. the Climate*. New York: Simon & Schuster.

Klop-Toker, Kaya, Simon Clulow, Craig Shuttleworth, and Matt W. Hayward. 2020. "Are Novel Ecosystems the Only Novelty of Rewilding?" *Restoration Ecology* 28 (6): 1318–20. https://doi.org/10.1111/rec.13241.

Knight, Will. 2023. "Some Glimpse AGI in ChatGPT: Others Call It a Mirage." *Wired*, April 18. https://www.wired.com/story/chatgpt-agi-intelligence.

Knighton, Mary A. 2019. "Guam, Un-Inc.; or, Craig Santos Perez's Transterritorial Challenge to American Studies as Usual." In *The Routledge Companion to Transnational American Studies*, ed. Nina Morgan, Alfred Hornung, and Takayuki Tatsumi, 338–46. New York: Routledge.

Knott, Gavin J., and Jennifer A. Doudna. 2018. "CRISPR-Cas Guides the Future of Genetic Engineering." *Science* 361 (6405): 866–69. https://doi.org/10.1126/science.aat5011.

Koch, Natalie. 2021. "*Whose* Apocalypse? Biosphere 2 and the Spectacle of Settler Science in the Desert." *Geoforum* 124 (August): 36–45. https://doi.org/10.1016/j.geoforum.2021.05.015.

Kolbert, Elizabeth. 2014. *The Sixth Extinction: An Unnatural History*. London: Bloomsbury.

———. 2021a. "CRISPR and the Splice to Survive." *New Yorker*, January 11. https://www.newyorker.com/magazine/2021/01/18/crispr-and-the-splice-to-survive.

———. 2021b. *Under a White Sky: The Nature of the Future*. New York: Crown.

Konstantinou, Lee. 2019. "Something Is Broken in Our Science Fiction." *Slate*, January 15. https://slate.com/technology/2019/01/hopepunk-cyberpunk-solarpunk-science-fiction-broken.html.

Koppes, Clayton R. 1982. *JPL and the American Space Program: A History of the Jet Propulsion Laboratory*. New Haven, CT: Yale University Press.

Kornfeldt, Torill. 2018. *The Re-Origin of Species: A Second Chance for Extinct Animals*. Translated by Fiona Graham. New York: Scribe.

Kosaka, Kris. 2013. "Ozeki's Work Reflects Her Complex Identity." *Japan Times*, November 23. https://www.japantimes.co.jp/culture/2013/11/23/books/ozekis-work-reflects-her-complex-identity.

Krainin, Todd. 2015. "Jurassic Pigeon." *Reason: Free Minds and Free Markets*, July 5. https://reason.com/2015/07/05/jurassic-pigeon-2.

Kralicek, Karin, Jay M. Ver Hoef, Tara M. Barrett, and Hailemariam Temesgen. 2023. "Spatial Bayesian Models Project Shifts in Suitable Habitat for Pacific Northwest Tree Species under Climate Change." *Ecosphere* 14 (3): e4449. https://doi.org/10.1002/ecs2.4449.

Lai, Paul. 2011. "Discontiguous States of America: The Paradox of Unincorporation in Craig Santos Perez's Poetics of Chamorro Guam." *Journal of Transnational American Studies* 3 (2): 1–28. https://doi.org/10.5070/T832011622.

Lakhani, Nina. 2019. "The Lost River: Mexicans Fight for Mighty Waterway Taken by the US." *The Guardian*, October 21. https://www.theguardian.com/environment/2019/oct/21/the-lost-river-mexicans-fight-for-mighty-waterway-taken-by-the-us.

Lan, Yifan, Cuicui Zhang, and Hao Wei. 2023. "Projection of Future Long-Term Aurelia Coerulea Biomass Variability by Regional Moderate-Temperature-Duration Approach in the Bohai and Yellow Seas." *Ecological Indicators* 150 (June): 110257.

Landecker, Hannah. 2007. *Culturing Life: How Cells Became Technologies*. Cambridge, MA: Harvard University Press.

Lander, Joan, and Puhipau, dirs. 2006. *Mauna Kea—Temple under Siege*. https://vimeo.com/ondemand/maunakeatempleundersiege.

Land Report. 2024. "Land Report 100: Who Is America's Largest Landowner?" https://landreport.com/land-report-100.

Lanier, Jaron. 2010. *You Are Not a Gadget: A Manifesto*. New York: Knopf.

Lee, Felicia R. 2013. "What the Tide Brought In." *New York Times*, March 12. https://www.nytimes.com/2013/03/13/books/ruth-ozekis-new-novel-is-a-tale-for-the-time-being.html.

Lee, Stephan. 2011. "'A Visit from the Goon Squad': First a Pulitzer, Now an HBO Show." *Entertainment Weekly*, April 29. https://ew.com/article/2011/04/29/visit-goon-squad-first-pulitzer-now-hbo-show.

LeMenager, Stephanie. 2014. *Living Oil: Petroleum Culture in the American Century*. Oxford: Oxford University Press.

———. 2017. "The Humanities After the Anthropocene." In *The Routledge Companion to the Environmental Humanities*, ed. Ursula K. Heise, Jon Christensen, and Michelle Niemann, 473–81. New York: Routledge.

Lesk, Michael. 1997. "How Much Information Is There in the World?" https://www.lesk.com/mlesk/ksg97/ksg.html.

Levin, Jonathan. 2011. "Contemporary Ecofiction." In *The Cambridge History of the American Novel*, ed. Leonard Cassuto, Clare Virginia Eby, and Benjamin Reiss, 1122–36. Cambridge: Cambridge University Press.

Levy, David M. 2016. *Scrolling Forward: Making Sense of Documents in the Digital Age*. 2nd ed. New York: Arcade.

Levy, Steven. 2012. "Google Throws Open Doors to Its Top Secret Data Center." *Wired*, October 17. https://www.wired.com/2012/10/ff-inside-google-data-center.

———. 2018. "Jeff Bezos Wants Us All to Leave Earth—for Good." *Wired*, October 15. https://www.wired.com/story/jeff-bezos-blue-origin.

Linton, Jamie. 2010. *What Is Water? The History of a Modern Abstraction*. Vancouver: University of British Columbia Press.

Liptak, Andrew. 2017. "Annihilation Author Jeff VanderMeer on How His Next Novel Is Inspired by Our Dystopian Present." *The Verge*, October 3. https://www.theverge.com/2017/10/3/16387840/annihilation-jeff-vandermeer-hummingbird-salamander-borne-science-fiction-climate-change.

Liu, Alan. 2004. *The Laws of Cool: Knowledge Work and the Culture of Information*. Chicago: University of Chicago Press.

Lohr, Steve. 2020. "Cloud Computing Is Not the Energy Hog That Had Been Feared." *New York Times*, February 27. https://www.nytimes.com/2020/02/27/technology/cloud-computing-energy-usage.html.

Long Now Foundation. n.d. "The Clock of the Long Now." https://longnow.org/clock. Accessed July 15, 2024.

Lorimer, Jamie. 2015. *Wildlife in the Anthropocene: Conservation after Nature*. Minneapolis: University of Minnesota Press.

Los Angeles County Public Works. n.d. "Water Supply: Imported Water." https://dpw.lacounty.gov/landing/wr/watersupply/importedWater.cfm. Accessed July 15, 2024.

Louis, David. 2015. "Oil Shaped the History of Parco/Sinclair." *Rawlins Times*, August 15. https://www.wyomingnews.com/rawlinstimes/news/oil-shaped-the-history-of-parco-sinclair/article_5215be1f-a65a-5c52-bc59-7f02ca1d6099.html.

Luce, Henry. 1941. "The American Century." *Life Magazine*, February 1941.

Lummi Nation Natural Resources. n.d. "Salmon Enhancement." https://www.lummi-nsn.gov/Website.php?PageID=43. Accessed July 16, 2024.

Malarcher, Patricia. 2013. "Utopia Now: Saya Woolfalk's Magical World." *Surface Design Journal* 37 (4): 6–11.

Mancuso, Cecilia. 2021. "Multiplicative Speculations: What We Can Learn from the Rise and Fall of Hopepunk." *ASAP/Journal* 6 (2): 459–83. https://doi.org/10.1353/asa.2021.0031.

Markley, Robert. 1997. "Falling into Theory: Simulation, Terraformation, and Eco-economics in Kim Stanley Robinson's Martian Trilogy." *Modern Fiction Studies* 43 (3): 773–99.

Marris, Emma. 2011. *Rambunctious Garden: Saving Nature in a Post-wild World*. New York: Bloomsbury.

Marris, Emma, Peter Kareiva, Joseph Mascaro, and Erle C. Ellis. 2011. "Hope in the Age of Man." *New York Times*, December 7. https://www.nytimes.com/2011/12/08/opinion/the-age-of-man-is-not-a-disaster.html.

Marshall, Kate. 2015. "What Are the Novels of the Anthropocene? American Fiction in Geological Time." *American Literary History* 27 (3): 523–38.

———. 2016. "The Old Weird." *Modernism/Modernity* 23 (3): 631–49.

Mars Society. n.d. "About the Mars Society." https://www.marssociety.org/why-mars. Accessed July 16, 2024.

Martin, Paul S. 1992. "The Last Entire Earth." *Wild Earth* 2 (4): 29–32.

———. 2005. *Twilight of the Mammoths: Ice Age Extinctions and the Rewilding of America*. Berkeley: University of California Press.

Martine, Arkady. 2019. "Clarity Isn't the Point in Confusing, Absorbing 'Dead Astronauts.'" NPR, December 7. https://www.npr.org/2019/12/07/785536098/clarity-isnt-the-point-in-confusing-absorbing-dead-astronauts.

Marvier, Michelle, Peter Kareiva, and Robert Lalasz. 2011. "Conservation in the Anthropocene: Beyond Solitude and Fragility." *Breakthrough Journal* 2:1–6.

Masanet, Eric, Arman Shehabi, Nuoa Lei, Sarah Smith, and Jonathan Koomey. 2020. "Recalibrating Global Data Center Energy-Use Estimates." *Science* 367 (6481): 984–86. https://doi.org/10.1126/science.aba3758.

Masco, Joseph. 2004. "Mutant Ecologies: Radioactive Life in Post–Cold War New Mexico." *Cultural Anthropology* 19 (4): 517–50. https://doi.org/10.1525/can.2004.19.4.517.

Mason, Ben Young, and Justin Wilkes, creators. 2016–18. *Mars*. Television series. National Geographic. https://www.nationalgeographic.com/tv/shows/mars.

Massenberg, Julian R., Johannes Schiller, and Christoph Schröter-Schlaack. 2023. "Towards a Holistic Approach to Rewilding in Cultural Landscapes." *People and Nature* 5 (1): 45–56. https://doi.org/10.1002/pan3.10426.

Maunakea Observatories. 2020. "About." https://maunakeaobservatories.org/about.

Maxwell, Richard, and Toby Miller. 2012. *Greening the Media*. Oxford: Oxford University Press.

———. 2020. *How Green Is Your Smartphone?* Cambridge: Polity.

McKenzie, James. 2021. "Powering the Beast: Why We Shouldn't Worry about the Internet's Rising Electricity Consumption." *Physics World*, January 13. https://physicsworld.com/powering-the-beast-why-we-shouldnt-worry-about-the-internets-rising-electricity-consumption.

McKibben, Bill. 1989a. *The End of Nature*. New York: Random House.

———. 1989b. "The End of Nature." *New Yorker*, September 3. https://www.newyorker.com/magazine/1989/09/11/the-end-of-nature.

———. 2011. *Eaarth: Making Life on a Tough New Planet*. New York: St. Martin's Griffin.

McLaughlin, Katherine. 2022. "You Won't Believe Work Gets Done at These Three Google Offices." *Architectural Digest*, December 7. https://www.architecturaldigest.com/story/inside-google-offices.

McMillan, Robert. 2012. "Wired Scores Exclusive Aerial Photos of Apple's 'Area i51.'" *Wired*, April. https://www.wired.com/2012/04/apples-secret-data-center.

Meehan, Mary Beth, and Fred Turner. 2021. *Seeing Silicon Valley: Life inside a Fraying America*. Chicago: University of Chicago Press.

Meltzer, David J. 2015. "Pleistocene Overkill and North American Mammalian Extinctions." *Annual Review of Anthropology* 44 (October): 33–53. https://doi.org/10.1146/annurev-anthro-102214-013854.

Messeri, Lisa. 2016. *Placing Outer Space: An Earthly Ethnography of Other Worlds*. Durham, NC: Duke University Press.

———. 2017. "Gestures of Cosmic Relation and the Search for Another Earth." *Environmental Humanities* 9 (2): 325–40.

Meta. 2021. "Sustainability Report." https://sustainability.fb.com/wp-content/uploads/2022/06/Meta-2021-Sustainability-Report.pdf.

———. n.d. "What Is the Metaverse?" https://about.meta.com/what-is-the-metaverse. Accessed July 16, 2024.

Metz, Cade, and Tripp Mickle. 2024. "OpenAI Completes Deal That Values the Company at $80 Billion." *New York Times,* February 16. https://www.nytimes.com/2024/02/16/technology/openai-artificial-intelligence-deal-valuation.html.

Microsoft. n.d. "About." https://www.microsoft.com/en-us/about. Accessed July 16, 2024.

Microsoft Unlocked. n.d. "Water Works." https://unlocked.microsoft.com/water-works. Accessed July 16, 2024.

Milburn, Colin. 2012. "Greener on the Other Side: Science Fiction and the Problem of Green Nanotechnology." *Configurations* 20 (1–2): 53–87. https://doi.org/10.1353/con.2012.0008.

Miles, Jonathan. 2016. "T. C. Boyle's New Novel Taps the Biosphere's Erotic Potential." *New York Times,* November 11. https://www.nytimes.com/2016/11/13/books/review/t-c-boyle-terranauts.html?_r=0.

Miller, Laura. 2017. "Jeff VanderMeer Amends the Apocalypse." *New Yorker,* April 17. https://www.newyorker.com/magazine/2017/04/24/jeff-vandermeer-amends-the-apocalypse.

Minteer, Ben A. 2019. *The Fall of the Wild: Extinction, De-extinction, and the Ethics of Conservation.* New York: Columbia University Press.

Mitchell, Robert. 2010. *Bioart and the Vitality of Media.* Seattle: University of Washington Press.

Moncada Storti, Anna M. 2020. "Scenes of Hope, Acts of Despair: Deidealizing Hybridity in Saya Woolfalk's World of the Empathics." *Frontiers: A Journal of Women Studies* 41 (3): 147–77. https://doi.org/10.1353/fro.2020.0032.

Moore, Lorrie. 2003. "Bioperversity: Margaret Atwood's Genetically Engineered Nightmare." *New Yorker,* May 11. https://www.newyorker.com/magazine/2003/05/19/bioperversity.

Moore, Mike. 2022. "A Brief History of Corte, Forestry and Mosaic." *Cortes Currents* (blog), March 15. https://cortescurrents.ca/a-brief-history-of-cortes-forestry-and-mosaic.

Moore, Ronald D., developer. 2004–9. *Battlestar Galactica.* Television series. NBC Universal Television.

Morse, Nathaniel B., Paul A. Pellissier, Elisabeth N. Cianciola, Richard L. Brereton, Marleigh M. Sullivan, Nicholas K. Shonka, Tessa B. Wheeler, and William H. McDowell. 2014. "Novel Ecosystems in the Anthropocene: A Revision of the Novel Ecosystem Concept for Pragmatic Applications." *Ecology and Society* 19 (2): 12.

Morton, Adam. 2022. "De-extinction: Scientists Are Planning the Multimillion-Dollar Resurrection of the Tasmanian Tiger." *The Guardian,* August 16. https://www.theguardian.com/australia-news/2022/aug/16/de-extinction-scientists-are-planning-the-multimillion-dollar-resurrection-of-the-tasmanian-tiger.

Mueller, Tom. 2009. "Recipe for a Resurrection." *National Geographic,* May. https://www.nationalgeographic.com/magazine/article/cloned-species.

Murcia, Carolina, James Aronson, Gustavo H. Kattan, David Moreno-Mateos, Kingsley Dixon, and Daniel Simberloff. 2014. "A Critique of the 'Novel Ecosystem' Concept." *Trends in Ecology and Evolution* 29 (10): 548–53. https://doi.org/10.1016/j.tree.2014.07.006.

Murphy, Patrick D. 2009. "Engineering Planets, Engineering Ourselves: The Ethics of Terraforming and Areoforming in an Age of Climate Change." *Journal of Ecocriticism* 1 (1): 54–59.

Musk, Elon. 2015. "Terraforming a new home (Mars) is a far better use for nuclear weapons than genocide." @BoredElonMusk. Twitter, September 10, 10:36 a.m. https://twitter.com/BoredElonMusk/status/641998719378808832.

———. 2016. "Making Humans a Multiplanetary Species." Presented at the Sixty-seventh International Astronautical Congress, Guadalajara, Mexico, September 27. https://nss.org/elon-musk-making-humans-a-multiplanetary-species.

———. 2017a. "GNF Elon Musk Presentation." Presented at the Sixty-eighth International Astronautical Congress, Adelaide, Australia, September 29. https://www.iafastro.org/media/videos/gnf-elon-musk-presentation.html.

———. 2017b. "Making Humans a Multi-planetary Species." *New Space* 5 (2): 46–61.

Nakamura, Lisa. 2007. *Digitizing Race: Visual Cultures of the Internet*. Minneapolis: University of Minnesota Press.

NASA. 2008. "Cone Nebula." Image article, March 23. https://www.nasa.gov/image-article/cone-nebula/.

———. 2020a. "Artemis Plan: NASA's Lunar Exploration Program Overview." September. https://www.nasa.gov/wp-content/uploads/2020/12/artemis_plan-20200921.pdf?emrc=f43185. See also https://www.nasa.gov/specials/artemis/index.html.

———. 2020b. "Veggie." NASA Fact Sheet. https://www.nasa.gov/sites/default/files/atoms/files/veggie_fact_sheet_508.pdf.

———. 2023. "Growing Plants in Space." Exploration Research and Technology. Updated December 8. http://www.nasa.gov/content/growing-plants-in-space.

———. 2024a. "HI-SEAS: The Hawai'i Space Exploration Analog and Simulation, Mauna Loa, Hawai'i." Goddard Earth Sciences Division Projects. Updated July 25. https://earth.gsfc.nasa.gov/acd/campaigns/hi-seas.

———. 2024b. "Hubble Science Highlights." Updated June. https://science.nasa.gov/mission/hubble/science/science-highlights.

———. 2024c. "Hubble's Deep Fields." Updated March. https://science.nasa.gov/mission/hubble/science/universe-uncovered/hubble-deep-fields.

———. 2024d. "Kepler/K2 Overview." Updated February. http://www.nasa.gov/mission_pages/kepler/overview/index.html.

———. n.d. "Missions: Pioneer 10 & Pioneer 11." Archived February 28, 2024, at the Wayback Machine. https://web.archive.org/web/20240228030517/https://rps.nasa.gov/missions/10/pioneer-10-11/.

NASA/JPL. 2020. "Visions of the Future." December 24. http://www.jpl.nasa.gov/visions-of-the-future.

NASA/OSMA. 2023. "Planetary Protection." Office of Safety and Mission Assurance. December 15. https://sma.nasa.gov/sma-disciplines/planetary-protection.

National Park Service. 2020. "The 'Underground' Air Force: Minuteman Missile National Historic Site." October 20. https://www.nps.gov/articles/mimiarmsrace-08.htm.

Neilson, Sarah. 2022. "A Conversation on Radical Acts with Award-Winning Sci-Fi Author Becky Chambers." *Seattle Times*, July 12. https://www.seattletimes.com/entertainment/books/a-conversation-on-radical-acts-with-award-winning-sci-fi-author-becky-chambers.

Next Nature. n.d. Home page. https://www.nextnature.net. Accessed July 16, 2024.

Nieves, Evelyn. 2018. "The Superfund Sites of Silicon Valley." *New York Times*, March 26. https://www.nytimes.com/2018/03/26/lens/the-superfund-sites-of-silicon-valley.html.

Nisbet, James. 2017. "Contemporary Environmental Art." In *The Routledge Companion to the Environmental Humanities*, ed. Ursula K. Heise, Jon Christensen, and Michelle Niemann, 301–12. New York: Routledge.

North, Michael. 2013. *Novelty: A History of the New*. Chicago: University of Chicago Press.

Nye, David E. 1994. *American Technological Sublime*. Cambridge, MA: MIT Press.

OCLC. 2018. "'Ti:Biodiversity>1980 . . . 1988.'" WorldCat. https://www.worldcat.org/search?q=ti%3Abiodiversity&fq=yr%3A1980..1988+%3E&qt=advanced&dblist=638.

———. 2023. "'Ti:Biodiversity>1989 . . . 2022.'" WorldCat. https://www.worldcat.org/search?q=ti%3Abiodiversity&fq=yr%3A1989..2022+%3E&qt=advanced&dblist=638.

Ohman, Mark. 2019. "Voyager: How Are Jellyfish Connected to Climate Change?" Scripps Institution of Oceanography, October 29. https://scripps.ucsd.edu/news/voyager-how-are-jellyfish-connected-climate-change.

O'Malley, Michael, and Roy Rosenzweig. 1997. "Brave New World or Blind Alley? American History on the World Wide Web." *Journal of American History* 84 (1): 132–55.

O'Mara, Margaret. 2019a. "The Church of Techno-Optimism." *New York Times*, September 28. https://www.nytimes.com/2019/09/28/opinion/sunday/silicon-valley-techno-optimism.html.

———. 2019b. *The Code: Silicon Valley and the Remaking of America*. New York: Penguin.

OpenAI. 2023. "Planning for AGI and Beyond." February 24. https://openai.com/blog/planning-for-agi-and-beyond.

Oreskes, Naomi. 2004. "The Scientific Consensus on Climate Change." *Science* 306 (5702): 1686. https://doi.org/10.1126/science.1103618.

———. 2007. "The Scientific Consensus on Climate Change: How Do We Know We're Not Wrong?" In *Climate Change: What It Means for Us, Our Children, and Our Grandchildren*, ed. Joseph F. Dimento and Pamela Doughman, 65–100. Cambridge, MA: MIT Press.

Oreskes, Naomi, and Erik M. Conway. 2010a. "Defeating the Merchants of Doubt." *Nature* 465 (7299): 686–87. https://doi.org/10.1038/465686a.

———. 2010b. *Merchants of Doubt: How a Handful of Scientists Obscured the Truth on Issues from Tobacco Smoke to Global Warming*. New York: Bloomsbury.

Owen, David. 2017. *Where the Water Goes: Life and Death along the Colorado River*. New York: Riverhead.

Oxford English Dictionary. 2023a. "Bio- (comb. form)." December. https://doi.org/10.1093/OED/2063768136.

———. 2023b. "Footprint (n.)." July. https://doi.org/10.1093/OED/5563219722.

———. 2024. "Cloud (n.)." June. https://doi.org/10.1093/OED/1057708127.

Ozeki, Ruth L. 1998. *My Year of Meats*. New York: Penguin.

———. 2003. *All over Creation*. New York: Penguin.

———. 2013a. "A Crucial Collaboration: Reader-Writer-Character-Book." *Poets and Writers*, June. http://www.pw.org/content/crucial_collaboration_readerwritercharacterbook.

———. 2013b. *A Tale for the Time Being*. New York: Viking.

———. 2016. "Foreword." In *Scrolling Forward: Making Sense of Documents in the Digital Age*, by David Levy, xiii–xvi. New York: Arcade.

———. 2022. *The Book of Form and Emptiness*. New York: Penguin.

Pak, Chris. 2016. *Terraforming: Ecopolitical Transformations and Environmentalism in Science Fiction*. Liverpool: Liverpool University Press.

Parks, Lisa, and Nicole Starosielski, eds. 2015. *Signal Traffic: Critical Studies of Media Infrastructures*. Champaign: University of Illinois Press.

Pellow, David N., and Lisa Sun-Hee Park. 2002. *The Silicon Valley of Dreams: Environmental Injustice, Immigrant Workers, and the High-Tech Global Economy*. New York: New York University Press.

Perez, Craig Santos. 2008. *from unincorporated territory [hacha]*. Kaneohe, HI: TinFish.

———. 2010. *from unincorporated territory [saina]*. Richmond, CA: Omnidawn.

———. 2011. "'*from* achiote'; '*from* tidelands'; '*from* The Micronesian Kingfishers.'" *Journal of Transnational American Studies* 3 (2). https://doi.org/10.5070/T832011623.

———. 2014. *from unincorporated territory [guma']*. Richmond, CA: Omnidawn.

———. 2015. "Transterritorial Currents and the Imperial Terripelago." *American Quarterly* 67 (3): 619–24. https://doi.org/10.1353/aq.2015.0044.

———. 2016. "A Testimony Before the United Nations." *Diálogo* 19 (1): 153–56. https://doi.org/10.1353/dlg.2016.0016.

———. 2017. *from unincorporated territory [lukao]*. Richmond, CA: Omnidawn.

———. 2020. "Love in a Time of Climate Change." In *Habitat Threshold*. Richmond, CA: Omnidawn Publishing.

———. 2021. *Navigating CHamoru Poetry: Indigeneity, Aesthetics, and Decolonization*. Tucson: University of Arizona Press.

———. 2023. *from unincorporated territory [åmot]*. Oakland, CA: Omnidawn.

Philadelphia Zoo. n.d. "Guam Kingfisher Conservation." https://www.philadelphiazoo.org/guam-kingfisher-conservation. Accessed July 15, 2024.

Pierce, Daniel J. 2016. "Prehistoric Trees Could 'Future-Proof' Forests against Climate Change." *Vice* (blog), October 24. https://www.vice.com/en/article/kb7xde/prehistoric-trees-could-future-proof-forests-against-climate-change.

Platt, Kalvin. 2008. "Foster City—a New City on the Bay: A Tribute to Professor McDougall." *Focus* 5 (1). https://doi.org/10.15368/focus.2008v5n1.3.

Poinar, George O. 1992. *Life in Amber*. Stanford, CA: Stanford University Press.

Poinar, George O., and Roberta Hess. 1982. "Ultrastructure of 40-Million-Year-Old Insect Tissue." *Science* 215 (4537): 1241–42.

Polyak, V. J., Yemane Asmerom, Stephen Burns, and Matthew S. Lachniet. 2012. "Climatic Backdrop to the Terminal Pleistocene Extinction of North American Mammals." *Geology* 40 (11): 1023–26. https://doi.org/10.1130/G33226.1.

Poynter, Jane. 2006. *The Human Experiment: Two Years and Twenty Minutes inside Biosphere 2*. New York: Thunder's Mouth.

Press, Gil. 2013. "A Very Short History of Big Data." *Forbes*, May 9. https://www.forbes.com/sites/gilpress/2013/05/09/a-very-short-history-of-big-data.

Preston, Christopher. 2018. *The Synthetic Age: Outdesigning Evolution, Resurrecting Species, and Reengineering Our World*. Cambridge, MA: MIT Press.

ProPublica. 2021. "Revive and Restore: Form 990: Return of Organization Exempt from Income Tax." Nonprofit Explorer. https://projects.propublica.org/nonprofits/organizations/814576399/202201369349311015/full.

———. 2023. "Revive & Restore." Nonprofit Explorer, November 30. https://projects.propublica.org/nonprofits/organizations/814576399.

Quammen, David. 1998. "Planet of Weeds." *Harper's Magazine*, October. https://harpers.org/archive/1998/10/planet-of-weeds.

Radford, Tim. 1996. "Mammoth Task or White Elephant?" *The Guardian*, August 20.

Rathi, Akshat. 2016. "What Could Wreck Elon Musk's Plan to Colonize Mars Isn't Science, Technology, or Money—It's Ethics." *Quartz* (blog), September 28. https://qz.com/794307/what-could-wreck-spacex-founder-elon-musks-plan-to-colonize-mars-is-not-technology-politics-or-money-but-ethics.

Reilly, Charlie. 2009. "An Interview with Jennifer Egan." *Contemporary Literature* 50 (3): 439–60.

Reisner, Marc. 1986. *Cadillac Desert: The American West and Its Disappearing Water*. New York: Viking.

Revive and Restore. 2023. "Annual Report." https://reviverestore.org/wp-content/uploads/2023/12/2023-RR-Annual-Report_OPTIMIZED-1.pdf.

———. n.d.-a. "Passenger Pigeon Project." https://reviverestore.org/about-the-passenger-pigeon. Accessed July 15, 2024.

———. n.d.-b. "What Is 'Genetic Rescue'?" https://reviverestore.org/what-we-do/genetic-rescue-toolkit. Accessed July 15, 2024.

Rich, Nathaniel. 2014. "The Mammoth Cometh." *New York Times Magazine*, February 27. https://www.nytimes.com/2014/03/02/magazine/the-mammoth-cometh.html.

———. 2021. *Second Nature: Scenes from a World Remade*. New York: MCD/Farrar, Straus & Giroux.

Robinson, Kim Stanley. 1993. *Red Mars*. Mars Trilogy, bk. 1. New York: Bantam.

———. 1994. *Green Mars*. Mars Trilogy, bk. 2. New York: Bantam.

———. 1996. *Blue Mars*. Mars Trilogy, bk. 3. New York: Bantam.

———. 2013. "California: The Planet of the Future—the *Boom* Interview." *Boom: A Journal of California* 3 (4): 3–11. https://doi.org/10.1525/boom.2013.3.4.3.

Romano, Aja. 2018. "Hopepunk, the Latest Storytelling Trend, Is All about Weaponized Optimism." *Vox*, December 27. https://www.vox.com/2018/12/27/18137571/what-is-hopepunk-noblebright-grimdark.

Roose, Kevin. 2023. "A Conversation with Bing's Chatbot Left Me Deeply Unsettled." *New York Times*, February 16. https://www.nytimes.com/2023/02/16/technology/bing-chatbot-microsoft-chatgpt.html.

Roosth, Sophia. 2017. *Synthetic: How Life Got Made*. Chicago: University of Chicago Press.

Rosetta Project. n.d. "About." https://rosettaproject.org/about. Accessed July 16, 2024.

Rothman, Joshua. 2015. "The Weird Thoreau." *New Yorker*, January 14. https://www.newyorker.com/culture/cultural-comment/weird-thoreau-jeff-vandermeer-southern-reach.

———. 2022. "Can Science Fiction Wake Us Up to Our Climate Reality?" *New Yorker*, January 24. https://www.newyorker.com/magazine/2022/01/31/can-science-fiction-wake-us-up-to-our-climate-reality-kim-stanley-robinson.

Roush, Wade. 2005. "Amazon: Giving Away the Store." *MIT Technology Review*, January 1. https://www.technologyreview.com/2005/01/01/231797/amazon-giving-away-the-store-2.

Rowling, J. K. 2001. *Fantastic Beasts and Where to Find Them*. New York: Arthur A. Levine.

Royal Swedish Academy of Sciences. 2020. "Press Release: The Nobel Prize in Chemistry 2020." October 7. https://www.nobelprize.org/prizes/chemistry/2020/press-release.

Ruas, Carla. 2020. "Report: Oil and Gas Drilling on Public Lands Is Fueling Climate Change." *Wilderness Society* (blog), February 12. https://www.wilderness.org/news/blog/report-oil-and-gas-drilling-public-lands-fueling-climate-change.

Rubenstein, Dustin R., and Daniel I. Rubenstein. 2013. "From Pleistocene to Trophic Rewilding: A Wolf in Sheep's Clothing." *Proceedings of the National Academy of Sciences* 113 (1): E1.

Rubenstein, Dustin R., Daniel I. Rubenstein, Paul W. Sherman, and Thomas A. Gavin. 2006. "Pleistocene Park: Does Re-wilding North America Represent Sound Conservation for the 21st Century?" *Biological Conservation* 132 (2): 232–38.

Rubenstein, Mary-Jane. 2022. *Astrotopia: The Dangerous Religion of the Corporate Space Race*. Chicago: University of Chicago Press.

Ruzicka, James J., Elizabeth A. Daly, and Richard D. Brodeur. 2016. "Evidence That Summer Jellyfish Blooms Impact Pacific Northwest Salmon Production." *Ecosphere* 7 (4): 1–22. https://doi.org/10.1002/ecs2.1324.

Sahagun, Louis. 2013. "The L.A. Aqueduct at 100." *Los Angeles Times*, October 28. http://graphics.latimes.com/me-aqueduct.

Salam, Erum. 2023. "Bitcoin Is Terrible for the Environment: Can It Ever Go Green?" *The Guardian*, April 26. https://www.theguardian.com/technology/2023/apr/26/bitcoin-mining-climate-crisis-environmental-impact.

Salazar, Juan Francisco. 2017. "Microbial Geographies at the Extremes of Life." *Environmental Humanities* 9 (2): 398–417.

Sammler, Katherine G., and Casey R. Lynch. 2021. "Apparatuses of Observation and Occupation: Settler Colonialism and Space Science in Hawai'i." *Environment and Planning D: Society and Space* 39 (5): 945–65. https://doi.org/10.1177/02637758211042374.

Sawyer, Andy. 2009. "Space Opera." In *The Routledge Companion to Science Fiction*, ed. Mark Bould, Andrew M. Butler, Adam Roberts, and Sherryl Vint, 505–9. New York: Routledge.

Schiebinger, Londa L. 2004. *Plants and Empire: Colonial Bioprospecting in the Atlantic World*. Cambridge, MA: Harvard University Press.

Schlossberg, Tatiana. 2019. "Silicon Valley Is One of the Most Polluted Places in the Country." *The Atlantic*, September 22. https://www.theatlantic.com/technology/archive/2019/09/silicon-valley-full-superfund-sites/598531.

Schuler, Timothy A. 2019. "Open Office." *Landscape Architecture Magazine*, January 31. https://landscapearchitecturemagazine.org/2019/01/31/open-office.

Schwetman, John D. 2021. "'There Is No Plan B': Anthropocene Architecture in T. C. Boyle's *The Terranauts*." *Western American Literature* 56 (1): 55–79. https://doi.org/10.1353/wal.2021.0014.

SEADS (Space Ecologies Art and Design). n.d.-a. "Biomodd." https://seads.network/hyperproject/biomodd. Accessed July 15, 2024.

———. n.d.-b. Home page. https://seads.network. Accessed July 15, 2024.

———. n.d.-c. "Merapi Terraforming Project." https://seads.network/project/merapiterraformingproject. Accessed July 15, 2024.

———. n.d.-d. "Seeker." https://seads.network/hyperproject/seeker. Accessed July 15, 2024.

Seattle Art Museum. n.d. Articles referring to Saya Woolfalk on *SAM Stories* blog. https://samblog.seattleartmuseum.org/tag/saya-woolfalk/. Accessed July 25, 2024.

Seddon, Philip J., Axel Moehrenschlager, and John Ewen. 2014. "Reintroducing Resurrected Species: Selecting DeExtinction Candidates." *Trends in Ecology and Evolution* 29 (3): 140–47. https://doi.org/10.1016/j.tree.2014.01.007.

Sendur, Elif. 2020. "Undoing Bodies: Tentacular Spaces and Sympoiesis in Octavia Butler's *Lilith's Brood*." *Studies in the Humanities* 46 (1–2): 117–133.

Seymour, Nicole. 2012. "Toward an Irreverent Ecocriticism." *Journal of Ecocriticism* 4 (2): 56–71.

———. 2018. *Bad Environmentalism: Irony and Irreverence in the Ecological Age*. Minneapolis: University of Minnesota Press.

Shapiro, Beth. 2015. *How to Clone a Mammoth: The Science of De-extinction*. Princeton, NJ: Princeton University Press.

———. 2017. "Pathways to De-extinction: How Close Can We Get to Resurrection of an Extinct Species?" *Functional Ecology* 31 (5): 996–1002. https://doi.org/10.1111/1365-2435.12705.

———. 2021. *Life as We Made It: How 50,000 Years of Human Innovation Refined—and Redefined—Nature*. New York: Basic.

Shaw, Tamsin. 2022. "How Social Media Influences Our Behavior, and Vice Versa." *New York Times*, September 1. https://www.nytimes.com/2022/09/01/books/review/max-fisher-chaos-machine.html.

Sherkow, Jacob. 2015. "BioSci Fi: *Oryx and Crake*, Margaret Atwood, 2003." *Stanford Law and Biosciences Blog*, September 27. https://law.stanford.edu/2015/09/27/biosci-fi-oryx-and-crake-margaret-atwood-2003.

Shulevitz, Judith. 2021. "The Radiant Inner Life of a Robot." *The Atlantic*, March 2. https://www.theatlantic.com/magazine/archive/2021/04/kazuo-ishiguro-klara-and-the-sun/618083.

Siceloff, Steven. 2015. "HI-SEAS Team Completes 8-Month Isolation Mission." NASA, June 19. https://www.nasa.gov/feature/hi-seas-team-completes-8-month-isolation-mission.

Sinha, Indra. 2007. *Animal's People*. New York: Simon & Schuster.

Skipper, Joe, and Joey Roulette. 2023. "Elon Musk's SpaceX Set for Debut Flight of Starship Rocket System to Space." Reuters, April 17. https://www.reuters.com/business/aerospace-defense/elon-musks-spacex-set-debut-flight-starship-rocket-system-space-2023-04-17.

Smith, S. E. 2011. "Dirty, Dangerous and Destructive—the Elements of a Technology Boom." *The Guardian*, September 26. https://www.theguardian.com/commentisfree/2011/sep/26/rare-earth-metals-technology-boom.

Smith, Tracy K. 2011. *Life on Mars*. Minneapolis, MN: Graywolf.

Socolow, Robert H. 2012. "Truths We Must Tell Ourselves to Manage Climate Change." *Vanderbilt Law Review* 65 (6): 1455–78.

Solnit, Rebecca. 2003. *River of Shadows: Edweard Muybridge and the Technological Wild West*. New York: Penguin.

———. 2004. *Hope in the Dark: Untold Histories, Wild Possibilities*. New York: Nation.

———. 2010. *Infinite City: A San Francisco Atlas*. Berkeley: University of California Press.

Song, Min Hyoung. 2022. *Climate Lyricism*. Durham, NC: Duke University Press.

Soper, Kate. 1995. *What Is Nature? Culture, Politics, and the Nonhuman*. Oxford: Blackwell.

Souder, William. 2014. "100 Years After Her Death, Martha, the Last Passenger Pigeon, Still Resonates." *Smithsonian Magazine*, September. https://www.smithsonianmag.com/smithsonian-institution/100-years-after-death-martha-last-passenger-pigeon-still-resonates-180952445.

Soulé, Michael E. 1985. "What Is Conservation Biology?" *BioScience* 35 (11): 727–34.

Soulé, Michael E, and Reed Noss. 1998. "Rewilding and Biodiversity: Complementary Goals for Continental Conservation." *Wild Earth* 8:19–28.

Spielberg, Steven, dir. 1993. *Jurassic Park*. Based on the novel by Michael Crichton. Universal Pictures and Amblin Entertainment.

———, dir. 2018. *Ready Player One*. Based on the novel by Ernest Cline. Warner Bros. and Amblin Entertainment.

Springboard Research. n.d. *Accelerating Cloud in Asia Pacific*. https://farm6.static.flickr.com/5107/5692321314_5886bed37e_z.jpg. Accessed July 16, 2024.

Starosielski, Nicole. 2011. "Underwater Flow." *Flow: A Critical Forum on Media and Culture*, October 16. https://www.flowjournal.org/2011/10/underwaterflow.

———. 2012. "'Warning: Do Not Dig': Negotiating the Visibility of Critical Infrastructures." *Journal of Visual Culture* 11 (1): 38–57. https://doi.org/10.1177/1470412911430465.

———. 2015. *The Undersea Network*. Sign, Storage, Transmission. Durham, NC: Duke University Press.

———. 2019. "The Elements of Media Studies." *Media + Environment* 1 (1). https://doi.org/10.1525/001c.10780.

Starr, Kevin. 1986. *Americans and the California Dream, 1850–1915*. Oxford: Oxford University Press.

———. 2007. *California: A History*. New York: Modern Library.

Stephens, Elizabeth. 2020. "Speculative Biology: Precarious Life in Art and Science Resurrection Projects." *Continuum* 34 (6): 870–86. https://doi.org/10.1080/10304312.2020.1842128.

Stephenson, Neal. 1992. *Snow Crash*. New York: Bantam.

———. 1996. "Mother Earth Mother Board." *Wired*, December 1. https://www.wired.com/1996/12/ffglass.

Stewart, Dan. 2021. "Kazuo Ishiguro on How His New Novel *Klara and the Sun* Is a Celebration of Humanity." *Time*, March 2. https://time.com/5943376/kazuo-ishiguro-interview.

Stone, Brad. 2007. "Google's Next Frontier: Renewable Energy." *New York Times*, November 28. https://www.nytimes.com/2007/11/28/technology/28google.html.

Strasser, Bruno J. 2006. "A World in One Dimension: Linus Pauling, Francis Crick and the Central Dogma of Molecular Biology." *History and Philosophy of the Life Sciences* 28 (4): 491–512.

Studios Architecture. n.d. "Google Bay View Campus, Tech Workplace Interiors." Studios Design. https://studios.com/google-bay-view.html. Accessed July 16, 2024.

Sullivan, Heather I. 2020. "The Dark Pastoral: Material Ecocriticism in the Anthropocene." *Ecocene: Cappadocia Journal of Environmental Humanities* 1 (2): 19–31. https://doi.org/10.46863/ecocene.16.

Swart, Sandra. 2014. "Frankenzebra: Dangerous Knowledge and the Narrative Construction of Monsters." *Journal of Literary Studies* 30 (4): 45–70.

Sze, Julie. 2020. *Environmental Justice in a Moment of Danger*. Oakland: University of California Press.

Taylor, Jesse Oak. 2018. "The Novel after Nature, Nature after the Novel: Richard Jefferies's Anthropocene Romance." *Studies in the Novel* 50 (1): 108–33.

TED. 2013. "TEDx DeExtinction." March 15. https://www.ted.com/tedx/events/7650.

Teicher, Jordan G. 2012. "The Brain of the Beast: Google Reveals the Computers behind the Cloud." *Morning Edition*, NPR, October 17. https://www.npr.org/sections/alltechconsidered/2012/10/17/163031136/the-brain-of-the-beast-google-reveals-the-computers-behind-the-cloud.

Thomas, Julia Adeney, ed. 2022. *Altered Earth: Getting the Anthropocene Right*. Cambridge: Cambridge University Press.

Thomas, Russell. 2021. "Welcome to the 'Plastisphere': The Synthetic Ecosystem Evolving at Sea." *The Guardian*, August 11. https://www.theguardian.com/environment/2021/aug/11/welcome-to-the-plastisphere-the-synthetic-ecosystem-evolving-at-sea.

Thomas, Sue. 2013. *Technobiophilia: Nature and Cyberspace*. London: Bloomsbury Academic.

Thompson, Clive. 2020. "Monetizing the Final Frontier: The Strange New Push for Space Privatization." *New Republic*, December 3. https://newrepublic.com/article/160303/monetizing-final-frontier.

Thompson, Derek. 2023. "The AI Disaster Scenario." *The Atlantic*, February 27. https://www.theatlantic.com/newsletters/archive/2023/02/ai-chatgpt-microsoft-bing-chatbot-questions/673202.

Tolentino, Jia. 2017. "Finding Solace in Tracy K. Smith's Prescient Poem 'Solstice.'" *New Yorker*, March 6. https://www.newyorker.com/books/page-turner/finding-solace-in-tracy-k-smiths-prescient-poem-solstice.

Torchinsky, Rina. 2022. "Elon Musk Hints at a Crewed Mission to Mars in 2029." NPR, March 17. https://www.npr.org/2022/03/17/1087167893/elon-musk-mars-2029.

Truett, Joe, and Mike Phillips. 2009. "Beyond Historic Baselines: Restoring Bolson Tortoises to Pleistocene Range." *Ecological Restoration* 27 (2): 144–51. https://doi.org/10.3368/er.27.2.144.

Tuhus-Dubrow, Rebecca. 2013. "Cli-Fi: Birth of a Genre." *Dissent* 60 (3): 58–61. https://doi.org/10.1353/dss.2013.0069.

Turner, Fred. 2006. *From Counterculture to Cyberculture: Stewart Brand, the Whole Earth Network, and the Rise of Digital Utopianism*. Chicago: University of Chicago Press.

Turner, Frederick Jackson. 1920. *The Frontier in American History*. New York: Henry Holt.

Turner Endangered Species Fund. 2019. "Bolson Tortoise." http://tesf.org/project/bolson-tortoise.

Ulin, David L. 2013. "There It Is. Take It.: Mulholland Gave LA Water and a Motto to Live By." *Boom: A Journal of California* 3 (3): 28–37. https://doi.org/10.1525/boom.2013.3.3.28.

University of Arizona Biosphere 2. n.d. "About Biosphere 2." https://biosphere2.org/about/about-biosphere-2. Accessed July 16, 2024.

Urban Video Project. 2016. "UVP Insights: Saya Woolfalk on ChimaCloud." Short film, 1 min., 53 sec. https://vimeo.com/168981439.

US Census Bureau. 2020. "Sinclair Town, Wyoming." https://data.census.gov/profile?g=160XX00US5671150.

US Environmental Protection Agency. 2024. “Search for Superfund Sites Where You Live.” Updated June 17. https://www.epa.gov/superfund/search-superfund-sites-where-you-live.

US Fish and Wildlife Service. 2023. “Guam Rail.” February 2. https://www.fws.gov/species/guam-rail-rallus-owstoni.

Vaidman, Lev. 2021. “Many-Worlds Interpretation of Quantum Mechanics.” In *The Stanford Encyclopedia of Philosophy* (fall 2021 ed.), ed. Edward N. Zalta. https://plato.stanford.edu/archives/fall2021/entries/qm-manyworlds.

Vance, Ashlee. 2023. *When the Heavens Went on Sale: The Misfits and Geniuses Who Put Space within Reach*. New York: HarperCollins.

VanderMeer, Ann, and Jeff VanderMeer, eds. 2008. *The New Weird*. San Francisco: Tachyon.

———. 2010. *The Kosher Guide to Imaginary Animals: The Evil Monkey Dialogues*. San Francisco: Tachyon.

VanderMeer, Jeff. 2010. *The Third Bear*. San Francisco: Tachyon.

———. 2014. *Area X: The Southern Reach Trilogy: Annihilation; Authority; Acceptance*. New York: Farrar, Straus & Giroux.

———. 2017. *Borne*. New York: Farrar, Straus & Giroux.

———. 2018. *The Strange Bird: A Borne Story*. New York: Farrar, Straus & Giroux.

———. 2019. *Dead Astronauts*. New York: Farrar, Straus & Giroux.

———. 2021a. *Hummingbird Salamander*. New York: Farrar, Straus & Giroux.

———. 2021b. “My Five Summer Yard Hacks.” *Orion Magazine*, July 27. https://orionmagazine.org/2021/07/my-five-summer-yard-hacks.

———. n.d. “The Yard.” Jeff VanderMeer. https://www.jeffvandermeer.com/yard. Accessed July 16, 2024.

VanderMeer, Jeff, and Eric Nyquist. 2017. “The Borne Bestiary.” New York: MCD/Farrar, Straus & Giroux. https://www.mcdbooks.com/features/borne-33-bestiary.

VanderMeer, Jeff, and Mark Roberts, eds. 2005. *The Thackery T. Lambshead Pocket Guide to Eccentric and Discredited Diseases, 83rd Edition*. New York: Bantam.

van Dooren, Thom. 2019. *The Wake of Crows: Living and Dying in Shared Worlds*. New York: Columbia University Press.

van Dooren, Thom, and Deborah Bird Rose. 2017. “Keeping Faith with the Dead: Mourning and De-extinction.” *Australian Zoologist* 38 (3): 375–78.

Vasanta Studios. 2017. “Life in the Broken Places: Interview with Jeff VanderMeer.” Farrar, Straus & Giroux. Short film, 4 min., 50 sec. https://www.mcdbooks.com/features/life-in-broken-places. Also available at https://www.youtube.com/watch?v=05stee_pAAU.

Vermeulen, Angelo. 2007. “Art Projects: Biomodd.” https://www.angelovermeulen.net/?portfolio=biomodd.

———. 2011. “Art Projects: Merapi Terraforming Project.” http://www.angelovermeulen.net/?portfolio=merapi-terraforming-project.

———. n.d. “Art Projects: Seeker.” http://www.angelovermeulen.net/?portfolio=seeker. Accessed July 16, 2024.

Vertesi, Janet. 2015. *Seeing like a Rover: How Robots, Teams, and Images Craft Knowledge of Mars*. Chicago: University of Chicago Press.

———. 2020. *Shaping Science: Organizations, Decisions, and Culture on NASA’s Teams*. Chicago: University of Chicago Press.

Vitale, Daniel. 2023. “One Surprising Source of Hope for Climate Change?” *Los Angeles Times*, March 5. https://www.latimes.com/opinion/story/2023-03-05/climate-change-crisis-fiction-novels-dystopia-books.

Vopson, Melvin M. 2021. “The World’s Data Explained: How Much We’re Producing and Where It’s All Stored.” *The Conversation*, May 4. http://theconversation.com/the-worlds-data-explained-how-much-were-producing-and-where-its-all-stored-159964.

Wachowski, Lana, and Lilly Wachowski, dirs. 1999. *The Matrix*. Warner Bros.

Wainwright, Oliver. 2023. “How Solar Farms Took Over the California Desert: ‘An Oasis Has Become a Dead Sea.’” *The Guardian*, May 21. https://www.theguardian.com/us-news/2023/may/21/solar-farms-energy-power-california-mojave-desert.

Wallace, Molly. 2009. “Reading Octavia Butler’s *Xenogenesis* after Seattle.” *Contemporary Literature* 50 (1): 94–128.

Wallbank, Jessica A., Gavin Lear, Joanne M. Kingsbury, Louise Weaver, Fraser Doake, Dawn A. Smith, François Audrézet, et al. 2022. “Into the Plastisphere, Where Only the Generalists Thrive: Early Insights in Plastisphere Microbial Community Succession.” *Frontiers in Marine Science* 9:1–16. https://doi.org/10.3389/fmars.2022.841142.

Wasko, Janet. 2020. *Understanding Disney: The Manufacture of Fantasy*. Cambridge: Polity.

Watson, James D., and Francis H. Crick. 1953a. “Genetical Implications of the Structure of Deoxyribonucleic Acid.” *Nature* 171 (4361): 964–67. https://doi.org/10.1038/171964b0.

———. 1953b. “Molecular Structure of Nucleic Acids: A Structure for Deoxyribose Nucleic Acid.” *Nature* 171 (4356): 737–38. https://doi.org/10.1038/171737a0.

Wenzel, Jennifer. 2020. *The Disposition of Nature: Environmental Crisis and World Literature*. New York: Fordham University Press.

Werner-Jatzke, Chelsea. 2020. “SAM Book Club: Empathy Lives On in Parable of the Sower.” Seattle Art Museum, *SAM Stories* (blog), June 17. https://samblog.seattleartmuseum.org/2020/06/sam-book-club-empathy-parable-of-the-sower/.

White, Richard. 2011. *Railroaded: The Transcontinentals and the Making of Modern America*. New York: Norton.

Whole Earth. 1968. “Purpose.” *The Whole Earth Catalog*. Archived April 21, 2018, at the Wayback Machine. https://archive.org/details/1stWEC-complete.

———. 1986. “The Essential Whole Earth Catalog: Access to Tools and Ideas.” Whole Earth Catalog Records, 1968–1986, ser. 6, box 35, no. 6, Stanford University Library.

Whyte, Kyle Powys. 2017. “Our Ancestors’ Dystopia Now: Indigenous Conservation and the Anthropocene.” In *The Routledge Companion to the Environmental Humanities*, ed. Ursula K. Heise, Jon Christensen, and Michelle Niemann, 206–15. New York: Routledge.

———. 2019. “Too Late for Indigenous Climate Justice: Ecological and Relational Tipping Points.” *WIREs Wiley Interdisciplinary Reviews: Climate Change* 11 (1): 1–7.

———. 2021. “Time as Kinship.” In *The Cambridge Companion to Environmental Humanities*, ed. Jeffrey Cohen and Stephanie Foote, 39–55. Cambridge: Cambridge University Press. https://doi.org/10.1017/9781009039369.005.

Wilderness Act. 1964. Public Law 88-577, 16 U.S.C. 1131–36, 88th Cong., 2nd Sess. https://www.nps.gov/subjects/wilderness/upload/W-Act_508.pdf.

Wilderness Society. 2021. "Why Protecting 30% of Lands and Waters Is Critical." *Wilderness Society* (blog), March 5. https://www.wilderness.org/articles/blog/why-protecting-30-lands-and-waters-critical.

Williams, Mary I., and R. Kasten Dumroese. 2013. "Preparing for Climate Change: Forestry and Assisted Migration." *Journal of Forestry* 111 (4): 287–97.

Wilson, Edward O., and Frances M. Peter, eds. 1988. *Biodiversity*. Washington, DC: National Academy Press.

Wingfield, Nick. 2016. "Forget Beanbag Chairs: Amazon Is Giving Its Workers Treehouses." *New York Times*, July 10. https://www.nytimes.com/2016/07/11/technology/forget-beanbag-chairs-amazon-is-giving-its-workers-treehouses.html.

Witze, Alexandra. 2024. "Geologists Reject the Anthropocene as Earth's New Epoch—after 15 Years of Debate." *Nature* 627, no. 8003 (March 6): 249–50. https://doi.org/10.1038/d41586-024-00675-8.

Wolfe, Allison L., and Jack M. Broughton. 2020. "A Foraging Theory Perspective on the Associational Critique of North American Pleistocene Overkill." *Journal of Archaeological Science* 119 (July). https://doi.org/10.1016/j.jas.2020.105162.

Wolfe, Audra J. 2002. "Germs in Space: Joshua Lederberg, Exobiology, and the Publish Imagination, 1958–1964." *Isis* 93 (2): 183–205.

Woolfalk, Saya. 2016. *ChimaCloud*. Light Work UVP. Video installation. https://www.lightwork.org/archive/saya-woolfalk-chimacloud.

———. 2019. *Expedition to the ChimaCloud (March 1–Sept. 1, 2019)*. Nelson-Atkins Museum of Art, Kansas City, MO. https://kcstudio.org/saya-woolfalk-expedition-to-the-chimacloud-march-1-sept-1-2019.

———. n.d. "Bio." http://www.sayawoolfalk.com/bio. Accessed July 16, 2024.

Wray, Britt. 2017. *Rise of the Necrofauna: The Science, Ethics, and Risks of De-extinction*. Vancouver, BC: Greystone Books.

Wright, Robyn J., Morgan G. I. Langille, and Tony R. Walker. 2021. "Food or Just a Free Ride? A Meta-analysis Reveals the Global Diversity of the Plastisphere." *ISME Journal* 15:789–806. https://doi.org/10.1038/s41396-020-00814-9.

Wyss, Robert. 2016. *The Man Who Built the Sierra Club: A Life of David Brower*. New York: Columbia University Press.

Yamashita, Karen Tei. 1990. *Through the Arc of the Rainforest*. Minneapolis, MN: Coffee House.

Yeung, Peter. 2019. "The Toxic Effects of Electronic Waste in Accra, Ghana." *Bloomberg News*, May 29. https://www.bloomberg.com/news/articles/2019-05-29/the-rich-world-s-electronic-waste-dumped-in-ghana.

Yudkowsky, Eliezer. 2023. "Pausing AI Developments Isn't Enough: We Need to Shut It All Down." *Time*, March 29. https://time.com/6266923/ai-eliezer-yudkowsky-open-letter-not-enough.

Yu Zong, Emily. 2021. "Anachronism in the Anthropocene: Plural Temporalities and the Art of Noticing in Ruth Ozeki's *A Tale for the Time Being*." *LIT: Literature Interpretation Theory* 32 (4): 305–21. https://doi.org/10.1080/10436928.2021.1977568.

Zettler, Erik R., Tracy J. Mincer, and Linda A. Amaral-Zettler. 2013. "Life in the 'Plastisphere': Microbial Communities on Plastic Marine Debris." *Environmental Science and Technology* 47 (13): 7137–46. https://doi.org/10.1021/es401288x.

Zhang, Sarah. 2016. "A Huge Solar Plant Caught on Fire, and That's the Least of Its Problems." *Wired*, May 23. https://www.wired.com/2016/05/huge-solar-plant-caught-fire-thats-least-problems.

Zimmer, Carl. 2013. "Bringing Them Back to Life." *National Geographic*, April. https://www.nationalgeographic.com/magazine/2013/04/species-revival-bringing-back-extinct-animals.

———. 2014. "Century after Extinction, Passenger Pigeons Remain Iconic—and Scientists Hope to Bring Them Back." *National Geographic*, August 31. https://www.nationalgeographic.com/adventure/article/140831-passenger-pigeon-martha-deextinction-dna-animals-species.

———. 2019. "The Lost History of One of the World's Strangest Science Experiments." *New York Times*, March 29. https://www.nytimes.com/2019/03/29/sunday-review/biosphere-2-climate-change.html.

Index

Page numbers in italics refer to figures.